BMC and Leyland B-series Engine Data

BMC and Leyland B-series Engine Data Lindsay Porter

Comprehensive data and how-to guide to the popular B-series 4-cylinder engine used by Austin, Morris, MG, Riley and Wolseley 1954–81

I'd like to dedicate this book to the man
behind the B-series engine and a true
gentleman, Eric Bareham.

Published in 1985 by Osprey Publishing Limited
12–14 Long Acre, London WC2E 9LP
Member company of the George Philip Group

British Library Cataloguing in Publication Data
Porter, Lindsay
    'BMC' B-series engine data book.
    1. Automobiles—Motors
    I. Title
    629.2'5   TL210
ISBN 0-85045-597-9

Editor Tim Parker
Design Roger Daniels

Filmset by Tameside Filmsetting Limited,
Ashton-under-Lyne, Lancashire
Printed in Great Britain by
Butler & Tanner, Frome and London

Whilst great care is taken to ensure that the information
in this book is accurate neither the author, editor or
publisher can accept any liability for loss, damage or
injury caused by errors in or omissions from the
information given.

Contents

PART ONE

B-series: one of the family

1 From Chevrolet truck engine . . .

'Some people think you sit down and design a whole engine, but you never do—you evolve *an engine.'—Stan Johnson, Executive engineer, Advanced Engine Design at Longbridge in 1984.*

·Herbert Austin had always seen the necessity for building a range of motor cars rather than specializing in one model. Austin's first motor car (as distinct from those which he had been responsible for at Wolseley) appeared as early as 1906, yet by 1908, his model range extended to three cars ranging down in size from the gargantuan 8.8-litre Austin 60 to the more 'modest' 4.4-litre 18/24. Of course, power available per litre quickly increased, making such monsters an unnecessary irrelevance, but Austin continued with his policy of producing a full model range right the way through the threatening inter-war period. By the early 1930s, the Austin range consisted of the big Austin Twenty with its so very tall 3.4 engine, the Sixteen (2.5 litres), a couple of Twelves with 1861 cc or 1535 cc engines and the 10/4 of 1125 cc, as well as the famous Seven. All of these cars were introduced in what must have been a year of frenzied activity at Longbridge, in 1932. A year later, the Austin Seven was re-launched in revised form, giving Austin a formidable car range, matched only by the arch-rivals over at Morris, who in fact beat Austin in the league of top sellers, producing around 50,000 cars to Austin's 44,000 in 1932.

In 1932, Austin's top seller was the ubiquitous Seven, of which 20,000 were built, but in 1933, the success of the Ten reflected the changing tastes of the British motoring public and proved once again that Sir Herbert Austin had a genius' flair for spotting what the public would buy and providing them with it. The Seven sold a few hundred more in 1933 than it had the previous year, but the new Ten, whose production did not get properly under way until mid-1932, actually outsold the Seven in its first full year of production, with 20,937 cars built*. What is more, Austin decisively beat Morris into second place in the same year, selling 57,741* to Morris' 44,000.

As R. J. Wyatt points out in his book *The Austin 1905–52*, 'Austin had chosen exactly the right time to bring the Ten on to the market. In 1933, cars of 8 hp took 25.6 per cent of sales, and the 10 hp class reached 26 per cent, a position which it was to hold for a number of years at the expense of the larger cars of 11–16 hp. Buyers still wanted an 8 hp car at about £120, but the feature for the middle years of the 1930s was the 10 hp car costing about £170.'

The Autocar greeted the new Ten with a sense of enthusiasm that was only to be expected, when no fewer than 39 pages of advertising were devoted to the car. They published a three-page description of the new Austin, fully illustrated it with photographs and drawings and threw in a full road-test report and a double-spread sectioned drawing. It must have been difficult for *The Autocar*'s scribes to sound excited about what was a fairly conventional-looking motor car, but they did point out that 'the outward appearance is unmistakable Austin [which was a polite way of saying 'old-fashioned and upright'] and this should prove to be a hallmark of dependability'.

A number of features were mentioned by all the magazines which road tested the car, such as the rear axle, which was placed well back to improve the ride, the low-slung chassis giving easier access through the doors, but the part-cable-, part-rod-

---

*R. J. Wyatt, *The Austin 1905–52*, David & Charles.

operated brakes were mentioned only from the point of view of how they operated, no mention being made of how *well* they operated!

The new 10/4 engine received the ritual descriptions of engine layout, but the testers of the day cannot have known just how influential the general arrangement of the engine's bottom-end would be. In general layout, the engine had a strong resemblance to the Austin 12 six-cylinder engine, but whereas the 12/6 was a sales flop, the 10/4 sold in large numbers. The main feature of the engine was its stout crank and equally stout crankcase in the modern idiom, with a pressed-steel sump and separate head. The layout, which was to become the norm at Austin (and is still seen over half a century later on the A+ engine), followed that of the 12/6: the camshaft/valves were on the left-hand side of the engine, the

manifold consisted of a one-piece casting with a hot-spot, while the distributor was on the 'dry' side of the engine and was driven by a shaft running between numbers one and two cylinders with a skew gear on to the camshaft. An AC pump was also operated from the camshaft, the pump itself being placed beneath the carburettor. The oil pump plunged down into the sump and was driven off the same skew gear as the distributor. The camshaft was chain driven from the front of the crankshaft.

As usual, Austin used a Zenith carburettor, while in 1933 a V-type Zenith was substituted

Although there are few, if any, lineage connections between the Austin Seven and the B-series engine, the small car was the precursor answer to Austin's large-scale production philosophies of the Fifties

until the downdraught Zenith, so familiar a sight on postwar Austin engines, was fitted later in the decade after it had been found to give the Ripley Sports 10 an extra power boost.

The Austin Ten was a winner in no uncertain terms, even though there was a fair amount of competition around. At £168, the 1125 cc car, developing all of 28 bhp, was bettered in price only by the Morris Ten, which sold at £165. Only the Hillman Minx among the rest of the 10 hp class was priced below the £200 barrier, at £175, while comparable Rover, Standard and Peugeot models sold at the £225–£235 mark, the Crossley went for £288, and the relatively luxurious Lanchester attacked a different market altogether at a whopping £315. The Austin, on the other hand, had one of the lowest top speeds on offer, although not by any great margin (56 mph compared with the average 59 mph of the Hillman), it was the equal slowest with the Standard in terms of acceleration and, worst of all, it took a considerable distance to stop from 30 mph. While the Morris took 33 ft, which was pretty average, the Austin Ten gently decelerated over all of 45 ft. Not one road test of the day pointed out these shortcomings, preferring to make no comment at all rather than make criticism, and the car's value for money and undoubted longevity meant that it found a ready market. In 1932 it was said by *The Motor* that Sir Herbert Austin's decision to build 'an entirely new 10 hp 4-seater car was partly prompted by his determination not to enlarge the famous Sevens'. But by introducing the Ten at only £40 more than a de-luxe Austin Seven saloon, its success was assured.

Minor improvements were carried out to the Ten over the years, including revised brakes and synchromesh on second gear for 1935.

By the end of the 1930s, one Harry Weslake was consulted by Austin with a view to improving their cars' 'breathing', and in 1938 the Ten received an aluminium cylinder head. However, the Ten was completely redesigned as the Ten Cambridge for 1939, receiving a new body with semi-chassisless construction, a much more modern appearance and improved front suspension, while the new Girling brakes were still rod operated. Most of the 'old' Ten's mechanical parts were carried over into the new car and the good old 1932 engine now developed 33 bhp. On the face of it, the 1932 Austin Ten engine may not seem to have any relevance to the 'B-series' story. However, the Ten, the immediate predecessor to the A40 Devon and Dorset which followed it shortly after the war, had the crank size of all Ten engines: $3\frac{1}{2}$ in. stroke, or 89 mm: that measurement was to be etched on the minds, the drawing boards and even the computer VDUs of literally

The Austin Ten developed a reputation for solid, stolid reliability that Austin mid-range family cars were never to lose. It also bequested something of the structure of its engine to the B-series unit

generations of Austin, BMC, Leyland and Austin/Rover designers to come!

The war hit plans for the new Ten to become as big a success as the Austin Eight, on which it was modelled, but civilian production of the Ten continued until 1941, albeit at only half the level of pre-war production, and then, from 1941 onwards, production was maintained as a variation of Henry Ford's famous theme: 'Any colour as long as it's drab army green.'

Austin were well placed to restart production at the end of the war, much to the annoyance of many at Morris, some of whom muttered that while the Nuffield group had been prepared to give their all to the war effort, Austin had fought their own commercial battles at the same time. Whatever the rights or wrongs of the situation, Austin Eight and Ten production was simply stepped up from 1945 and Austin re-entered the commercial fray as first in the market for new cars with, in addition, the 1939 Twelve and a Sixteen with a new engine added to the range. In all, the Austin Ten itself saw production for civilian use from July 1945 to October 1947 in the postwar period.

Just before the war, in 1939, another piece in the B-series jigsaw fitted into place when Austin launched their first ever overhead-valve engine. It was a 3.5-litre six-cylinder engine with what some have described as a more-than-coincidental similarity to the Bedford truck engine of the period. Legend has it that the very designer who had worked on the Bedford truck engine with General Motors 'went over' from Luton to Longbridge, where he designed for Austin another version of the same engine. However, although the two engines do seem similar, Bob Grice, retired joint MD of Jaguar and ex-head of testing at Longbridge, refutes the idea.

Bob Grice was 'spotted', as he puts it, by Lord Austin before the war and became close to Leonard Lord, too. He explained that, 'A lot of commercial engines in those days looked similar from the outside, but what went on inside them could be quite different. In any case,' he went on to say in the manner of one whose honour had been slightly questioned, 'we had people to do everything that needed doing ourselves. *All* Austin engines were designed at Longbridge!'

In fact, Austin are said to have made use of diesel experts from MAN and Daimler-Benz when attempting to design a diesel engine pre-war, and it is undoubtedly true that a freelance designer like Harry Weslake was called in on numerous occasions and certainly contributed to the 'breathing' of the new truck engine, working from his newly built workshop on the site of the Alta car factory, where Geoffrey Taylor, who ran Alta, went into partnership with him. So the idea of 'pinching' an engine was far from being a new idea in the 1930s as Ford 8 and Morris 8 enthusiasts will know! And, after all, Austin were trying to take two very big steps at once: they were attempting to break into the truck market in a meaningful way, and they were attempting their first overhead-valve engine. And if it meant repositioning the camshaft on the 'other' side of the engine to differentiate the engine from the Bedford unit and to suit normal Austin practice, so be it!

The 'standard' 3460 cc truck engine developed 67 bhp, and Eric Bareham, whose name will figure very largely as this story progresses, remembers the truck engine being bored out and restroked (3.35×4 in. originally; $3\frac{7}{16} \times 4\frac{3}{48}$ in. in revised form) to give 3995 cc in 1940. The engine became known as the 'high-speed' engine, giving 87 bhp, but it was not put into car production until 1947 (although it saw military service), when, fitted with a Stromberg carburettor in place of the original Zenith, it gave 100 bhp in the huge Austin Sheerline and 110 bhp from three SU carburettors in her sister ship, the Princess. Jensen also bought the 4-litre 'high-speed' engine for their 541, 541R and 541S cars, and Boats & Engines Ltd of Weybridge adapted them for marine use.

Austin's pre-war experience with their new ohv engine stood them in good stead after 1945, when, unlike many other manufacturers, they had a coherent plan to follow. As already explained, Eights, Tens and Twelves rolled off the lines and the pre-war sixteen was wheeled out, but in place of the old 1930's side-valve long-stroke thumper was a shining new ohv engine, descended directly from the truck engine. This four-cylinder unit had been developed during the war and had seen military service and was essentially a four-cylinder version of the six-cylinder truck engine, even to the extent of utilizing the same stroke, which meant of course that the same machinery for producing blocks and cranks could be used for both engines. A $3\frac{1}{8} \times 4\frac{3}{48}$ in. bore × stroke ratio gave 2.2 litres and the engine became one of the stalwarts of the Austin engine range in those postwar years, being fitted immediately to the

Austin 25 cwt van, the 16 hp saloon and then going on to be used in all sorts of mundane and unsung areas such as the Austin Taxi, the Hire Car, the Clark fork-lift truck (after a period of considerable development by Eric Bareham) and to Boats & Engines Ltd marine products.

Even though Austin's chief designer since 1941, Jules Haefli, a man of Swiss extract, was 'given the boot' it is said for having come up with the hideously old-fashioned Sheerline limousine, Austin's engine range was starting to take shape from the top down. The 'ex-Bedford' truck and limousine engine had been followed by Eric Bareham's design for the four-cylinder 16 hp engine and the layout for all ohv Austin engines to come had taken form. The rationale, as Eric Bareham explained to me, was as follows: the camshaft and manifolds, the mechanical fuel pump and, of course, the carburation and exhaust pipe were all on the same side of the engine (the left-hand side—looking from the rear), while the 'electrics', the distributor, spark plugs and the coil and dynamo could then all be placed on the cooler, 'dry' side of the engine. This practice—following the pre-war 12/6 and 10/4 approach, except that then, of course, the dynamo could go above the head—had a number of advantages. It

The 1947 Austin A40 Devon was the company's first post-war car and used an engine that was directly descended from two sources: the Austin 10 sidevalve which bequeathed its block layout and leading dimensions, and the 1939 truck engine, which was Austin's first ohv unit and which set the pattern for the overhead valve layout right up to the present day. The Devon was accompanied in production by the very similar but 2-door A40 Dorset. The engine was known simply as 'the 1200' or sometimes as 'the 1000/1200' by those who remembered the design of the stillborn smaller capacity option

meant that none of the electrics could be affected by the heat of the exhaust nor be anywhere near the petrol supply, which had obvious safety considerations. The lengths of the plug leads were kept to a minimum, which increased their efficiency, and, because of the fact that the exhaust and inlet manifolds lay next to one another, it was possible to employ a 'hot-spot'. This means that inlet and exhaust manifolds share a common casting wall, semi-detached style, which gives much quicker warming up and so gives greater economy than cross-flow heads or water-jacketed inlet manifolds, expecially for short journeys. Also, the heat generated by the exhaust 'wall' helps petrol droplets to vaporize in a highly successful way—but that really belongs to a later part of the story.

Life being what it is, there were snags, of course. One was that the camshaft-driven distributor had to be driven by a shaft which passed between two of the bores until it reached the skew-gear on the camshaft—which was also used to drive the oil pump. Another snag, which seems much more serious at first sight, and which still tends to make some non-Longbridge engineers shudder, is that all the ports except the two end exhaust ports have to be siamesed so that, as Eric Bareham says, 'you can get the pushrods, ports and holding-down studs all the way along the engine.' In other words, there is only so much length in any given engine, and if you want to cram so much along one side of it, there just is not enough room to do it all in the conventional way. Siamesing the ports is, according to Bareham, 'theoretically 'orrible!' because with numbers 1 and 2 cylinders sharing one inlet tract and 3 and 4 cylinders sharing another, the induction pulses of an engine firing in the order of 1, 3, 4, 2 should cause all sorts of problems. In practice no such problems occur and it has been argued that the volume within siamesed inlets is greater than that which could be obtained from any one of a pair of separate inlets and that siamesing can actually help to smooth out the flow of fuel/air mixture. Mind you, any engineer would point out that no one would ever *seek* to siamese the inlet ports: it's simply fortuitous that it happens to work so well!

The centre exhaust ports were also siamesed, and this could have led to heat build-up and burned-out exhaust valves. However, as Bill Appelby, Haefli's successor, said in late 1983, a few months before he died, 'At Longbridge we used the very best materials: our materials really

LINDLEY SEARLE

This is the early B-series engine, identified in its infancy by the lack of external oil pipe running to the oil filter housing. The layout was very similar to that of the A40 1200 cc engine, but the whole thing was enlarged and there were many refinements so that there was a considerable step taken between the two engine's designs

were Rolls-Royce standard—that's why Austin engines lasted 100,000 miles'—unlike Ford engines of the day, which were notorious for their desperately low life-expectancy, sometimes as low as a quarter of the Austin figure. Appelby claimed that Ford used reclaimed materials, whereas Austin only ever used new. Certainly, the problem of burned-out exhaust valves was a minor problem—no pun intended—although the sound of a Morris Minor's exhaust valves 'popping' through the exhaust on the overrun is a familiar one and proves that the system could give problems. Eric Bareham was asked why the problem was not simply side-stepped at the design stage: perhaps Bedford's idea of putting the camshaft on the other side of the engine was a good one! The pushrods would have been moved out of the way, which would have left more room for the ports without jettisoning a single one of the advantages of the Austin layout. He explained that fitting pushrods through the spark plug side of the cylinder head would have meant letting tubes into the head through which the pushrods could pass, which would have added appreciably to production costs. However, perhaps it would be best to remember Stan Johnson's comments shown at the head of this chapter '. . . you *evolve* an engine. . . .' Austin's 'modern' 10 hp side valve engines (as opposed to the vintage flatmates with which they shared the 1932 range) had a block which was recognizably similar to those of postwar engines. Perhaps it was easier for Austin to think along the same layout lines as that of their first 'modern' engine, the 10 hp unit with camshaft on the left; perhaps the plant machinery was constructed in such a way that it could only handle this type of layout; or, to be cynically speculative, perhaps there was a political need to keep the Austin engine distinct in some way from the Bedford/Chevrolet truck engine, which was actually still in production in the 1950s.

So, compromises and all, Austin had started to reorganize their engine range from the top down. The D-prefixed 4-litre engines, later to be known apocryphally as the 'D-series' engines (although they were never officially given the title, it would seem) and the 2.2-litre four-cylinder engine (later to become 2.6 in 1948 for the Atlantic, civilian Champ and then the Healey 100) both provided Austin with a pattern for what was to follow.

Part of the pattern was the input of Harry Weslake. Weslake began his entrepreneurial career during the First World War, when he (or rather his father, because Harry was under 21 years of age) patented and produced the Wex carburettor. Not long afterwards the young Weslake was approached by J. E. Greenwood, Sunbeam's engine designer, who presented him with three apparently identical 500 cc engines and the request that he find out why they were all giving different power outputs. His solution was to form the basis for all his future work; he measured the amount of air which was passed through each cylinder head in a given time and found that there was a direct relationship between the power of an engine and the efficiency of the gas flow through the head. Weslake's arrival into the B-series story comes via one of those quirks of coincidence that make life so interesting. Once again Eric Bareham enters the story, but this time from a very different angle. In 1935, the London-born but partly Birmingham-bred engineer went to work for Alta in Tolworth, Surrey, near London.

'Who should turn up in 1936', he was to say when recounting his early days, 'but Harry Weslake—the first time I'd seen him.' Eric wasn't to know it at the time, but Weslake had scored a notable hit with an overhead-valve conversion of the Standard Motor Company engine that SS were using in their Jaguar cars. He formed a partnership with Geoffrey Taylor, who ran Alta with an eye to a fast buck rather than any automotive ideals according to Bareham, who was by then Alta's chief, indeed *only*, designer!

'They [Weslake and Taylor] built a new shop alongside the existing one, about 100 ft long. He put in his air flow apparatus, brought along his bloke Jack Connor who did all the work, and started business there.'

Eric Bareham was not especially happy in the shoe-string existence that spelled Alta, but consoled himself by doing drawing-board work at home for Weslake and worked on the Jowett and Austin Ten heads from 1937 on. He described how Weslake, the businessman, would find work for Weslake, the engineer. He would, it seems, take his ideas to manufacturers, along the lines of, 'I can make your engine run better than it's ever run before—give me the chance.' To put it in workshop language, and with a chuckle, Bareham describes Weslake's ability to sell himself as 'an old bull-shitter of the first order' and says that both he and Taylor were 'sharp cookies'. It is no wonder then, that their partnership should break up before the war, but not before Weslake had carried out work on the head of the new-for-1939 Austin ohv truck engine.

In late 1938, Eric Bareham could stand Alta no longer, so he joined Austin after a very brief spell at Electricar, Hall Green, Birmingham. Throughout most of the war, he worked at Austin on the wide variety of projects undertaken at that time, but, under Johnny Rix, carried out many of the original layouts for the 2.2-litre Austin Sixteen engine to be introduced to 'civvy street' after the war. Just before the war ended, however, Bareham felt drawn again to London, so he left Austin for a second spell at Lagonda, this time under Chas Sewell, the chief designer, who was under chassis expert Don Bastow, who in turn was under W. O. Bentley himself. 'He was sort of God', Eric remembers.

While Eric Bareham was away from Austin, Haefli and the real inspiration of the time, Johnny Rix, were designing the Austin Ten replacement. The bodywork was to be of a modern design,

although, amazingly, after having designed and built the highly successful Ten Cambridge with semi-chassisless construction, the new cars, to be called A40 Devon in four-door form and A40 Dorset in two-door, were founded on a separate chassis again. The shadow of Lord Austin's conservatism still fell darkly over Longbridge! The car almost cost the company its existence, explained Bob Grice, who had been with the company since the Herbert Austin era, rose to chief of testing after the near débâcle of the A40 and finally became joint MD of Jaguar. The front suspension, known in latter years for its

First to appear with the B-series engine was the MG ZA Magnette fitted with a tuned version of the engine in 1500 cc form, the extra capacity being easily possible because of the block stretching that had been carried out (Photo Paul Skilleter)

The Magnette was built to a body design by Gerald Palmer and was a modified version of the Wolseley 4/44. In 1956, the Wolseley, which had previously used a 1250 cc engine was also fitted with the B-series unit and re-christened the 'Fifteen-Fifty'. This car belongs to enthusiast Richard Phillips

wallowing qualities, allowing the blubbery-looking car with fat wings to rise and fall on an undulating road like the approach of a walrus out of water, gave great problems. On British roads there were no severe difficulties, but on continental pavé and particularly in Belgium the front suspension would quickly break up. This cost the company millions of pounds in the years following the A40 launch in 1947 and, it is said, Austin almost foundered.

Before the war, car tax had been based upon the 'horsepower' rating of the engine: the higher the hp rating, the higher the tax. This commendably egalitarian ideal was poorly conceived, hp ratings being based upon a hypothetical figure not at all connected with the actual bhp, or power output. In order to increase the sizes of their engines, manufacturers resorted to producing 'tall' engines, with a long stroke and narrow bore, which kept the car within certain hp limits. As a result, engines became increasingly inefficient, and after the war Sir Miles Thomas, then running the Nuffield show, approached the Labour Government's Chancellor of the Exchequer, Hugh Dalton, complete with working diagrams, to make his point. 'We finally prevailed,' says Sir Miles in his book *Out On A Wing*. 'Freedom from bore-tax meant that an engine could be built

squat, sturdy, light and cheap', which meant that once again business principles took precedence over Socialist principles, although this time for the soundest of engineering and indeed commercial reasons, and the old hp basis of levying car tax was withdrawn from January 1948.

Consequently, the new A40 had a slightly larger bore than the old Ten and, because the 'Ten hp' rating had become irrelevant, the bhp rating was used in the car's nomenclature instead.

An interesting amount of the old Ten engine was retained. Shell bearings, in preference to white-metal run into the conrods, had been used before the war, and these were continued. The block was essentially very similar, although of course the old side-plate for access to the side-valves was supplanted by a pair of simple tappet chest covers. No separate adjuster was fitted for the timing chain because, as on the Ten engine, camshaft and crankshaft sprockets were at the correct centres when the chain was new. The block height, main crank sizes, bore centres and other leading dimensions were largely unchanged between Austin Ten and A40 except that, of course, it was ohv along the exact lines of the truck and 2.2-litre engines as developed by Haefli, Rix, Bareham, Weslake and others. The engine developed 40 bhp from a 7.2:1 compression ratio, which was deliberately set low because of the low octane rating of the 'pool' petrol, which was the only petrol to be had at the time, although in fact it seems surprising today that some contemporary road testers considered the compression ratio to be on the high side! *The Motor*, perhaps following Austin marketing terminology, dubbed the car a 'Phase III' model, which meant that it was a true postwar car and not 'Phase I' or 'Phase II', which were interim and essentially pre-war cars introduced after the war ended (or, as in Austin's case with the Sixteen, launched in 1944 in anticipation of its ending!)

The magazine commented, 'Those who follow policy, as well as actual design, will find much that is significant in this new Austin. Motoring history, politics and manufacturing history can all be traced in its evolution. Politics (and economics) are traceable in the concentration on a single light-car model of 1200 cc in the place of the existing 900 cc and 1125 cc types, this concentration being dictated by the urge for greater standardization and made possible by the new flat-rate taxation, which takes no account of engine size.

Improved performance

'Austin manufacturing history is marked in the general conception as well as the details. Sound design has always been the characteristic that mattered above all else at Longbridge and out of it grew a certain natural conservation which tended to place the accent more on reliability and comfort than on performance. The latter tended to be adequate rather than notable.

'With the introduction of the Sixteen with its 75 mph maximum, immediately after the war, a new element began to creep into Austin characteristics, and that element was continued in the six-cylinder models, in which performance—as an aid to journey comfort rather than as an end in itself—was noticeable. Now that same characteristic is to be observed in the new "A40" model, which, while in no sense a sports car, should have a

performance appreciably brisker than is normally expected from cars of its class.'

It is interesting to compare the power outputs of the Ten and A40 engines. The former engine developed 32 bhp at 4000 rpm, representing 28.5 bhp per litre, while the overhead-valve revved more freely and at 4300 rpm gave 40 bhp. Although it was a few hundred cc larger than the Ten engine, its output was up to 32 bhp per litre, an increase of 16.8 per cent. Even when the extra 1 cwt in weight of the Devon was considered when compared with the Ten, top speed was up from just over 60 mph to around 70 mph, while 0–15 mph acceleration times were down from 27.4 seconds to 20.5 seconds.

The engine's overhead-valve gear carried forward an interesting idea from the Sixteen and truck engines, whereby the adjustable ball at the end of the rocker was drilled and connected to the pressurized oil feed. The idea was that oil would form a 'cushion' between the rocker ball and the cup at the top of the pushrod and so keep down tappet noise. (In view of the A40 and also the B-series engines' reputation for rocker box noise, the system cannot have been too successful!) The oil feed system in general was changed in the A40 engine when compared with the Ten unit. The earlier car had used pipes to carry the main oil feeds around, whereas the A40 engine used a system of drilled oilways, the oil passing internally through the engine castings. The oil pump sat on the base of the block and extended down into the sump. As already pointed out, it was driven by a vertical shaft from the same skew gear on the camshaft as the distributor. From the pump, the oil passed diagonally upwards through the block to the other side of the engine, where, at the rear right-hand side, it went through the oil pressure release valve. From there it went forwards along the main oil gallery, where it branched off to the main, big end and camshaft bearings through drillings in the crankshaft. From the rear camshaft bearing the oil passed upwards through drillings in the block and head to lubricate the rocker shaft and rockers, while the tappets were given their squirts of oil via the centre camshaft bearing. A feed was taken from the front camshaft bearing to lubricate the timing chain. 'Loose' oil then drained back into the sump. The engine was fitted with a by-pass filter, which meant that only a proportion of the oil that passed along the main gallery actually went through the filter. By-pass filters are finer because they can afford to be slower, but they operate best with white-metal bearings, where any tiny particles not picked out by the filter will bed into the soft white metal rather than scoring the face, as was the case with later, harder bearing materials. The bearings on the A40 were thin-walled but still lined with white metal, which explains why it was still possible to get away with the by-pass type of filters. Oil from the main gallery was fed through the filter via external pipes—or, *infernal* pipes if you had one stick while trying to change the filter!

Unlike the Austin Ten engine, where the water circulated by syphonic action, a water pump was fitted to the front of the engine block, and this, with special attention being given to the flow of the water in the head to make sure that the spark plug and valve areas were well cooled, made the cooling system a highly efficient one.

The new (or 'evolved'—*pace* Stan Johnson) engine had also received the Weslake treatment to the cylinder head, where the combustion chambers were described by *The Motor* as 'kidney shaped, with the valve heads occupying the "bumps" of the kidney'.

However, at the time of launch the Weslake head was still not completely developed, as Eric Bareham's Longbridge notebooks show. On 5 December 1947, Bareham drew for Weslake a 'recess' to extend the otherwise equal 'bumps' so that the inlet side of the kidney shape became greater. He calculated that this reduced the compression ratio from 7.24:1 to 7.04:1 (because the volume inside the head was of course increased) and he issued a new black and white drawing the same day, reg. no. 6141. This, it would seem, was the first time that Weslake settled on the non-symetrically-shaped combustion chambers and it could be that the Devon and Dorset ran with a lower compression ratio than the published figure from some time early in 1948. (Should anyone be enthusiastic enough to take a pipette to their removed cylinder head—provided it has never been refaced, of course—the old volume is given by Bareham as 34 cc while the modifications added a nominal 1.41 cc.) This new head was actually fitted first to the A40 Sports and it's not certain whether it actually found its way into the standard models as well.

Most Dorset saloons, the two-door model, were to sell overseas, while the Devon was the staple of the home market. The importance of exports to British industry in the wake of the

Second World War, the need to repay huge US loans, which had enabled Britain economically to survive the war and its aftermath, and the rigid austerity at home, were emphasized by the fact that Austin actually launched the new models in New York rather than in London. The A40 range (which also included from 1948 a Sports model, rebodied for Austin in aluminium by Jensen Motors on the other side of Birmingham at West Bromwich) sold extremely well and in 1950, for instance, around 110,000 A40s were sold, a figure which very comfortably beat the 60,000 or so that the whole of Austin sold in its record-breaking pre-war year of 1938.

In August 1951, the Devon received hydraulic brakes, Dorset production having stopped in 1949 after 15,939 had been built, and in early 1952 the Devon was dropped after 273,958 cars were built—this car, incidentally, represented only the first of many instances of the marketing people at Austin in the 1950s completely and utterly misunderstanding what 'export' markets actually wanted from their cars.

One year after the introduction of the Devon/Dorset, which replaced in one fell swoop the old Eight, Ten and Twelve models, the 'Phase II' Sixteen was replaced by the 'Phase III' A70 Hampshire, clothing the ohv engine in bodywork which was less stylish, more bulbous than the Devon's although identifiably of the same lineage. When the Devon was replaced by the Somerset, its new styling led *The Motor* to say, 'Anyone seeing an example of the new Austin A40 Somerset saloon on the road for the first time might well mistake it for an A70 Hereford model.'

Austin now proclaimed the fitting of the Weslake/Bareham head formerly fitted to the Sports, with inlet valves increased to $1\frac{3}{8}$ in. from $1\frac{5}{16}$ in., the pistons given concave crowns and the manifold redesigned. With a Zenith VIG carburettor now fitted, an extra $2\frac{1}{2}$ bhp was obtained, an increase of 6 per cent, while *The Motor* commented that the new engine 'pinked' less than the old one, which could confirm that the compression ratio was indeed lower, although it was still quoted at 7.2:1. A minor change was the fitting of an oil filter with internal oilways to the block instead of the external pipes previously fitted. The rear axle ratio was raised a little to make best use of the increased power, but the added body weight probably threw away most of the benefit. As *The Autocar* pointed out, the styling was such that the Somerset looked bulkier

than it actually was, although it was 6½ in. longer than the Dorset, gave extra passenger space and was said to be a more rigid structure. The Somerset sold roughly about as well as its predecessor, still at levels undreamed of before the war. And all the while its engine, the immediate predecessor to the B-series engine, was proving itself in terms of reliability, durability and high efficiency for the day.

Karma

'*We have to keep reminding ourselves that we are not in business to make cars, but to make money.*'—Roy Brocklehurst, ex-general manager at Abingdon, during the middle of BL's fight for survival in 1981, the Michael Edwardes era.

It is important to remember that all an engine does is pull a car along, and all a car does is make money for a company. And all a company exists for *is* to make money! Those of us who are enthusiasts, whether like Stan Johnson and John Wheatley, Longbridge engineer/enthusiasts or you or me, may have a different perspective, but there are always those who see no mystical qualities in the products of a car company, or any company for that matter. And they are usually the people at the top! For those *running* companies their jobs represent the culmination of many years of ambition, which has driven them forward in

In 1954, an all-new Austin appeared fitted with the 'cooking' versions of the B-series engine. The Cambridge could be had in 1200 cc A40 version or, as the A50, with the 1½-litre unit. The 1200 cc version was underpowered when fitted to the Cambridge, even though the chassis-based construction re-adopted for the A40 Devon, Dorset and Somerset had been dropped, and from 1957 the 1200 cc option was dropped

competition with others until, after the same combination of luck, fine judgement and determination as the winners of the Cup Final or the County Cricket Championships, they find themselves at the top.

The men (and handful of women who have the opportunity) who survive and even thrive on the rarefied but often exposed and lonely upper slopes are not, in spite of this description of their qualities, to be the least bit despised. Indeed, they should be greatly and genuinely admired, because their capacity to achieve what they do is given to very few of us. But nevertheless, in asking 'Why did they decide to do X and not Y,' it is important to remember what motivates them. People like Eric Bareham reveal their enormous talents on the drawing board, the Weslakes and to a wider extent Issigonis (there is only one!) showed theirs in a flair for three-dimensional results, but none of them either aspired to or came remotely near the top of a huge company or corporation.

On the other hand, Herbert Austin, Leonard Lord and very much later Michael Edwardes were utterly determined men chasing an ideal which was bound up with personal success, either like Lord, as the working-class man with an inferiority complex determined to 'prove something', or because of whatever else it is that drives such men. All three achieved a very great deal while the gentler, genteel man with all the right connections, George Harriman, presided over a period of steady decline at BMC and, in the end, the decline of the company and the controversy of the Leyland takeover broke him and he died a disappointed man.

These points are important because if one stops looking at cars and engines from the enthusiasts' point of view and looks at them from the point of view of power, politics and big business, the picture, although of course a simplistic one because nothing can be totally categorized, becomes interesting. Rather like bas-relief illuminated from a different angle you see something which is still the same but with a whole lot of different highlights and different shadows.

Just two companies carved up between them a large part of the British motor car market in 1932: Austin and Morris. In that year, which was not untypical, they built over 50 per cent of all cars produced in the UK. In some ways, the companies were similar, but in others they were quite different. William Morris began in 1913 and brought for the first time American mass-production methods to car manufacture in this country. He concentrated on building and selling cars and bought in almost every component; rather than build a vast operation making everything from wheel nuts to windscreen wipers, he used his companies' profits (and apart from Morris Motors (1926) Ltd they remained his personal property) to buy ailing companies like Wolseley, Riley, SU and others and turn them to profitability, often by using the advantages brought by economies of scale to share major components, although to nothing like the extent of 'badge engineering' in the 1950s and 60s.

By way of contrast, Herbert Austin, who had started even earlier in the lifetime of the motor car, back in 1906, carefully founded his empire upon a wide production base and ensured that his company made literally everything that went into his cars, except the rubber and glass. Naturally enough, this made Austin's potential as a profit earner that much higher in the good years but left it looking vulnerable in the slack ones. Whereas Morris could cut down on supplies at no cost to his company, Austin had to maintain the overheads that went with his empire in bad times as well as good. In 1921 and 1922, the company had been within an ace of bankruptcy and a representative of the Midland Bank sat on the board from then on. In 1924, Austin and Morris talked of a merger, but Morris turned the idea down, and in 1925 Austin attempted to sell his company to General Motors, but again was rebuffed.

Both companies passed through the 1930s vividly aware of each other's presence but obstinately unaware of the threat of Ford, who lifted their UK market share from around 5 per cent at the start of the decade to a figure comparable with those of Austin and Morris by the time the war came. But perhaps the biggest similarity of the two companies was that each had been made huge, powerful businesses by the initial inspiration of one man, and as so often happens the man who is swift, decisive and efficient when a business is being built up becomes dogmatic and inflexible as he becomes older and the business matures. An instance of Herbert Austin's intransigence, idiocy even, is his refusal to allow designers to rake back the windscreen of a car by more than 8 degrees because he believed it could harm the driver's eyes. Morris displayed his own inflexibility after the war when he refused his chief executive, Miles Thomas, permission to introduce the Morris Minor as early as he wished, and replace the Morris 8, because as far as he, Lord Nuffield (as he became), was concerned, there was nothing wrong with the 8!

In 1926, Morris bought the bankrupt Wolseley company, which dated back to 1896 in terms of car production and which had initially been put on its feet by none other than Herbert Austin, who left Wolseley in 1905 to form his own company. Austin also attempted to bid for Wolseley, but was outbid by his much larger rival, who that year had produced exactly twice as many cars. His failure to take over his old firm was said to have wounded Austin and the fact that his company had earlier been rejected by Morris when he had suggested a merger also still rankled. In the same year in which he obtained Wolseley, Morris turned Morris Motors into a company quoted on the stock exchange. The company became known as Morris Motors (1926) Ltd. and 5 million £1 shares were issued, the personal fortune which Morris accrued from the sale being largely placed into the charitable Nuffield Foundation, which was to establish many a worthwhile cause, some of which are still around today in the form of Nuffield hospitals, all of which are private concerns, and Nuffield Science Courses for schools. However, ironically enough, Morris, or Lord Nuffield as he became, was not noted for any generosity of spirit in his personal or business life.

He seemed to lose interest in the business from the late 1920s on, and as a result, Morris market share dropped, to be overhauled by Austin. Morris increasingly spent long periods away from his business—as much as seven months on one occasion—and yet he bitterly resented any major decisions being taken in his absence. As Graham Turner describes in *The Leyland Papers*, 'As the business grew Lord Nuffield seemed less and less able to comprehend it. His company was his only offspring and when the offspring became too big for him to control, he sometimes appeared to hate it while wanting still to be acknowledged as its sole inspiration.' When the Morris share slumped to 27 per cent in 1933, another barb was added to the strands that were to cause so many snags in years to come, when Leonard Lord was placed in charge of Morris Motors after having made a great success of reorganizing the newly launched Wolseley. Lord has often been described as both crude and uncouth, but mainly by those who were sacked by him and who, by definition, he considered failures. Those with whom he got on well have nothing but praise for him. And to rubbish a man because he swore a great deal is to have little insight into the macho world of Midlands industry and is in fact a rather petty kind of snobbery. Lord was a hard, efficient man and he soon pulled Morris round, so that from 1935 until the war Morris once again outsold the products of the old 'enemy' at Longbridge. However, in August 1936, Lord quarrelled with Morris, and then resigned when Morris refused to increase his share of the profits. He almost immediately regretted his action and asked Morris through an intermediary for his job back. Morris merely patronized him with a job as manager of a fund he had set up to help areas of high unemployment, the irony of the job probably appealing to Morris while increasing the gall within Lord. He was to

say to Nuffield executive Miles Thomas, 'Tommy, I'm going to take that business at Cowley apart brick by bloody brick.'

As already explained, Morris began by buying in all of his components, including engines. His first, before the First World War, was a White and Poppe engine, but war broke out before he could properly launch his new cars. During the war he assembled munitions, gaining experience of production-line assembly as he did so. After the war, he persuaded the White and Poppe works manager, Hans Landstad, to join him, and together, but with Landstad taking a special interest, they studied line flow production at the Continental Engine Company of Detroit. As a result, the postwar Morris Cowley was fitted with an imported Continental Red Seal engine and gearbox. Later, Hotchkins & Co., one time gunmakers, made the engines under licence in Coventry and eventually the engine was extended to six cylinders. Thanks to his Americanized production techniques, which maintained rapid assembly and kept stocks to a minimum, the business thrived.

In rapid order, Morris began to utilize both the money his cars were making and his excellent credit rating with the banks, and started to buy out his suppliers, choosing his timing with great subtlety and perhaps exerting the sorts of pressure that only a very major customer can exert on a major supplier when they want to reduce them to a low ebb. First he bought the Hotchkiss engine factory, followed by E. G. Wrigley & Co. of Smethwick, his axle supplier, and later the SU carburettor company. The acquisition of Wolseley in 1927, as well as bringing Len Lord on to the scene, also introduced some of the Wolseley engineering excellence and one of the first fruits was the 8 hp overhead-camshaft engine, whose design was actually based upon the Hispano-Suiza aero-engine that Wolseleys had made during the war. The engine was excitingly advanced but not a little delicate, one of the worst features being the way in which its camshaft drive spewed oil, a problem due simply to the inadequacy of contemporary oil seals, compared with their modern-day equivalents. The engine was de-designed to lose its overhead cam and became a more reliable unit for use in the first Morris Minor, although the OHC unit still alternately delighted and drove to despair owners of the new little MG Midgets. With Morris' ascendancy being lost to Austin, there was an urgent need to compete with a cheaper and more rugged car. Lord at the Wolseley factory pulled the Morris 8 engine out of the hat in record time by the simple expedient of copying the new Ford 8 hp engine! The 918 cc side valve engine was to prove the mainstay of the company through the 1930s, but the company also produced long-stroke side valve 10 and 12 hp four-cylinder engines and a range of sixes. The Morris 6 engine of 1928 was expanded and developed until it was converted to overhead valve in 1936, while the 1921 Axford Six engine, similarly stretched and developed, saw out the whole pre-war period, this engine also receiving its overhead valve conversion in 1936. As a result, Morris' engine line-up, while appearing quite modern, had benefited little from Wolseley's range of advanced ohc engines, William Morris' cloying conservatism restricting them to a range of ohv engines which were built largely as conversions to existing and venerable side-valve engines plus the Leonard Lord 'Ford-type' 8 engine, which was undoubtedly the saviour of the company, but without Lord's progressive influence even that in time was to become just another millstone.

During the war, Morris Motors under the effective control of Miles Thomas, gave its all to the production of war goods, although Alec Issigonis and a small group of colleagues beavered away on their plans for the Mosquito, or Minor as it was to become. From 1940, after a particularly bruising encounter with one of the ministries, Nuffield's mood began to change even more rapidly for the worse and, as Thomas put it, 'began to sulk in his tent'. With no inspiration from the 'old man' and a vice-president in Thomas who clearly wished to see no further ahead than the war itself, albeit for the most patriotic or perhaps blinkered of reasons, Morris were very slow off the ground when war ceased. Then, when Thomas finally wanted to launch the Mosquito, Morris demurred, saying that since there were still plenty of orders in hand for the Morris 8, why bother? Eventually, however, the Mosquito/Minor was launched in 1948. Morris engines used in the pre-war period up to 1952 did not include the antique ohv pre-war, six-cylinder jobs and only one ohv engine at all, which was the 918 cc Wolseley ohv conversion itself, discontinued in 1948.

In 1946, Miles Thomas, unhappy with the increasingly poisoned atmosphere at Nuffield, left to become chairman of BOAC. In short order, the managing directors of Engines branch, SU Carburettors, Morris Commercial and Victor Riley of Riley Motors had followed, and, in addition, Lord Nuffield purged several other top men from their posts. Almost pathetically, Lord Nuffield attempted to involve himself again in the detail design of motor cars with A. V. Oak, his chief engineer of long standing, but as quickly as Oak or a designer like Alec Issigonis suggested something, Nuffield turned them down. Oak took retirement and Issigonis moved to Alvis. As Thomas later reported, 'This wholesale clearance of men who had been pillars of strength in the development of Nuffield's wonderfully profitable business . . . was later to have wide-scale repercussions on the structure of the whole British motor trade. . . .'

Meanwhile Austin were pressing ahead with great élan and Lord Nuffield could see that a merger between the two great companies was essential while Morris' stock remained, in every sense of the word, still high. He agreed to a merger in 1950, but his board turned him down because they wanted time to improve Morris Motors' position. In 1952, by which time the pressures for merger were such that it looked inevitable, William Morris, Lord Nuffield, railroaded his board into the merger with Austin from which came the British Motor Corporation.

An important footnote to the story of the Nuffield empire must include the three car companies that Morris owned. The oldest established was based on the premises at Longwall Street, Oxford, where William Morris had set up a retail garage in 1903, known as the Morris Garages. In 1921, Cecil Kimber, a man whose name has since been revered by MG enthusiasts, was appointed as sales manager to the Morris Garages, who had moved from being general motor traders to specializing, reasonably enough, in Morris cars. In 1922 the general manager took his own life and Kimber, 34 years of age, was asked to take his place. Kimber quickly arranged to build more attractively-bodied versions of the rather mundane Morris cars, and public reaction fed by Kimber's flair quickly propelled matters along until, in 1924, the MG Super Sports was launched without the use of the Morris prefix. In 1928 the MG Car Company was registered in its own right and the 18/80 Six and the highly significant 'baby' sports car, the Morris Minor-based M-type Midget with Wolseley ohc engine, was launched. Through the 1930s, a wide

range of MG sports cars both open and closed were built, culminating in the production of the TA and for a short while the TB. The Abingdon factory was widely recognized as being efficient, purposeful although rather small, and Kimber had ensured that his cars were sporting even when not downright quick, and invested heavily in motor sport and other promotional activity. As a result, MG's profits were always low. Kimber was a man of flair and individuality who ran MG as though he owned it. Somehow, Morris never stepped in to prevent him from running things as he saw fit, but after Miles Thomas moved into the driving seat, things changed. Thomas asserted that individuality was all very well during peace time but 'when Kimber wanted to maintain his acute individualism after the war had broken out and adopt a policy of nonconformity when he was supposed to be working to Ministry specification . . . (I told him) he had better look for another outlet for his energies.' Interestingly, Thomas gave Kimber full credit for conceiving the MG, but described earlier in his book *Out On a Wing* how one Alfred Keen, who was said to have worked for Morris at Longwall Street since 1903,

The Morris versions of the car were similar in shape, size and function and, even though the B-series engines were of course shared, the bodies were totally different and the 'Series II Oxford' range used torsion bar front suspension while the Austin stayed with coil springs. A downmarket Oxford was built and known as the Cowley, was offered with either the smaller or larger engines. Unlike the Cowley pictured here, the Morris Oxford was externally distinguished by its all-chrome grille and plated side-strip

had built a hotted-up Morris Cowley at the Morris Garages in the early 1920s, but there is nowhere any suggestion that this was an 'MG'. Incidentally, all MG engines had always been, right from the very start, taken from the standard cars of the day and adapted for a form of tuning which was still compatible with production methods.

The story of Wolseley, its first cars introduced by Herbert Austin, its bankruptcy and buy-out by Morris and the involvement of Leonard Lord at the first motor car company he ever controlled has been told elsewhere in this book and also the story of a manufacturer of advanced engines, most of which were ignored by the sluggish parent. Riley,

23

however, came on the scene a little later. It fell into the hands of the Nuffield organization in 1938, which left insufficient time for Nuffield to blunt the edge of sharp performance coupled to engineering excellence which had been the hallmark of the company. Because, under Miles Thomas, little thought was given within Nuffield to peace-time car production, Riley were allowed to produce postwar, improved versions of their new-for-1938 cars and achieved a reasonable degree of success with more stylish bodies, new chassis with torsion bar suspension and the 1938 $1\frac{1}{2}$ and $2\frac{1}{2}$-litre engines from 1946 until the time of the BMC merger.

Events at 'the Austin', as Longbridge has always been known by locals, were still dominated by its founding light, but whereas William Morris retained the energy to involve himself (however negatively) in the running of his brainchild, by the time of the 1930s, Herbert Austin was ageing. He had started his own business in 1905 when 38, so by 1930 he was past his prime at the age of 63; in fact he died eleven years later.

Right from the start, Austin based himself at Longbridge and right from the start built Austin engines to his own design. Like other manufacturers of the day, Austin built cars individually and to order, but when the war came and he went over to munitions work, he learned a great deal about primitive mass-production methods, methods which had to be implemented after the war to get over the acute manpower shortages which cursed Europe after four years of trench fighting. In 1919, Austin launched the Austin Twenty with the advanced feature of a monobloc block casting (although still with a separate crankcase, rather than the separate cylinders that had gone before) copied from the American Hudson that Herbert Austin had used during the war.

The success of the Twenty led to a period of rapid expansion, with the emphasis on production rather than the buying-in of parts, but throughout the 1920s there was an air of expectancy that Austin may at any time be merged or bought out. Herbert Austin himself had no compunctions on that score and tried and failed on a number of occasions to bring about just such an outcome.

It was in the 1930s that the Austin Motor Company achieved its greatest successes, by which time Herbert Austin, though still as obstinate, opinionated and strong-willed as ever, was beginning to fade. Engine design was

perhaps slightly more forward-looking than it was at Morris, with the new 12/6 and 10/4 coming to pass, without any desperate need to copy the opposition as Morris had done with their 'Ford-type' 8 engine. However, Austin could easily have slumped into that intermediate phase where there is success based on past success but no innovation or drive to ensure that the momentum is maintained, had it not been for the row between Morris and Lord at Cowley. When Lord was cast into the wilderness, Herbert Austin must have felt in two minds about taking him on. Lord was a match for either of the two great men, but at the same time Austin knew that he was ten years older than Morris and would need someone to carry the business forward. In addition, Lord's talents must have been obvious, while best of all, perhaps, he had left Morris, and here was a chance for Austin to find some small consolation for having been spurned when he suggested alliance, and for losing the scavengers' scrap over the carcase of the Wolseley company.

After leaving Morris in 1936, taking a visit to study production techniques in America and then accepting the humiliating post Morris offered him—perhaps he saw it as a way of sidling back into his old position, although to be frank it was not his style—Len Lord joined Austin in 1938. He replaced the ageing and partially sighted Englebach, who had been Works Director since 1922, and his impact was so immediate and no doubt disturbing to those working under him that it is said that some wag scrawled on the wall, 'Oh Lord, give us Engle back!'

Even though Herbert Austin must have been sorely tempted to 'interfere' at Longbridge, it is said by those who worked there when Lord arrived that he made a deliberate effort to pull back and to leave Lord to run things his own way and from the time of Lord's arrival, Herbert Austin spent less and less time at the factory.

It was in early 1938, according to Wyatt, when the Austin board decided to go for the medium-sized commercial market, an area in which Austin had had conspicuously little success in spite of being for a time the country's largest car maker. By 1939, the new ohv $3\frac{1}{2}$-litre truck engine was built and ready after an incredibly short gestation period. After all, the engine was Austin's first ever ohv and broke new ground in respect of size and type (although not block arrangement). The answer must surely be that Austin *did* copy the Bedford truck engine, which appears so similar to the Austin unit. And the catalyst? Leonard Lord! Remember that it was Lord, the man of action rather than scruples, who was behind the Wolseley design for the Morris 8 engine and which was most certainly copied from the Ford 8 unit. Then, Morris had needed an engine in a hurry; this time Austin needed one quickly and, in both cases, Lord was the man who made the decisions. The Bedford truck engine was itself based on the Chevrolet 'Stove-Bolt' engine of 1932 (both Chevrolet and Bedford were part of General Motors of America, of course) and so, since A-series, B-series and ultimately O-series were descended from Austin's $3\frac{1}{2}$-litre truck engine, it would seem that there exists a very interesting transatlantic lineage in the murky past, although such a connection could never be acknowledged because it looks as though the $3\frac{1}{2}$-litre engine was born the wrong side of the blanket.

It was lucky for Austin that their first ohv engine was produced before the war because it is unlikely that a 'new' engine design could have been produced during wartime. The lack of an ohv engine of any description would surely have left Austin in an even worse position than Morris come the end of the war because they at least had the pick of the Wolseley ohc engineering and their own ohv-converted side valves. However, it is

This 'Cowley' LCV has survived the passage of time to find service in the 'eighties with Practical Classics *magazine. It is still a remarkably durable and capacious workhorse*

And, at last, this is how it looked in situ! Inside a Cowley engine bay, this B-series engine demonstrates the enviable amount of access afforded around both Morris and Austin models. The SU carburettor was only fitted to Nuffield-derived models while Austins used the less elegantly simple Zenith carburettor

inconceivable that Len Lord would have allowed Austin to have wallowed its way through the war years as Miles Thomas allowed Morris to drift. Especially after Herbert Austin's death in 1941, the ruthless but effective Lord ensured that Austin developed ideas and thought out ideas for the postwar period, so that after the war finished there was a coherent strategy to follow.

It should not be assumed that Austin's contribution to the war effort was insignificant; far from it. Longbridge produced a huge range of munitions, and Eric Bareham remembers having to draw a Hispano machine-gun magazine which, even to this master draughtsman, was 'the hardest thing I ever had to draw; like an enormous Swiss roll'. The newly bodied 'Lord' Austin Eight and Ten remained in production throughout the war (although the Twelve, introduced in 1939, did not) and a steady stream of military/commercial

vehicles was built. The Longbridge drawing office was maintained and there was no problem, according to those who worked there, in finding people to spend 'odd moments' on new projects that could be justified both in terms of the war effort and civilian projects to come. So it was that the Austin 16 hp ohv engine was developed via the 4-litre version of the truck engine with, no doubt, some thought being given to the smaller-yet A40 engine which was to follow.

By 1952, Austin's car range was taking considerable shape with the dynamic influence of Leonard Lord fully visible. A40 Devons and Dorsets had given Austin a flying start once the old pre-war stopgap models had been phased out in 1947 and sold well until 1952, when the A40 Somerset came out to replace them; A40s had replaced the Austin Eight, Ten and Twelve in one fell swoop. The Sixteen was replaced by the A70 Hampshire, using the new 2199 cc four-cylinder ohv engine produced during the war for the Sixteen, and both Hampshire and its successor from 1951, the Hereford, used an enlarged form of the bulbous 'family' styling adopted for the A40. This 2.2-litre engine was also fitted to civilian versions of the Austin Champ jeep-type vehicle which Austin built for the Government. In military form, a Rolls-Royce engine (built at Longbridge) was used, but in the commercially unsuccessful civilian versions, Austin's own engine was used. (Nowadays, the vast majority of Champs in captivity are ex-War Department and so are fitted with the Rolls-Royce engine.)

Austins had designed a couple of pre-war prototypes as replacements for the old 28 hp Limousine, but both of these were discarded after the war. In 1941, Hancock, the chief designer, had been replaced by Jules Haefli, and he was given responsibility for a limousine replacement. In the event, two body styles were developed, the Princess, with elegant frontal styling, and the Sheerline, which had a more olde worlde charm (not at all to Lord's liking!), both using the 4-litre engine developed in 1940. Sheerlines were built at Longbridge and used a single Stromberg carburettor, 100 bhp 4-litre engine, while the Princess was built at Vanden Plas and used three SU carbs, developing around 110 bhp. In the same year that the cars were launched, Austin bought out Vanden Plas lock, stock and barrel.

The A40 engine designed by Bill Appleby, who was later to succeed Jules Haefli when he was reportedly sacked for the disappointing design of the Sheerline, was at that time Austin's smallest development of the series of engines that had started with the 1939 $3\frac{1}{2}$-litre truck engine. Although it is of course simpler to say it than to do it, all that had happened was that the engines were scaled down, first from six to four cylinders to give 2.2 litres, then right down to 1200 cc. In 1951, the Austin A30 was launched, with bodywork styled in the same well-rounded family style to become the 'baby' of the family. Its 803 cc engine (not known at that point as 'A-series') was again a scaled-down version of what had gone before. There is no doubt that Eric Bareham was one of the leading figures in the design of the A-series engine and his notebooks show that the first design brief was drawn up on 24 May 1949 but that the engine under consideration at that stage was a side-valve engine, extremely simple and cheap to produce and with syphonic water circulation (i.e. without even a water pump). Also under consideration was a two-cylinder horizontally opposed unit, but after a side-valve experimental AS3 engine was completed on 31 March 1950, complete with aluminium head, a change in the design approach took place. Perhaps having built the engine, it became clear that performance was not going to be adequate and on 9 September 1949, following a page spent considering some problem with '7 hp Inlet Ports', still in the side-valve mode, Eric Bareham's notebook makes first reference to '7 hp ohv' and deals with the major dimensions involved.

The A30 was launched in 1951, and following hard upon its launch, Eric Bareham began to carry out work on the 'B'-series engine, the first reference being made in his notebooks on 18 January 1952.

2 Designing the B-series

'We had a meeting in Mr Rix's office and someone said, "What shall we call the new range of engines?" I suggested "A"-series for the smallest one and the others just followed from there.'—Eric Bareham.

Many people have, over the years, confused the 1200 cc A40 engine with the B-series unit, thinking that they are one and the same engine. However, there is no doubt that, as Eric Bareham himself says, 'The B-series engine is a completely different engine, being both longer and heavier.' The confusion comes about because of the identical capacity and bore/stroke of the A40 engine and the smaller of the B-series engines and because they look superficially similar. The two engines are *not* interchangeable and David Garrett of the Cowley/Oxford Club confirms that neither a Cambridge nor Cowley B-series engine will fit into the earlier cars without engine mounting modifications, although the gearbox/engine attachment remains the same.

The A40 engine had proved to be tough and reliable with few problems in service. It did have its limitations though, and Bob Grice, who was to become BMC's chief of testing, explained that Len Lord told him, before they got down to designing the B-series engine, that he wanted Austin to have an engine that was as reliable as the old Heavy 12. 'He said he wanted a universal engine,' Bob Grice was to say, 'one that could be used in LCVs (Light Commercial Vehicles) and which would be capable of being developed as a diesel.' The engine was to form a cornerstone of Austin's engine line-up and, since it was to become increasingly obvious as the 1950s drew near that there would have to be a merger between Austin and Morris, the engine would complete the modern range of Austin engines. Lord could

see that Nuffield had absolutely nothing to compare with the Austin engines and it must have been clear to him that, when and if a merger took place, there would be an opportunity for Austin totally to dominate the partnership. Other commentators have taken the comment made to Miles Thomas in 1936 literally, as though when he said, 'I'm going to take that business at Cowley apart brick by bloody brick,' Len Lord actually meant it. Of course, Cowley was an enormous asset and one that Lord, the great tactician, would never have dreamed of destroying. Instead, Leonard Lord went one better.

At Longbridge, Lord was doing all he could to make Austin a leading motor company. He had the model range modernized; he had got production up to a high level very early on in peace-time and so he had ensured a high capital inflow at a time when other manufacturers were struggling to get going; and he aimed to use the capital he generated to expand the company. He made an enormous leap forward for Austin when his new car assembly building and offices were completed in July 1951. (The offices quickly became known as 'The Kremlin', a name which has stuck until today.) The assembly plant was designed to be the most efficient and advanced in the world at that time and involved a great convergence of finished components along vastly long tunnels and covered ways and all controlled by a punched card system, the contemporary equivalent of the computer. These tracks were completed initially, one being used for the A40, one for the A70 and another for the new AS3/A30. The system was designed to be infinitely flexible and significant problems did not arise until much later when it was realized that the new Austin-Healey Sprite could not be built there, in 1957, because the lines only took engines from below the track, whereas the Sprite engine would only go in from above!

Over at Morris, Miles Thomas was replaced by Reg Hanks as chief executive, following which there was a mass of resignations. Issigonis had been beavering away on the Mosquito/Minor, which he had designed around a flat-four side-valve engine, making the engine bay low and wide to suit. Morris Engines Branch at Coventry built prototypes of the engine, but, according to Paul Skilleter in his book *Morris Minor*, Issigonis, and Jack Daniels who worked with Issigonis, claimed that the Engines division did not really want to make the engine and so did everything they could to prevent its being built. In fact, Morris would have been very hard pushed to find the capital for an all-new engine with a high risk of service failures. It was to have been built in 800 cc or 1100 cc alternative sizes, the great advantage being that capacity could have been modified simply and cheaply by a change of cylinder barrel. However, Lord Nuffield was antipathetic towards the new car in particular and Issigonis in general and the Miles Thomas arguments that the old Morris 8 engine was not only available but tried and tested carried forwards into the Hanks era and the Minor was launched in 1948, its highly effective body and chassis design in stark contrast to the venerable side-valve engine bolted up-front.

On the success of the Minor, Morris' profits rose sharply in 1950 to match those at Austin (although, of course, the latter company had poured huge sums into modernization, sums not met by the Nuffield group). But relations between Hanks, who wanted, not unnaturally, to run the business his way, and Lord Nuffield were becoming strained. At the same time, the general feeling was that Austin and Morris were bound to merge. It seemed increasingly that their competitive struggle was becoming internecine rather than constructive and the first steps towards merger were taken when Len Lord 'dropped in' on Nuffield on 10 October 1950 to pass on his best wishes on the old man's seventy-third birthday. After a considerable amount of back-door negotiating at which Lord seemed to excel, Lord Nuffield finally approved the merger, even though Reg Hanks, who stood to lose most, was strongly against it. From the first meeting in 1950, the process took until November 1951, during which time Lord had played one of his cards in the game when, with the knowledge of Nuffield, he

approved the go-ahead of the Minor competitor, the Austin A30.

The new organization brought together two empires, their combined forces totalling a labour force of 42,000, an output of 300,000 cars per year and assets of £66,000,000 (worth around ten times that figure in 1980s terms) and that made them the fourth largest car manufacturer in the world and the largest outside the USA. The British Motor Corporation included Austin's plants in Australia, New Zealand, Mexico, Eire, India and South Africa and the ex-Nuffield names of Morris, Wolseley, Riley, MG, Morris Commercial, SU Carburettors and the Nuffield Press. However, BMC was formed only as a holding company, which meant that each one of the 'names' within the company was run as a separate entity, and in some ways this was to store up problems for the future.

Other problems were to occur. The chairman of the new group was Lord Nuffield; Leonard Lord was deputy chairman, Reg Hanks vice-chairman of Morris Motors and George Harriman was deputy managing director at Austin. The atmosphere that had pervaded Morris while Miles Thomas was there had been unhappy. Thomas said of Nuffield that, 'Although W.R. had said long before that he was going to leave the running of the business to the Board, he still persisted in exercising what was inappropriately, if undeniably, his right of destructive criticism.' That had been in 1947, and now, four years later, Lord Nuffield, a stubborn and wrong-headed 74-year-old, faced in Len Lord a deputy chairman who undoubtedly bore the need to prevail over the man who had humiliated him before the war. Something had to give. Inevitably it was Nuffield himself, and when Leonard Lord threatened to resign unless he could run the company his way, the old man knew that this was a bluff that could not be called; that whether Lord stayed or went through the motions of leaving, it would be the end for him, and so in the stoical manner of one who knows that his past has opened up a choiceless future, he said farewell at his last AGM, which lasted all of $6\frac{1}{4}$ minutes, leaving no time for the prepared fine phrases and walking out 'a sad and lonely man', in the words of Graham Turner.

OVERLEAF
It was in a drawing office like this one at Longbbridge where the B-series engine was 'schemed'. At the time, Austin were justifiably proud of the modernity of their entire design and production facilities

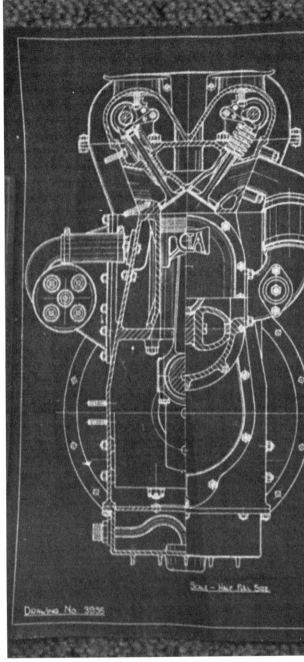

Eric Bareham the man behind the B-series engine and, according to one of his senior contemporaries, much else besides, was pictured here in 1969 (the earliest surviving picture of him at work) in Tokyo at the Champion (spark plugs) conference, at which time he had risen to Chief Designer, Engines at Longbridge, a post which the internal politics of the Leyland clique ensured that he did not keep for long

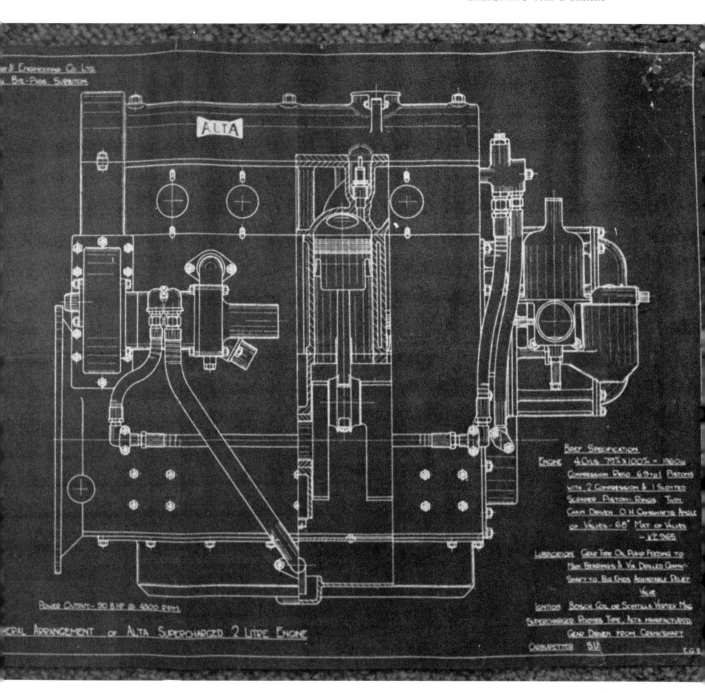

Included in Eric Bareham's pre-war 'apprenticeship' had been a period at Alta where, as sole draughtsman, his methodical mind had set about installing some order, no mean feat for such a young man. This is a photograph of one of his blueprints for the 2-litre Alta engine with overhead camshaft but lacking some of what Eric Bareham saw as basic sound engineering features

'B' Series Valve Rocker. 162293/A   15. 4. 53

Oilway drillings modified to same as A33. at request of Mr. Randal, . . T.D.O.

1200cc 'B' Series Engine Cyl. Head modification   6. 5. 53

Experiments carried out with division in inlet ports to try & improve power at low speeds.

1st. Step. $\frac{1}{16} \times \frac{1}{16}$ groove milled down ⅛ of inlet ports & plate inserted

2nd step.   Port area increased as shown :—

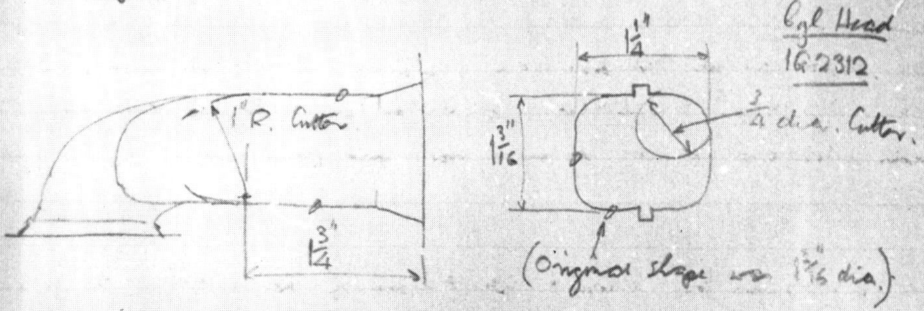

Cyl Head
162312

1" R. Cutter

$\frac{3}{4}$ dia. Cutter.

(Original shape was $1\frac{5}{16}$" dia.)

Two-stroke Engine   12. 5. 53.

References :—   Automotive Industries for July 1, July 15, Aug 15, Sep 1. Nov. 1. 1940.

A.. N°. 3492.   621.432.4. (Section thru DKW racing engine.)

Lord was now truly master of all that lay before him, much to the resentment of those from the old Morris companies. Lord ensured that Austin people were placed in charge of most of the key areas, such as design and testing, which was not surprising in view of the poor postwar performance in terms of innovation by the Lord Nuffield-staffed group and the mass exodus of Morris people such as Issigonis before the time of the merger. All the same, ill-feeling ran high and some Austin personnel did nothing to placate it. Bob Grice, who was Lord's chief of testing and over the BMC Motorsports programme, was an Austin man, based at Longbridge. When he travelled to Cowley to hold sway over the testing of vehicles in production, he needed an office, so he took over Lord Nuffield's, which had remained vacant since the old man's departure. Talk about salt in the wounds! No wonder that Morris engine workers refused to fit gaskets because they were stamped 'Austin' and that apparently C-series engines would arrive at Longbridge from Coventry, where they were built, with their insides vandalized!

Not only was there a strong feeling of identity with an individual marque name within the company, there was a strong streak of brand-orientated consumer loyalty from those who bought the cars too. Lord cleverly met this demand and utilized it to his company's advantage, drawing on his pre-war experience with Wolseley but taking things a whole lot further. At Wolseley, Lord had been used to fitting Morris bodywork and other leading components together with a relatively small input from Wolseley themselves, and cleverly disguising the cars with 'superior' fittings and trim. As a result, Wolseley became identified with an up-market image and the cars sold with a higher added value because of it. Now, at BMC, Lord faced the same problem multiplied by a large

factor. He had a large network of separate, fiercely independent and very powerful dealers to contend with a number of factories whose workers still identified with the 'old' company rather than with the new holding company of BMC, and a buying public who wanted both the economies of scale which result from large-scale production and the sort of variety that only a number of small companies can produce. He *had* to commonize component usage and he had to offer the dealers and the public what they wanted, and the way he did it was a masterstroke.

The first step was to do something about the range of engines used by the companies operating under the BMC umbrella. In late 1951/early 1952, there were fourteen different models of car being produced by the companies concerned, using no fewer than *eleven* different engines! By mid-1956, the range of models available had increased by one, but by then only seven engines were employed. Even more striking was the fact that three out of the seven engines were used to power 11 out of the 15 models, and one of these three engine types was employed in six out of the eleven and was also used in the American Nash Metropolitan and the range of Austin $\frac{1}{2}$-ton Commercials. That engine was the mainstay of the fleet, the B-series engine.

The B-series engine was conceived around the time of the formation of BMC for the specific purpose of fitting to the whole of BMC's range of medium-sized saloons and also the sports cars. At the time of its arrival, in 1954, many people expressed surprise at the apparent similarities between the A40 engine and B-series, so much so that they wondered whether it really was a new engine and, if it was, why Austin had not simply re-bored or re-stroked the A40 unit in order to obtain larger capacity. However, there were significant differences. It is not generally known that the A40 engine was originally designed in

More of Eric Bareham's work, this time at Longbridge in April and May 1953, where his notebooks showed that last-minute modifications were being carried out to B-series valve rocker oilway drilling 'to same as AS3' while he was applying his mind to a possible solution to the problem of the relatively inefficient siamesed inlet ports by toying with an idea for splitting them up. It was never followed through

OVERLEAF
Here, bottom-ends are being assembled in another part of no. 5 machine shop, the labour-intensive nature of the work in stark contrast to the early automation in evidence on the transfer machine lines. This shot was taken in December 1955

both 1200 cc and 990 cc forms (in fact Stan Johnson, currently a very senior Longbridge engineer, still refers to it as the '1000/1200 engine'). Consequently, there were problems in enlarging the engine to $1\frac{1}{2}$ litres to suit Lord's demands for a 'universal' engine.

As already explained, the A40 unit was essentially a shrunken version of the war-developed 16 hp engine, but because the engine was so compact but still used the same layout, there were one or two technical problems to overcome. First, there was the problem of the distributor position. On the truck engines there was plenty of block height and also plenty of room between the cylinders, so running the distributor drive through from the right-hand side of the engine to the left-hand camshaft presented no difficulties, and the same was true of the four-cylinder version of the engine, the Sixteen, where the lower end of the distributor shaft was carried in the outer wall of the block casting in exactly the same manner as with the larger 'Sixes'. On the A40, the block was much shorter and so, in order to position the distributor drive beneath the bottoms of the cylinders and the base of the adjacent pistons when at bottom dead centre, the distributor drive and thus the distributor body had to be angled lower, which had the unfortunate side-effect of making the distributor harder to service.

This design had first been adopted after the experimental, potentially inexpensive side-valve engine, which was dropped in favour of the ohv A-series unit. There, the distributor was to have been on the end of the camshaft (an idea that has relatively recently found favour at Austin) and the oil pump was to have been driven via a very short shaft. In the end, the A-series engine continued the Austin practice of putting the distributor on the opposite side of the engine to the camshaft and the B-series Design followed suit. The oil pump was mounted tight up against the bottom of the distributor drive bottom-end bearing with the pick-up low in the sump and protected by a gauze filter to keep back the crudest of the oil's pollutants.

The mounting for the end of the distributor shaft became invisible from outside the engine on the A40 as the shaft was carried in a lug cast into the inside of the crankcase wall. The same position was retained on the B-series engine, the skew gear on the end of the distributor shaft being driven off the bottom of the camshaft in exactly

the same way as in the engine's predecessors, and the shaft skimming the bottom of numbers 1 and 2 cylinders. (The Sixteen ohv distributor drive had passed between numbers 2 and 3 cylinders, but positioning the unit further back made it easier to sit the dynamo alongside the front of the block on the smaller A40 and B-series units.) However, the oil pump on the B-series was redesigned so that it sat higher up in the crankcase and pushed oil straight into the cast-in oil galleries rather than sitting low in the sump as in the A40 engine.

Two other technical problems encountered in the A40 engine, especially when it was intended to increase its capacity, were in one case solved and in the other alleviated in the B-series unit. The first was that in order to increase capacity, it was necessary to increase the engine's bore. The stroke could not be altered because the distance between crankshaft and camshaft were unchanged between the 10 hp, A40 and B-series (and A-series, too, incidentally, although that never caused problems because it was a much smaller engine with a smaller stroke to start off with). In fact the crankshaft sweep was already as large as it could be and the crank already passed between the cam lobes and within $\frac{1}{16}$ in. of the camshaft. In cases such as this it is sometimes possible to squeeze a little more stroke from an engine by splitting the big-end bearings diagonally so that the bottom of the big-end rather than the protruding stud head or nut skimmed the camshaft, but that had already been done on the original design. Consequently, as long as Austin/BMC were stuck with the same production equipment and the same crankshaft/camshaft centres, the stroke could not be changed. But the A40 engine had been designed as a 1000 or 1200 cc, with nothing larger envisaged, and so the water jackets between bores were large for the still-born 990 cc engines but narrow for the larger-sized unit, so there was no room to expand capacity widthwise without striking water. It would have been possible to have siamesed 1 and 2; 2 and 3 cylinders, but that would have left little extra capacity to create Lord's 'universal' engine and would have required considerable re-engineering of the engine in any case. Far better, it seemed, to go the whole hog and redesign the engine all over again.

It was decided that the length of the block would have to be increased so that the spaces between the cylinders (the water jacket) on 1200 cc engines would be wider apart than had been the case on the A40 unit, thus allowing the cylinders to be opened out to give 1500 cc while still retaining plenty of cooling capacity. Rather than having to pay the penalty of having a longer engine, because the A40 was considered to be compact for its day, the Longbridge engineers devised a simple but interesting way of shortening the engine's effective length. Several commentators at the time claimed that Austin had sunk the B-series water pump back farther into the block so as to reduce the engine length, but in fact it would seem that the length of the 'nose' carrying the water pump bearings internally and the pump pulley and cooling fan was simply shortened and made more compact. In fact the A40 engine's water pump had already been well recessed with the impellers near to no. 1 cylinder wall, so there was little room for improvement there. At the same time, the A40-type water pump seal was improved by being given extra graphite content, a modification which was also aimed at making the pump run more quietly.

From the pump, the cooling water was fed first into the water jackets around the cylinders, from where a combination of the force of the pump and the natural convection currents of the water fed it through openings into the cylinder head. Obviously, the need for cooling is greatest around the top of the engine and the retention of siamesed centre exhaust ports meant that particular attention had to be given to cooling that area adequately. At the lower end of the engine, the water jackets extended below the bottom line of the piston rings when at their lowest point. From there, the water was drawn into the chamber at the front of the cylinder head housing the thermostat. If the thermostat was closed because the temperature was low, the water circulated only within the engine until the point came when water heat opened the thermostat and allowed water to pass through the thermostat and into the top of the radiator. Once in the radiator, it cooled, became denser, and was drawn back into the engine through the bottom of the radiator, all of which is orthodox practice. From the outside, the B-series engine was yawn-makingly orthodox in most respects—until you look more closely, that is! The B-series cylinder head benefited from the fact that the block was made slightly longer. By insisting upon placing the camshaft on the same side as the ports, Longbridge engineers made the head look like a mass of ports, pushrods and holding-down studs, all jostling for position

down one side of the head. Eric Bareham, the man most responsible for the engine alongside Johnny Rix, explained to me how he went about engine design—this or any engine.

1 You decide upon the bore × stroke ratio.
2 The crankshaft is designed to suit.
3 Crank design determines cylinder centres.
4 Position the cylinder head studs to ensure an even pull-down—you can usually accept 3 studs per cylinder, but some engines need 4, then:
5 Determine the pushrod positions and . . .
6 Port positions, but accepting that you may have to play around with 4, 5 and 6 to achieve a reasonable compromise between them.

In the case of Austin engines, where layout was predetermined by accepted practice, the job of cramming 4, 5 and 6 studs, pushrods and ports down one side of the engine was made slightly easier when the block was lengthened a little, but even so, it was the wizardry of Harry Weslake which made such a 'theoretically 'orrible' layout, in Eric Bareham's words, work so well. The siamesed inlet ports were of the special Weslake so-called 'three-zone' type. Zone 1, where the port first entered the head from the inlet manifold, was tapered so that the speed of the incoming fuel–air mixture was increased, reducing drop-out of the heavier petrol spray. Zone 2 took the mixture through 90 degrees and around the valve stem, while Zone 3 was the area around the valve seat. The famous heart-shaped Weslake combustion chambers were used, of course, with the spark plug at the base of the heart. The non-symmetrical shape devised by Weslake and engineered by Bareham was used again because, as with the A40 Sports model, the inlet valve was larger than the exhaust. The B-series head differed from the A40 in that there was a step at the base of the heart shape which improved the swirl of the mixture through the head and also helped to deflect the incoming mixture away from the hot exhaust valve, which could easily have caused pre-

OVERLEAF
Rotary 'running-in' engine stands were used for both A- and B-series engines to ensure that everything turned over freely and that the oil pump was pumping oil all through the engines. They were 'turned over' electrically, not under their own power

ignition and running-on. (In fact, 'running-on' or 'dieseling' of MGB B-series engines was a common problem on models up to the mid-1970s, when anti-run-on devices were fitted, and could very well have been caused by the problem of red-hot exhaust valves at the centre of those cylinders with siamesed exhaust ports.) Excess heat build-up was never a problem on these early engines and another step to prevent it from causing trouble was to make the exhaust valve guides protrude into the port. One would have thought that the effect would have been negative, as the super-hot exhaust gases cut into the end of the valve guide, but it was claimed that the technique aided valve cooling without affecting flow through the exhaust ports.

The measurement of gas flow through a cylinder head was, of course, what Weslake was famous for. Working away from Longbridge—Weslake was once asked by Lord to work for Austin, to which he replied 'Not bloody likely!'; he remained an independent consultant all his life—Weslake measured the time it took for a given amount of air at standard temperature and pressure to flow through a wooden model of an inlet port which was modified by intuitively carving away bits of wood or adding Plasticine until the optimum flow rate was achieved. Then the exhaust port was similarly developed until its flow matched that of the inlet ports. The shape of the combustion chamber inside the head was developed through observation of gas flow. Weslake's engineers would clamp a sheet of glass over a model of one of the combustion chambers and pass smoke through an inlet valve and then out of the other side to observe how it flowed. This apparently crude approach was very much state-of-the-art of the day, when combustion chambers were just spaces where ignition took place and ports were little more than hosepipes, inefficiently carrying mixture and burned gases to and from the engine. Harry Weslake's experiments were developed and are still being developed by the inheritors of the Weslake Company so that the current state of high sophistication, which is at the very least matched by today's Austin-Rover engineers, owes an enormous (and widely acknowledged) debt of gratitude to Harry Weslake and particularly to the sort of work he carried out on engines like BMC's B-series.

With conditions in the exhaust valve department almost literally hellish, it was important that Austins used a very high grade of steel for their exhaust valves. Following Austin tradition, Austin made their own valves by extrusion from steel bars using EN59 steel, developed for its resistance to wear, corrosion and pitting, for the exhaust valves and silicon-chrome EN52 steel for the inlet valves. The latter had a diameter of 1.37 in. while the exhaust valve was smaller at 1.182 in. The valves themselves were formed by the 'hot-upsetting' process whereby a heated valve 'stem' was gripped and the valve head formed by forging the top into the classical mushroom shape. Weslake designed the same head to suit both the 1200 cc and the 1500 cc engines, which gave the larger engine a lower compression ratio, of course. (In the same way, the A50 1200 cc and still-born 1000 cc engines would have had the same Weslake head, and many years later, O-series 1700 cc and 2000 cc units shared the same head, too.)

While on the subject of engine capacities, it is interesting to take a look at the capacities and bore-stroke ratios which were considered before any detail design began. Remember that the B-series was a new engine and so almost all the options were open regarding capacity.

The BMC merger finally took place on 23 November 1951. Plans for a 'universal' engine must have been outlined by Lord, in principle at least, before the merger took place: indeed, it would have been unthinkable for the man who pushed for the merger and who stood to gain personally out of it, *not* to have had an idea of what he wanted to do with the companies' products once he had brought them together. Virtually no time was wasted in getting Austin personnel involved in Nuffield engines. By 4 December 1951, Eric Bareham was involved in testing and producing the power curves of the Morris SEA/3 six-cylinder 4.2-litre engine and well before the end of the year Bareham, Johnny Rix, Bill Appleby and others attended a meeting at which it was decided, following Eric Bareham's suggestion, that the family of engines should be named A-, B- and C-series. (Interestingly, the original truck engine's serial number was prefixed 'D', but it never seems to have been called the 'D-series'; it is often loosely called by that name today.)

On 20 December 1951, Eric Bareham set out in his notebook the possible bore × stroke ratios and resulting capacity of a range of sizes, most using a bore of $3\frac{1}{2}$ in. for reasons already explained. His page was set out as follows:

1400 cc Austin-Morris Engine. 'B' Series

$2\frac{13}{16} \times 3\frac{1}{32} \times 4 = 86.976$ c.i. (cubic inches)

$71.437 \times 88.9 \times 4 = 1425.27$ cc

With bore opened out to $2\frac{7}{8}$ (max.)

$2\frac{7}{8} \times 3\frac{1}{32} \times 4 = 90.885$ c.i.

$73.025 \times 88.9 \times 4 = 1489.34$ cc

$2\frac{13}{16} \times 3.54 \times 4$

$71.437 \times 90 = 1440$ cc

$2.578'' \times 3.500'' \times 4 = 73.17$

$65.48 \times 88.9 \times 4 = 1200$ cc

$2\frac{5}{8}'' \times 3\frac{1}{2}'' \times 4 =$

$66.675 \times 88.9 \times 4 = 1240$ cc

$2\frac{21}{32}'' \times 3\frac{1}{2} \times 4$

$67.468 \times 88.9 \times 4 = 1270$ cc

$2.638 \times 3\frac{1}{2} \times 4$

$67 \times 88.9 \times 4 = 1251$

$3\frac{1}{8} \times 3 \times 4$

$76.2 = 1508$ cc

$2.78 \quad 3$

$70.8 \times 76.2 \times 4 = 1200$ cc

This direct copy from E.B.'s notebook illustrates how, just as he was to describe to me some 33 years later, bore × stroke make up the first stage in designing any engine. It also shows quite clearly that the B-series *was* conceived as a new engine and not just a revamped A40 unit. Interestingly, Bareham attempted to obtain 1200 cc by changing the stroke, which would also have given a 1500 cc engine (see bottom two formulae), but whereas the 1200 cc would have been nicely approaching a 1:1 bore × stroke ratio, $3\frac{1}{8}$ in. bore by 3 in. stroke would have been *over* square, which did not suit Lord's idea of a long-stroke, long-life slogger at all. Interestingly enough, the idea of a 1200 cc B-series engine with different stroke to that of the 1500 was raised again on 11 August 1952, when Eric Bareham's notebook, p.233, shows:

'Revised 1200 cc "B" Series Engine ($2\frac{7}{8}''$ bore)'
Under this heading, a range of engine sizes was considered, from 1195 cc obtained from $2\frac{7}{8}$ in. bore × $2\frac{13}{16}$ in. stroke, through 1224 cc, down to 883.1 cc (2.578 in. × 2.578 in.) and even 609.8 cc (2.28 in. × 2.28 in.). (Then again, further paper experiments were carried out on

'B series capacity with 1:1 bore/stroke ratio', but only *after* the engine was put into production, some time in 1955.)

But, back to December 1951: the interesting point is that within 27 days of the formation of

BMC, Eric Bareham had sketched in the first outline of a new engine, starting first, as he later described, with bore/stroke ratio. From then on, Eric's progress was amazingly rapid. In 1984, Stan Johnson, Austin-Rover's head of experimental engineering, who had worked under Bareham, said of him, 'He was very good indeed on a drawing board. He could put the layout of an engine up in very quick time and the important point was, he could *globally* see a problem. In other words, it would flow from him. The layout became very meaningful in a very short time, whereas a lot of people, like myself perhaps, have to labour at it in order to make the whole thing work. He was a wonderful foil for Johnny Rix. Johnny would come round and do a bit of a sketch and Eric would fill a board up in no time.' Bareham's notebooks were filled with sketches, notes, ideas and formulae relating to different aspects of the new engine, work continuing on the engine throughout 1951. Of course, other engineers were also working on different aspects of the unit: even by 1951, no one engineer could possibly design an engine in solitude, but even so, in those days it was often possible to point the finger at the man who was the creative inspiration behind it. Some, such as ex-head of testing Bob Grice, claimed that Bill Appleby, a personal friend of his until Appleby's death in early 1984, was the man behind the ideas for the B-series engine. Stan Johnson, who was closer to the design engineering side than Bob Grice, did not feel the same way. The author talked to Stan Johnson in the summer of 1984, when this kindly, courteous senior manager spoke about his beloved Austin and those who had worked there. 'Who really *did* design the B-series,' he was asked.

'It's awfully difficult, you know, to say these things,' he answered carefully and cautiously, 'but we none of us, in the end, do very much, do we? I mean, in a company you're part of a team. Influences come from all over, as to exactly how things turn out in the end.' He paused and sucked on his pipe.

OVERLEAF
This rather satanic view of no. 5 machine shop shows hoardes of very early B-series engines undergoing assembly. From the types of inlet manifolds fitted there is clearly a mix of MG and Austin engines going down the line at the same time

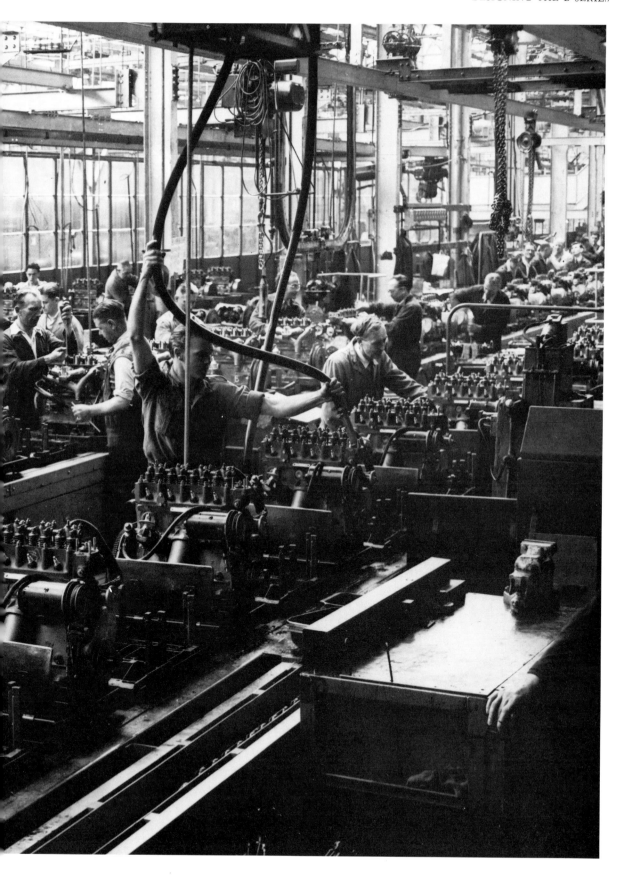

'Johnny Rix was a designer. What I *call* a designer. And Eric Bareham was a designer. Now, Appleby wasn't a designer in the same idiom, but he was a manager with some design understanding and design flair and a considerable amount of drive. Right?' And he stopped as though he wanted to be sure that what he said was absolutely clear. 'And I wouldn't be disrespectful to Appleby in any way.' He paused and re-lit his pipe, then spoke at first as if reconstructing memories to himself. 'But Johnny Rix was a designer. He was technical director after Haefli—he got the boot for the Sheerline—and did the job from 1948 to about '52 or '53. He was the kind of technical man who went from board to board; from a chassis to an engine, transmission to body in the course of a morning, in the course of an afternoon and made a contribution to every confounded board he went near. Ah, he was good. He was truly good. It upset me—it was funny how I felt about it—when I heard he got pushed out. Now, Johnny Rix thought a lot of Eric Bareham. It was Johnny Rix who really brought Eric Bareham back in 1947 (he had worked for a time at Lagonda) and it was Johnny Rix who did the 1000/1200 (the A40 engine). It was Eric Bareham and Johnny Rix; Johnny Rix and Eric Bareham that did the A30 engine in 1949.

'Then we had the BMC set-up with the Morris people, and then they decided they wanted a bigger engine. By that time, Bill Appleby was made chief engineer and Johnny Rix was made a broader sort of technical director, while Eric Bareham was made Appleby's assistant with a man named Benbow, who used to work with Eric at the same sort of level. There were a lot of bore/stroke ratio and a lot of bore centre things going on at Court House Green, where they had gone to 1500 already and they tried to use machinery that already existed, and Eric basically masterminded that. Although it was Eric and Bill Appleby that did it, it was essentially Eric's design. Eric did all the scheming (drawing up outline specifications) and all the actual design. Appleby did a lot of design work before the war and I'm sure during the war on the Austin Seven—the racing Seven for Murray Jamieson. But I would give Eric the credit, personally. In fact I would give Eric the credit for most of the 1947 to 1968 era.' He narrowed his eyes with introspective thought, drew on his pipe and nodded slowly. 'I really would.'

Immediately following Eric Bareham's en-gineering 'doodles' with engine sizes and bore/stroke ratios, he started carrying out calculations for a 1400 cc engine's gudgeon pin bearing loads, based on the weight of A40 flat-top pistons, and in very early 1952 work was done on valves, ports and valve springs for '1200 & 1425 cc' engines, which shows that it was by no means the case that Weslake was given a brief and came back with a complete head: it would seem that he was an improver rather than an originator, at least in the use that Austin made of him. On 10 January, Bareham designed a starter ring for the 1425 cc engine based on the A40 ring gear (he had used the same basis for AS3/A30), but by 16 January, the starter ring design was modified to take 1500 cc, which suggests that it was some time in that week that the engine size of 1500 cc was decided upon, 1200 cc having been regarded as the basic engine size all along.

Bareham worked on cylinder head design in January 1952 using the basic Weslake 'heart-shaped' combustion chambers, but he was not apparently involved with the engine again until March (it seems that there was still work to be done in the AS3/A30 engine) when work was carried out on the valve timing gear.

When the Johnny Rix-designed A40 engine replaced the old Austin 10 SV unit, several recognizable components remained. The cranks appeared very similar, so did the general block shape, and the crank/camshaft centres were unchanged. When the A30 engine came on the scene, it too used the same crankshaft/camshaft centres and so shared with the A40 its timing gears and timing chain, an obvious saving in cost over having to produce two sets of a rather expensive set of items.

When the B-series came along, there was no reason for the engineering point of view that all this could not have been changed. Those responsible for monitoring costs within a company, not unnaturally, see things slightly differently! B-series had exactly the same camshaft/crankshaft centres as the A40, which meant that, once again, the same timing gear could be utilized. The engine had a new crank, which was longer and considerably stronger than the A40 crank, having redesigned webs and improved oilways. To have changed the position of the camshaft would have allowed a larger stroke but would undoubtedly have made the whole design exercise very much larger. As Eric Bareham's initial notebook ideas show, 1500 cc with a $3\frac{1}{2}$ in. stroke gave a perfect bore/stroke ratio for the job in hand. There were evident cost savings to be made in the timing gear by leaving the camshaft where it was, and there was undoubtedly a saving in design effort in leaving certain points of the engine unchanged. It would be possible now to criticize the decision on the grounds that restricting the stroke of a new engine built in huge problems for the years ahead, especially since the engine was built on all-new machinery and it would surely not have been any more expensive to equip production facilities to produce a much-changed engine, but in all fairness, the B-series engine's life span was then thought to be in the order of five years, not the *thirty*-five years it is approaching.

The A40 had used a rather strange but cheap and simple timing chain tensioner. All the way around the centre of the timing chain sprockets was a radial slot and into this was fitted a rubber ring. The theory was that the rubber ring would push the chain outwards and so keep it tight and free from rattles. In practice, of course, as the chain stretched, the rubber tired and wore, and so achieved little and it was decided to try other systems. In April 1952, Bareham developed a gear-driven camshaft, based on Morris Oxford gears, the parts for which were not ordered until a year later. Experiments were carried out with the A40-type of rubber-faced tensioner on a proto-type engine and much later in 1955, after the engine had been put into production, there were even experiments with the Gilmer Toothed Rubber Timing Belt, but nothing seems to have got further than paper because Bareham's calculations showed that a belt measuring 1.75 in. in width would have been required to handle the driving torque required: the extra length it would have added to the engine was presumably deemed unacceptable. In the end a rather ingenious spring-loaded automatic tensioner developed by the Renold and Coventry Chain Co Ltd was fitted. Given final clearance as late as 13 January, 1954, the tensioner consisted of a shoe with a synthetic rubber face which was pressed against the chain by a spring inside the shoe housing. The shoe moved forwards automatically, using a spiral ratchet effect, to take up any slack in the chain and the face of the shoe was fed with lubricating oil at low pressure through a hole in the front plate and another in the face of the shoe.

The camshaft itself was a steel forging, because BMC designers preferred a case-hardened steel

camshaft rather than a cast-iron camshaft. Cast-iron cannot be case hardened (a process where the outer skin of the steel is toughened after the whole component is 'soaked' at high temperature in a bath of carbon particles, so increasing the carbon content of the skin) and so significantly larger gear teeth are required. The B-series camshaft skew gear, which drove the oil pump and distributor, were also case hardened, of course, and this permitted smaller gears with finer teeth. The camshaft ran in three thin-wall, steel-backed, white-metal bearings, pressed into the block, and it was held in position by a locating plate in front of the front bearing, the whole shaft being withdrawn or replaced through the front of the engine.

The cams themselves were of unusual shape, called the 'sine wave' shape, a pattern which was patented by BMC. The idea was to reduce valve spring surge, which could amount to $\frac{3}{16}$ in. on old-type cams but which was said to amount to no more than $\frac{1}{32}$ in. with 'sine-wave' pattern cams. It was said to be vital that tappet clearances were correctly maintained in order that this feature could actually work. In addition, the cam faces were slanted slightly, so if viewed from the side of the engine, the cams were at a very slight angle when compared with the line of the camshaft. The idea of this modification was that the tappets would rotate slowly, rather than be worn in one spot by the cams. In addition, new plant was installed to treat the tappets with 'Parco lubrization', which gave them inherent self-lubricating properties, which ensured that they slid easily in their bores in the cylinder block.

The 8.8 in. long pushrods were formed into cups on their top ends and these mated with the ball-shaped ends of the rocker adjusting screws. Just as on the A40, the oil feed was continued through the rockers and into the ball-and-cup arrangement with the aim of quietening running and cutting down on wear. The rocker arms ran in thin-wall, steel-backed, white-metal bushes and

OVERLEAF
One of the jewels in the Longbridge crown was the production facility which enabled vast numbers of A- and B-series engine to be produced. The key was the transfer line shown here at North Works with a stream of B-series cylinder blocks being transferred from one work station to another automatically, non-labour intensively and swiftly

were carried on a rocker shaft supported on four pillars. The pair of rockers for each cylinder was positioned on each side of a supporting pillar, the rockers for adjacent cylinders being kept separate by coil springs surrounding the rocker shaft. This layout was less than ideal because it meant that the outer rockers were overhung on the outsides of rocker shaft pillars, just as on the A40 and A-series engines. The reason for doing so was that there just was not felt to be enough room for extra holding-down studs in an already packed head. However, when Eddie Maher at Coventry Engines produced the racing Cooper S engine, engineered expensively to cope with vast increases in A-series engine output, it was felt necessary to squeeze in outrigger supports for the rocker shaft ends, but that is another story! Shortly after production and release, a Mr Turner at MG complained about the length of the ball pin thread on the rocker and the quality of the thread, and the length was increased by $\frac{1}{8}$ in. and the thread quality improved on all A- and B-series engines, which shows that feedback from MG was normal and accepted at Longbridge.

It has already been mentioned that the crankshaft was made both larger and stronger: it was forged, rather than cast, using EN16 steel, and was formed using the conventional type of counterbalance weights. Its oil feed drilling from the main journals to feed the big-end bearings were also conventional, except that an additional auxiliary hole was drilled in each crankpin, which fed oil to each big-end bearing $120°$ in front of the main oil hole and bottom dead centre. This was found to provide a cushion of oil for that period when the crankpin was under greatest pressure and was found to actually reduce crank wear and tear in practice. The crankpin and main journals were polished to a finish of 5–10 . The fillets at the ends of the bearings were regarded as a critical point and work was carried out by Bareham on ensuring that they were sufficiently strong, special care being taken to machine the fillets to a smooth blend without steps or ridges to act as fatigue points. In a talk presented to the Institute of Mechanical Engineers around 1960, by which time over 2,000,000 B-series engines had been produced, Eric Bareham pointed out a significant problem that had occurred in practice and one which should be carefully noted by today's B-series engine owners. He said, 'A reduction of (crankshaft) fillet radius from $\frac{3}{32}$ in. to $\frac{1}{16}$ in. will lower the crankshaft fatigue strength by some 15

per cent. This is a point which should be borne in mind when regrinding worn crankshafts, as the finished undersize component has obviously lost some of its original strength and so it is most important that the fillets are carefully formed and up to size.' One wonders just how many reconditioners would take note of this particular piece of advice! Crankshaft end-thrust was taken by a thrust washer on each side of the centre main bearing. They were split across their diameters, and each half had a lug which located in a recess in the main bearing.

The front crankshaft oil seal was a felt ring in the timing cover, but the rear seal was dramatically different. Going back to the Austin Ten 1932 design, the rear of the crank had a scroll or coarse-pitched thread cut into it where it passed through the rear of the block/rear main bearing cap. The idea was that oil which escaped behind the main bearing was 'screwed' forwards again by the scroll and into a reservoir in the rear of the main bearing cap, from whence it returned to join its legitimate route. Not unnaturally, some oil 'escaped' and one had to live with the odd drip of oil from the gearbox bellhousing which became progressively worse as the engine wore. Indeed, when the engine became 1800 cc some fifteen years later, the initial use of a three main bearing crank allowed rather too much crank whip. Then, if too much wear was allowed to go unchecked, the rear scroll would bash itself against both block and main bearing cap, damaging them and putting the engine beyond economic repair. But to be fair, the system was satisfactory for 1954, bearing in mind the lack of the modern type of efficient artificial-rubber seal. The crankshaft itself had main bearings of 2 in. diameter instead of the A40's $1\frac{7}{8}$ in. and crankpins of $1\frac{7}{8}$ in. diameter instead of $1\frac{3}{4}$ in. The white-metal Vandervell bearings were of the type fitted to the A40 and even to the Austin Ten in 1939, Austin being the first company in the world to use this now universal type of thin-wall bearing.

The B-series block design was in many ways a development of the A40 block, which in turn had an even greater superficial affinity to the Austin Ten block. Rather than follow the postwar trend towards ending the cylinder block/crankcase casting on the centre line of the crankshaft, the Austin designers felt that they would retain a great deal of strength by continuing the crankcase well below the crank centre-line. It had the disadvantage that the end main bearings were even more expensive than they otherwise would have been because they had to be machined to slide tightly into the crankcase end wall and up to the crank, but the extra depth gave the engine a good deal more rigidity, and it appreciably stiffened up the area of the connection to the gearbox, where there was of course a good deal of stress, the engine gearbox unit being held in position only at the front of the engine and rear of the gearbox. There was also the beneficial side-effect of the bottom of the crankcase presenting the sump with a smooth, level surface and making the sump pressing simpler and more potentially leak-proof, although there were plenty of other places on the typical B-series engine that seemed to more than make up for it! Because the first engines went into several models of car, different sumps were required. Different designs of cross-members, steering racks or steering boxes meant different sump shapes were required and these pressed-steel components were easily produced according to requirements.

The oil feed to the big-end bearings has already been mentioned and also the positioning of the oil pump, which was of the Hobourn-Eaton eccentric rotor type. Eric Bareham's notebooks show that Bill Appleby demanded a higher output from the oil pump than had previously been achieved and this no doubt contributed to the efficiency of the whole lubrication system. In turn, this certainly had a great deal to do with the long life expectancy of the engines. (Another factor was BMC's noted use of quality materials. Bill Appleby was to say that only the best, 'Rolls-Royce quality' materials were used, no reclaimed metals were considered acceptable 'Unlike those at Ford . . . !') From the pump, oil passed through internal oilways to a non-adjustable pressure relief valve situated on the right of the crankcase at the rear of the engine. The conical-shaped valve inside was held in position by a coil spring, itself positioned by two fibre washers and the domed screw plug.

From there, the oil was passed into the main oil gallery on the right-hand side of the engine at a pressure of between 55 and 60 lb per sq in. Cast integrally into the oil gallery part of the block was the oil filter mounting. The filter itself began as a by-pass type so that only a proportion of the oil received passed through it, although it was conventionally a very fine type of filter. From this main oil gallery, the oil passed through drillings to the main bearings, where oil was fed in at four

equidistant points. From the main bearings, oil entered drillings in the crankshaft, the end main bearings feeding numbers 1 and 4 big ends respectively and the centre main bearings feeding numbers 2 and 3. There, each crankpin received its oil in two doses, as already described. Oil was also fed along each connecting rod, the drilling ending in a hole at the base of each little end. The result was that oil was squirted out on to the cylinder wall, just as it had been on the A40, making sure that the cylinder walls were well lubricated, which is essentially important with an engine starting from cold.

From the main bearings, oil passed through further passages and up to the camshaft bearings. Oil from the rear camshaft passed upwards through a drilling in the block to the rocker shaft rear bracket, from whence it lubricated the rockers and pushrod cups before draining back through the pushrod apertures and back into the sump. The valve tappets were lubricated both by this draining oil and by oil pumped at low pressure from the centre camshaft bearing after passing along a cast-in gallery, while the front camshaft passed small quantities of oil into the timing case, where it lubricated the timing chains, gears and the Renolds tensioner. A drain hole was situated in the bottom of the timing case through which excess oil passed into the sump.

Just as on the A40, the timing cover was designed to fit both the Austin small- and medium-sized engines, which was logical in view of the fact that they shared most of their timing gear. In fact, because the B-series engine was fitted with the Renolds tensioner, the early A-series engine also had to have a timing chain cover with a bump in it—even though there was nothing inside the bump!

After a very short while in production, it was decided to fit lead-indium bearings to the B-series engine in place of the original white metal. In June 1952, lead-indium was pencilled in for the A90 engines; a month later an A30 engine was put

OVERLEAF
At the end of another ghostly transfer machine line, a developing flow of cylinder heads are coming to fruition. Here it would appear that one of the 'plattens', the cutter guides, is being lifted from the line, perhaps ready to be fitted with another head casting and returned to the start of the machine line

on trial with these bearings and in September Dr Weaving, who headed the experimental side of things over in East Works and who was carrying out work on a supercharged B-series prototype, requested lead-indium bearings for his speedy toys.

It later became apparent that it would be necessary to go to lead-indium on all B-series production engines. This meant that a more expensive full-flow filtration system would have to be fitted, because while white metal would tolerate tiny particles in the oil, the harder (but much harder wearing) lead-indium bearings would not. Unfortunately, the B-series oil filter housing had first been designed for the A40 Somerset engine as a way of doing away with the 10 hp and Devon/Dorset external pipework. Following the Somerset pattern, the B-series

engine internal oil gallery only allowed for a certain random percentage of oil to be pushed through the oil filter, while what was now needed was a system which would push all the oil through the filter. It meant going back to external pipework again! Instead of oil being allowed to pass along the main oil gallery down the right-hand side of the engine, with a proportion of the oil finding its way through the filter and the rest being fed through the engine at three points into the main bearings, it was necessary to pass the oil by a different route. The main feed from the pump was blanked off where it entered the rear of the oil gallery and instead the oil passed out of the block and into a large external pipe. The filter housing was modified by the not perfectly satisfactory means of fitting an adapter plate between the filter and filter housing into which the external pipe fed

Larger-than-life personality Bob Grice was, at the time of the B-series launch, responsible for all BMC's testing and as such bore a heavy responsibility for ensuring that the engine's life expectancy was satisfactory. Between them Bareham and Grice bequeathed one of the most reliable and long-lasting mass produced car engines of all time

the main stream of oil. This pushed the oil into the filter housing, where it passed through the filter before rising up through the filter body and back into the main internal oil gallery. Because the gallery had been blanked off at its rear end, there was no short-circuiting of oil and the oil was fed out of the gallery and into the main bearings in the normal way. The first full-flow filter elements were made of felt, but later ones were of the paper type which are used today.

Eric Bareham had been involved in adapting the original A40 block to accept an integral filter. Johnny Rix had told him, 'We'll build the filter on to the engine', and they did so, the filter projecting at an angle where the original filter had bolted on in an upright position. There had been no problem fitting it into the Somerset, but when the new Cambridge came out and the filter was left in the same position on the B-series engine as it had been on the A40 unit, it was necessary to cut a hole in the cross-member to accommodate it, Eric remembers. 'The original filter was easier to remove than the full-flow type,' he was to say.

B-series pistons were made in a low-expansion aluminium alloy and were of the split-skirt type with an anodized surface finish. They were made with alternative crown concavities to provide compression ratios of 7.2:1 on most cars and 8.3:1 on MGs. They were built slightly differently to the A40 type in that they were given an additional ring per cylinder, which was found to significantly improve oil consumption. In all, four rings were fitted: a chrome-faced parallel top ring, taper-faced 2nd and 3rd and a slotted scraper 4th ring. Eric Bareham felt in his lecture to the Institute of Mechanical Engineers that, 'This combination has been proved to give good oil control over extended periods, together with a minimum of blow-by. The chrome-faced type of top ring is a comparatively recent innovation, and while it takes rather longer than a plain-faced ring to bed into the cylinder wall, it does reduce cylinder bore and piston ring wear.'

MG engines, capable of higher revs, were fitted with solid-skirt pistons and also had rather narrower rings.

Pistons were held to the connecting rods by a clamped-type small end. High-performance engines used a floating type of gudgeon pin which was steadily being adopted by other manufacturers, which let BMC in for a bit of stick for holding on to the clamped type. Bareham defended the use of clamped gudgeon pins on

several grounds: floating gudgeon pins could rapidly become noisy as they wore; they needed selective (and time-consuming) assembly of parts to ensure the minimum initial working clearance; and the clamped type could be made smaller in diameter than a floating type owing to the solid support given to the central portion by the connecting rod boss. The gudgeon pins themselves were made from EN34 steel and their inner bores were reamed as well as drilled, as this was found to prevent them cracking from the inside. The connecting rods themselves were of H-section and were forged from 55-ton steel, which was then hardened and tempered.

Although other manufacturers commonly used a lower-quality steel for the con-rods in order to increase the life of the stamping dies, BMC design management were insistent that the steel used for the con-rods should be of a standard that would compare with the steel used for the manufacture of the crankshaft, while at the bottom of each con-rod, the tradition of splitting the big ends diagonally was continued. This meant that a slightly greater stroke could be squeezed out of the existing confines of the camshaft as already explained, and it also meant that the pistons could be pushed out and refitted through the tops of the bores, which made it much easier to compress the piston rings. The point was that if the big ends had been split horizontally the effective width of the big end would have been too great for it to pass upwards through the bore.

In May 1953, Eric Bareham carried out an experiment to de-siamese the B-series cylinder head inlet ports 'to try to improve power at low speeds,' as his notes at the time explained. The inlet ports began with a shape of $\frac{13}{16}$ in. diameter, but Eric's proposal was to pass a $\frac{3}{4}$ in. cutter down the ports to give a shape rather like a square but with rounded corners. Then a $\frac{1}{16}$ in. $\times$ $\frac{1}{16}$ in. groove was to be milled down the top and bottom walls of the tract and a plate inserted, dividing the port into two. This ingenious idea was never adopted, as the tradition of siamesed inlet ports, siamesed centre exhaust port but separate exhaust ports for the outer two cylinders was continued. Also, the combined inlet/exhaust manifold was carried forward from the A40 engine, including the use of a hot-spot. Interestingly enough, Austin were to continue to fit a Zenith down-draught carburettor right up until the 1959 A55 Mk II's time, when they joined the ex-Nuffield companies in using the semi-down draught SU carburettor. (Other, non-BMC users of the B-series engine chose between SU, Zenith or Solex carbs, while for certain industrial uses, where the engine was later developed to run on TVO fuel, a bi-fuel updraught carburettor was fitted.) MG models used an aluminium inlet manifold with twin hot-spots and a pair of SU HD4 carburettors.

Almost all of the ignition and electrical components were taken from the Lucas off-the-peg range, found on so many British cars. The coil was the Lucas LA12 oil-filled type, clamped to the dynamo body to ensure a good earth connection to the engine together with a minimum length of distributor HT lead, for the sake of efficiency and reduced radio interference, a problem that had hardly figured at all in earlier car designs. The distributor was the Lucas DM2, with centrifugal and suction advance mechanisms, and the spark plugs were Champion N5s. The first type of dynamo fitted, the Lucas C39, gave a charging rate of 19 amps, but this was rapidly superseded by the C40 with 22 amps, again an indication that these were the first days of the modern boom in in-car equipment and accessories with their ever-increasing demand upon a car's electrical output.

So, by a process of gradual development, deliberate conservatism in design coupled to a determination on the part of Austin to produce an engine to high standards of reliability, the B-series engine was made ready for fitting to the enormously important middle range of BMC cars. The cars themselves were the Austin A40 Cambridge and the Morris Cowley, both fitted with the 1200 cc engine, while the $1\frac{1}{2}$-litre version was used in the Austin A50 Cambridge, the Morris Oxford and the 'J' series of 10-cwt commercial vehicles as well as the Nash Metropolitan. In twin-carburettor form, the engine saw use in the MG Magnette and the MGA. Small wonder that, by as early as mid-1956, by which time more than a quarter of a million of the engines had been built, at a rate of more than 4500 per week, *The Motor* could say, 'It is probable that this engine is lurking under more British car bonnets than any other type,' and there had certainly never been a British motor car engine built in such prolific numbers.

3 Testing and introduction

With so much at stake, the engine had to be a success, right from the word go. Next to Johnny Rix and Eric Bareham, the engine's designers, the most important cog in the machine for ensuring that the engine did not fail was chief of testing, Bob Grice. He was a man who had started as an apprentice at Austin in the 1920s, and describes himself as having been 'spotted' by Herbert Austin as a rising star, from where he rose steadily up the hierarchy until he ended his days with BMH and BL as a joint MD at Jaguar. With BMC, he was very much in the ascendant, and explained that he had so many jobs, being responsible for testing, BMC motor sport and the royal family's BMC cars, that, 'I spent some days not knowing whether I was punched, bored or countersunk.' However, testing the cars was his main brief, and in the light of the almost disastrous fiasco of the A40 front suspension units, he says that neither Lord nor George Harriman ever queried his team's rejection of components because of doubts about their reliability, no matter how much it threw a spanner into the schedules: they knew that there was far more to lose if huge service costs were incurred. Bill Appleby, head of engine design, had no such inhibitions about letting Bob Grice know if he disagreed with the testers' decisions about a component's reliability. However, even he could get nowhere with Bob Grice, who had to formally 'sign-off' every new component or modification. As Bob Grice made clear with the B-series engine, there were no compromises! Talking about his close friend until his death in 1983, Bob Grice said with a chuckle, 'Appleby was the sort of fellow who got hot and bothered about such things—but *he* could never have the last say!'

The test schedule devised in the aftermath of the A40 failures was a gruelling one both for the cars and for the staff concerned, although the locations no doubt brought their own consolations! Prototype cars were sent off on a trial run lasting for six to eight weeks with a team of as many as forty-five to fifty people accompanying them, according to Bob Grice. From Longbridge, the entourage would drive to Dover, from where they would be shipped over to Boulogne. The first run was non-stop, all the way down to Bordeaux on the west coast of France, broken only by stops for fuel. Even in these days of comfortable motor cars and *autoroutes*, the trip is a long one, so in the early 1950s, it must have been quite a test of machines and men. After an overnight stay in Bordeaux, the team would drive down the coast, through Aquitaine and the now-trendy resort of Biarritz to cross over into Spain and on to San Sebastian. From there, the trip took them through Madrid and Seville and into the Rio Tinto mining area, where the dusty roads were used to check the vehicles for dust entry. Then they would move off to Algeciras, near Gibraltar, and Malaga, where they would stop for three days of endurance testing around Granada. The cars were taken up the Sierra Nevada mountains, where, as Bob Grice recalls, 'If you left a pen in your inside pocket, by the time you got to the top, the drop in pressure would smother your shirt in ink.' From Granada, they moved to Valencia, through Barcelona and back into France on the Mediterranean side of the border, passing through Perpignan, Carcassonne and then right back through central France to the port. 'I couldn't spend all my time in France and Spain, so I used to fly backwards and forwards, to and from Gib., Toulouse or wherever,' Grice said.

It would seem that a batch of prototypes was tested in this way, and then a batch of early production cars was put through the same

gruelling regime. As a further check, a sample of cars was taken from the production line every day and put through a somewhat less demanding schedule designed to pick up production rather than design problems. Three production vehicles would be taken out and each given three 200-mile runs, often out into Herefordshire and mid-Wales, to check oil, fuel and water consumption and so check that each B-series engine fell within certain performance and reliability limits. If problems were found, it was necessary to pin the fault down and if they were found to belong 'in-house', they were put right there and then, and, indeed, if a problem was potentially expensive enough, it was possible for the testing department to issue a red 'Stop' note, which instantly prevented further cars leaving the production line, according to Bob Grice, but of course a fault would have to be a very severe one before such a

MG fought fiercely to retain their individuality and succeeded in having a number of modifications made both to the engines for their own use and in some cases, right across the range as Eric Bareham's notebooks testify. The cast aluminium alloy chamber linking twin SU carburettors to air filter, decorated with a heavily raised MG badge added a touch of class to the ZA Magnette engine bay

dramatic step was taken. If a fault was found with a batch of bought-in components, such as distributors for instance, Bob Grice tells how that company's technical managers were called in and confronted with the evidence, the faulty components being compared with the 'master' specifications laid down when the component was originally designed.

As well as setting new production records, the

B-series engine joined the A-series with a more prosaic sort of 'first'. Its production methods were a radical improvement on anything that had gone before, forming part of Leonard Lord's pre-merger plans for a more streamlined, more efficient Longbridge. Once again, the antecedents for such developments went back to pre-war days and leaned heavily on the chance coming together of personalities who were to be working together in alignment after the war. When Morris, at the height of his expansionism, bought out his axle supplier, E. G. Wrigley & Co of Smethwick in the mid-1920s, he also 'acquired' Wrigley's general manager, Frank Woollard, a young and dynamic production engineer. Woollard became responsible for Morris' engine factory at Gosford Street, Coventry, and, although his ideas were ahead of the technology available to him, he revolutionized the production of engines. Miles Thomas one time Nuffield chief described the man and his achievements in saying, 'In Frank Woollard I saw the genius of a man who realized that, by arranging machine tools in a factory so that there was the minimum movement of a component like a heavy cylinder block between one operation and the next, manual effort, which meant time, which meant money, could be saved. Woollard was really the father of mass production machining in England. His ideas were the forerunners of the "transfer" multiple machine tool lines that today (around 1963, the time that Thomas was writing) are commonplace both in America and in this country.'

Woollard's influence may have had no direct bearing on the B-series story were it not for the fact that, as Thomas went on to say in his book *Out On a Wing*, 'And in the production planning office there was a sharp-faced young ginger-haired Yorkshire lad about the same age as myself, a tough far-sighted character named Len Lord, who recognized the philosophy behind Woollard's broad conceptions and who worked diligently on machine-tool layout and development to bring that idealism as near into effect as was possible. There was also a dynamic, fast-talking, fast-walking, bowler-hatted works manager called George Harriman, who strove to get the maximum output from the existing plant and manpower. He had a son of the same name. "Young George" Harriman and Len Lord struck up a friendship, a friendship that has blossomed over the years into a very great asset not only for the British motor industry but for the British

international economy as well.' How small the mills of God do grind!

In production terms, in terms of reliability, the new engines were a great success, but how good were the first cars they were fitted to? *The Motor* noted in their September 1954 feature on the new cars that the body was shorter, lower and narrower than the old A40 models, but with more room inside, the extra room coming about because of the space-saving chassisless construction and a longer wheelbase. 'Other modifications to the engine', they said, 'are of that unexciting type which so often mean all the difference between a trouble-free unit and one subject to minor bothers.' The all-new gearbox that accompanied the new engine was liked. 'Great pains have been taken to make the latest A40 gear change both light and instantaneous. To this end, the baulk-ring pattern of synchromesh has been adopted, and all gear wheels are now chamfered to ensure that there will be no difficulty in engaging first or second gear when the car is stationary.' The magazine also pointed out that the cable-operated column-gear-change mechanism had been improved by alteration to a rod linkage arrangement and that the final drive was higher on 1200 as well as 1500 models: up from the 5.28 of the Somerset to 5.125 for the smaller-engined car and 4.875 for the larger. The magazine's later full road test described the gearbox as 'an astonishing improvement', the engine's flexibility as 'most remarkable' and the steering as 'much improved' when compared with the model's predecessors, although a degree of understeer was noted, which was not the last time such comments were to be made about cars fitted with the B-series engine, excessive weight being one of its few faults.

Also in September 1954, *The Motor* put a Morris Oxford (Series II) with the B-series $1\frac{1}{2}$-litre engine through its paces saying, 'Superlatives can have little place in this report, for its subject is a car of all-round merit which sells at a moderate cost, invoking neither eulogistic praise of individual excellent features nor fierce condemnation of particular shortcomings.' Unlike the Cambridge, the new Oxford actually had a larger body than its predecessor, but nevertheless the new engine proved its worth in terms of overall fuel returns of 28.2 mpg for the new compared with the 25.7 of the old Oxford. Once again, understeer was the item picked out for greatest criticism, this tester going further with, 'Carrying its weight slightly farther forward than previously, this latest car understeers quite emphatically when travelling on dry roads, where it is stable but has to be pulled into a corner. Wet and slippery surfaces show up a slightly less predictable side of its character. . . .' Another criticism reflected typical dashboard design of the time, when neither aesthetics nor ergonomics seemed to count for much. 'Head-lamp switches which are on the fascia panel cannot be reached without leaning forward; pushing in the switch to turn off the self-parking windscreen wipers being most easily done with the left foot!'

Rather more excitement was generated by the B-series-engined car to be released first of all, the MG Magnette Saloon, which was first shown at the 1953 London Motor Show. But what were the BMC publicity people thinking of? *Autosport* tested their editor's own machine for the July 1954 issue, reporting that no demonstration cars had been made available by the company. By November, *The Autocar* had got hold of one and both magazines liked the car. The looks of the car were appreciated ('At the Motor Show it looked like the British equivalent of an expensive continental "Gran Turismo" machine'—*Autosport*), as was its gearbox ('. . . the practical, central gear lever can be moved from one position to another just as fast as the driver can move his hand. The synchromesh is good and cannot be beaten'—*The Autocar*) and its speed potential ('Make no mistake about it; the machine does qualify for the term "high performance"'). In fact, the extra power, superior handling and attractive MG interior made the Magnette a perfect family car with sporting pretensions, rather in the mould of the latter-day 3-series BMWs and Lancia Beta coupés.

In 1955, the MG MGA arrived on the scene at a time when the last of the Midgets—the TF—was out of production, and its open-topped successor had not begun. The MGA was praised by *The Motor* for its mechanical simplicity allied to performance that made it worthy of its famed initials with safety and comfort—in the terms of sports cars of its day—to boot. Its 68 bhp (raised to 72 bhp soon after the car's launch) and unladen weight of below 1600 lb made for performance that was 'interesting', while *The Motor* felt that its selling price of £595 would be 'highly competitive' when considering all that it had to offer.

*The MGA launched in 1955, demonstrated the sheer
versatility of the B-series engine. Not only could it power
the slogging, plodding Light Commercial Vehicles coming
from BMC, it could also cause a high-speed sensation when
tuned for sports car use!*

4 Phase 2—B-series to BL

From 1954 and throughout most of the next decade and a half, B-series engines were produced in quantity, sold to an increasing number of non-BMC users (outside sales were referred to as 'loose engine sales' within the company) and developed in ways that were possible because of the wisdom of having developed the B-series as such a robust engine with so much in reserve in the first place.

Since the engine could not be attributed to one marque name within BMC—each development of the engine was shared between models, apart from the special case of the MG twin-cam 1588 cc engine and the 1588 cc pushrod version that followed it—it makes sense to look at the engine's development chronologically rather than by a model name at a time.

1953

In October, the MG Magnette was introduced with a 60 bhp 1498 cc engine and a 7.2:1 compression ratio that was the norm when the B-series engine was fitted to later saloons but with twin SU carburettors. Complaints of valve crash at 5100 rpm led to use of stronger valve springs for all B-series engines. (Specified at Longbridge 12/11/53.)

A new Weslake-designed cylinder head with modified inlet ports, inlet valve guides and combustion chambers was issued by Longbridge 13/11/53. (1953 Magnettes presumably did not have this head fitted to them.)

On 24 November 1953, Eric Bareham set in train designs for a B-series diesel engine under the note '1600 cc B-type Diesel Engine', and considered the possibility of 1540 cc, 1600 cc and 1612 cc, none of which actually came to fruition.

On the same date, the 1498 cc, B-series engine with 8:1 compression ratio pistons was issued 'for MG Midget', although the compression ratio was to become 8.3:1 by the time the car was launched as the MGA.

1954

Throughout the early part of the year, a whole string of modifications was made to minor details, including increasing the length of the rocker arm ball pin after complaints from MG, deleting the ticklers from the SU carburettors (May 1954) and introducing the high-frequency induction hardening of all B-series bores. Also from May 1954, the oil pump was modified, and in September a change was made to the fuel pump mounting: studs were substituted for set screws to prevent damage to the gasket during assembly. Apart from the fuel pump business (the Magnette had a rear-mounted SU pump), it looks very much as though the Magnette was something of a test bed for the main but piecemeal introduction of B-series-engined cars in May 1954, when the 1500 cc Morris Oxford Series II appeared, in July 1954, when the 1200 cc Morris Cowley was launched and October 1954, when the 1200 cc Austin A40 Cambridge and 1498 cc Morris Cowley 1500 and Austin A50 Cambridge made their appearances.

OPPOSITE ABOVE
When the Morris Minor became a candidate for a larger engine, BMC went a step further and fitted new outer body panels to completely disguise the car's origins. The Wolseley Fifteen-Hundred was based on a Minor floorpan and used a B-series engine and gearbox

OPPOSITE BELOW
The Riley version of the car, known as One-Point-Five, had a twin-carburettor engine, larger brakes and a more luxurious interior

Estate car versions appeared in October 1954 as well, when the Morris Oxford Traveller and Austin A40 Countryman (note, there was no A50 Countryman, strangely enough) made their entrance.

In August 1953 the Nash Metropolitan 'sports' car, the result of a tripartite agreement between the Nash Corporation in the US, Austin in the UK and also Fisher & Ludlow, had emerged. Fisher & Ludlow were to build the bodies, Austin assemble them and Nash distribute them under the Nash and occasionally Hudson labels. When Fisher & Ludlow became part of BMC, the arrangements changed slightly, of course. Introduced with the A40 1200 cc engine, the car was enlivened with the 1500 cc B-series engine in August 1954 for the US market.

1955

In October, the MGA was launched with a 1498 cc engine, tuned with larger valves, thinner piston rings, solid-skirt pistons (in place of the lighter but weaker split-skirt type fitted to other models) and double valve springs, plus a higher compression ratio. No MG sports car had been available for some months, since the MG TF had been officially discontinued at the end of 1954.

1956

ZA MG Magnettes were supplanted by the ZB Magnette in October, available in plain or 'Varitone' twin-colour schemes and in manual or 'Manumatic' versions. The 'Varitone' version, incredible though it seems, had slightly different bodywork, with a larger rear window and chrome trim strips that extended along the bonnet sides, the door handle line and the rear wing and signalled the line where the two colours met. (Anders Clausager, British Motor Industry Heritage Trust archivist, has actually come across a handful of non-duotone Varitones and has found that the larger rear window was a 'knife and fork' job carried out on the basic bodyshell, which otherwise remained unchanged.) The ZB's engine was up from 60 to 68 bhp, to match the output of the original MGA, although the output of that car was now raised a little to 72 bhp. The ZB Magnettes also boasted a higher final-drive ratio.

The Wolseley 4/44, which had been introduced in 1952, looked very similar to the ZA Magnette (and in fact both were designed by the Nuffield man, Gerald Palmer), but actually shared only its roof panel, boot lid and front doors according to

RIGHT
Even the Wolseley was very comfortably fitted out with leather seats and a wooden dash. In their day, both cars were an excellent compromise between economy of space, comfort and performance

BELOW
In 1959, BMC took the logic of a common engine and gearbox a stage further and introduced a common body for Morris, Austin, MG, Riley and Wolseley saloons. It was designed by the Italian styling house of Pinin Farina but by 1961, the leading dimensions were subtly altered to give more rear seat room and truncated rear fins. Strangely, the MG and Riley versions of the car reverted to a more typically BMC defiance of logic and retained the old body style. Very strange!

Anders Clausager; since the ZA was two inches lower than the 4/44, its wheel arches, rear doors and then the remainder of the body had been modified. The 4/44 was *not* fitted with the B-series engine, however, until June 1956, when it then became known as the Fifteen-Fifty (Fifteen hundred cc; fifty bhp) but continued with the same body. In October, Manumatic transmission found its way on to that model, too. The B-series engine for the Fifteen-Fifty was in its standard non-MG form, but required a modified sump to enable it to fit over the Wolseley's cross-member, but then having to fit different sumps for different models was a familiar pastime for the BMC design engineers.

In December 1956, the 'Nash' Metropolitan became available on the UK and other non-US markets with a badge change to *Austin* Metropolitan which did nothing for its strange looks or diabolical handling, all available in fixed-head or drop-head form.

1957

Some time in 1954–55, Leonard Lord announced to the Cowley design office that he and Dick Burzi had designed a 'new' Morris Minor at Longbridge. The car arrived in April 1957, but the Minor continued much as before, while the new car, essentially a re-bodied Minor with B-series, 1489 cc engine, was called a Wolseley Fifteen-Hundred. In fact, few people recognized the car's Minor derived backbone at all! The plush interior, 'B-series' gearbox and high, 3.73:1, final drive ratio in the almost standard Minor rear axle made the car effortless and comfortable with an air of luxury. BMC went one better, when in November they introduced the Riley version with an engine in early-MGA stage of tune, the same gearbox but an even higher rear axle ratio and larger brakes, made by Girling, compared with the Wolseley's use of Lockheed units. *The Autocar* liked the car very much, describing it as 'amazingly smooth and willing' with an engine that would reach 6000 rpm without fuss.

At least one prototype Morris Minor replacement with a $1\frac{1}{2}$-litre engine and Wolseley-like bodywork was completed, but it was never introduced.

This Wolseley 16/60 belonging to Robert and Mary Thompson shows the later body styling which accompanied the use of an enlarged 1622 cc engine

The last production Austin A50 cars had been fitted with 13 in. wheels and these were continued on to the A55 Mk I, which was introduced in February 1957, its rear end having been redesigned to match those of the C-series six-cylinder-engined cars. The engine now had a compression ratio of 8.3:1, which knocked a couple of seconds off its 0–50 time, in spite of its having longer bodywork. Morris Oxfords continued unchanged except that the 'Traveller' estate car no longer had charming but expensive 'half-timbering' but became an 'all-steel' body. Strangely, no Austin A40, A50 or A55 Countryman was listed (one did not reappear until 1959) and the year saw the last of the under-powered and ill-equipped Cowley and the A40, marking the end of the B-series engine in 1200 cc form, although the 'economy' version of the Oxford, the Cowley 1500, was to continue until 1959.

1958

The Morris '1½-litre Minor' prototype was put to use when the Austin Lancer and Morris Major were built in the BMC factory (ex-Nuffield) at Victoria Park, Sydney, Australia, in a new £A13 million plant, representing a step towards local production rather than assembly. The Austin had utilitarian trim with A55-style instrument panels and instruments in front of the driver, and it carried an upright Wolseley-like grille. The Morris Major had an oval grille, different sidelights and centrally mounted instruments. Both models were relatively unsuccessful, despite being redesigned for 1959 with more massive bodywork, and were withdrawn in 1962 when their B-series engines were taken over by a rather more spectacular B-series venture, the 'Blue-Streak' six-cylinder unit.

For a couple of years, Morris' engine plant at Coventry under Eddie Maher and Austin's experimental engineering under Dr Weaving at Longbridge's East Works had been experimenting with exciting overhead-cam versions of the B-series engine, and in fact both were run in the 1955 TT race in Northern Ireland and speed record attempts in 1956 and 1957. The Longbridge engine used gear-driven camshafts, while the

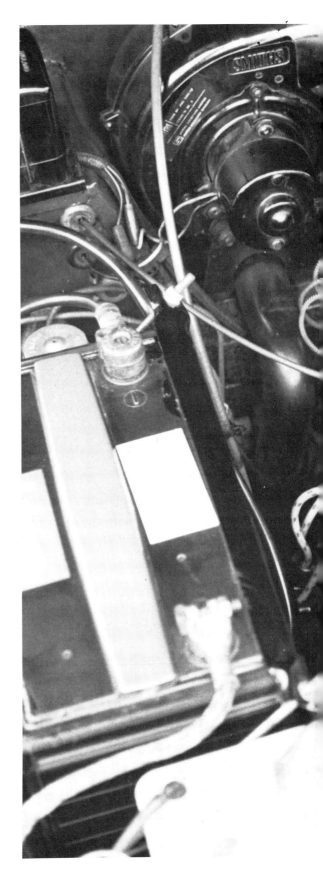

MG Magnettes soon stopped looking as good as this! Although the air filter and twin carbs disguise the fact, access to the engine was actually remarkably good . . .

. . . as shown by this shot of a Cambridge with most ancillaries removed

Morris engine, based on a 1954 design by Gerald Palmer, was chain driven, and it was that engine that found favour for use in the MGA Twin-Cam, introduced in July 1958. The engine was *based* upon the B-series engine, but was dramatically different. With a bore of 1588 cc, the engine was bored out and the water jackets re-cored, the old camshaft becoming simply a jack shaft driving the distributor and oil pump. The head was entirely different, of course, and was made of aluminium alloy with carburettors mounted on the opposite side to the normally situated exhaust manifold. This meant that the distributor had to be moved, and so it was placed on the large, cast front cover, while the dipstick was mounted at the left-rear of the engine and stretched all the way down to make a direct entry into the special cast, finned aluminium alloy sump. The twin $1\frac{3}{4}$ in. SU carburettors, bucket-type tappets and valves at an included angle of $80°$, and the high 9.9:1

compression ratio, topped off the formidable package, formidable that is, in terms of cost and complexity and in terms of fickleness, but in the end only giving around 108 bhp, which sounded a lot but certainly was not a very cost-effective way of gaining such power. To make matters worse, the engine had a habit of gobbling pistons, slight imperfections in ignition timing or a drop below the 100 octane fuel necessary to keep the thing cool leading to burned-out pistons. It was dearer than the faster Austin-Healey 100/6, much dearer than the Triumph TR3A, which was also faster to around 80 mph, and owners would not put up with the high oil consumption record of the first 345 engines, caused by using chromed piston

rings with chrome molybdenum treatment for the cylinder bores, while BMC's acknowledgement that the compression ratio was too high by the introduction of 8.3:1 pistons in mid-1959 came too late. Morris Engine's unhappy reputation had continued, and by the time the car ceased production in early 1960, only 2111 Twin-Cams had been built.

In December 1958, a highly significant new model the Wolseley 15/60 was launched, but the story of the Farina-bodied cars belongs fully to the following year:

1959

Leonard Lord's BMC had attempted to commonize components as far as possible, but it was taking time to get the expensive trappings of the individual marque out of the system. In December 1958, a new body style had been launched on the Wolseley 15/60, designed by

Later in the day with the head taken off, the increased bore size shows that cylinder 1 and 2; 3 and 4 were felt to be already too close to allow very much more enlargement (although the Indian Hindustan Ambassador B-series engines are at around 1750 cc with the same bore centres and no apparent problems) and so the block was redesigned to allow BMC to get to 1798 cc

OVERLEAF
The 1800 engine was fitted to the Austin (and later Morris 1800 car, known colloquially as the Land-Crab) but gained most fame in the MGB, several examples of which are shown here at an early MG Owners Club meeting

Pinin Farina in Italy, and the same basic style was seen across the range of BMC medium-sized saloons on the Austin Cambridge Mk III (January 1959), the MG Magnette Mk III (February 1959), the Morris Oxford Series V (March 1959) and the Riley 4/Sixty-Eight (April 1969). All used the same body, although with slight panel differences to give styling changes, and different trim, and the same mechanical components, although the 1489 cc B-series engine was in twin-carburettor, higher-powered form in the Riley and MG cars. This model also marked Austin's break with a very long-standing tradition, when Zenith carburettors were dropped and SU carburettors used instead, the SU company being part of BMC, of course. This era saw the start of the height of BMC's rationalization policy coming into effect, with the greatest possible choice coming from the smallest possible use of components, apart from minor changes, of course. In 1959 and the following year, the B-series 1500 engine saw the widest possible use within the corporation. The Austin/Nash Metropolitan, an Austin, a Morris, an MG saloon and briefly an MG sports car, two models of Riley and two models of Wolseley all used exactly the same engine with only minor changes to the more powerful MG and Riley models. However, going rather against the current, the MGA went over to the Twin-Cam block size of 1588 cc from July 1959, an engine size that was never to be used in any other car! Admittedly, it allowed MG sports cars to compete more competitively in the under-1600 cc class and it gave an extra 7.5 bhp, but at what cost in production terms? No one at BMC at that time seems to have known the answers to such questions and there appears to have been little will to control such maverick exercises.

1960

In September, an Austin Cambridge Estate reappeared when the A55 Countryman was introduced, while, amazingly, BMC got their publicity act together for once and announced the Morris Oxford Series V Traveller at the same time.

At this time, both the 1622 cc version of the B-series engine and the 1798 cc version were under development. The 1622 engine was by now in its final stages, the development, according to Eric Bareham, being a very straightforward job of re-coring the water jackets to make room for larger bores on the same bore centres as before. The

1800 engine, an altogether more ambitious project, was brought forward in the development programme, reportedly because the Sid Enever-designed MGB in which it was to be placed was turning out to be heavier than anticipated and so would have been too slow if fitted with a smaller power source, while the ill-fated Twin-Cam was clearly not a realistic option as a way of increasing the car's power. The wisdom of Eric Bareham and others in having over-designed the B-series engine in the first place could now be seen in perspective. The block, extended over its A40 dimensions, had sufficient meat in it to allow expansion to a much greater capacity than was originally envisaged—aided partly by improvements in block casting techniques; but the curse of a $3\frac{1}{2}$ in. stroke already at its maximum was a problem that was now making its presence felt.

Bob Grice's son, Bob Grice junior, was also employed by BMC at this time and was involved in proving the 1800 engine on the roads. It was fitted to a Cambridge and driven up and down the new M1 motorway from one end to the other at a speed of just over 100 mph, he remembers. 'Then, when I got back, a relief driver would take over, and that's how it went until the end of the shift, when it was back to Longbridge, where another two drivers would take over. To the best of my memory, we would "prove" an engine by saying that it had to do 50,000 miles under flat-out driving conditions on something like a motorway or abroad on the German *autobahnen*—then I think it was 50,000 miles on the circuit to guarantee that the car could be driven flat-out the whole time, with no real interruptions, and there was also 50,000 under normal use, 50,000 at full throttle on the test bed and 50,000 going "through the cycles", where a cam, driven by a windscreen wiper motor, opened and closed the throttle, taking the engine through all its bad vibration frequencies.' Of course, as Bob Grice pointed out, no one engine could possibly do all of that, but BMC 'wanted 50,000 miles from all conditions from any one given assembled unit'.

1961

As so often in the past, the first from the stable with a new B-series engine was an MG. The MGA

Access to the engine in the MGB is 'finger-trappin', spanner-droppin', loud cursin' close, though nowhere near as difficult as in the MGA with its inadequately small bonnet opening

1600 Mk II was launched in June, superseding the anachronistically-engined 1588 cc car, and the Magnette Mk IV followed in September with the same capacity engine. The Cambridge, renamed as an A60, the Morris Oxford Series VI, Riley4/Seventy-Two and Wolseley Sixteen-Sixty in their various automatic, duotone and estate forms also received the beefier engine in October 1961. BMC took the opportunity to uprate the performance of the engines quite considerably, making changes to combustion chambers, valve sizes and ports, and pushing the MGA compression ratio up to 8.9:1. That the 1622 cc engine was so much of an improvement was borne out by the fact that it was only 2 per cent larger than the MGA's 1588 cc engine, but it was 12 per cent more powerful. The MG Magnette and Riley body styles, incidentally, were the only ones in the range not face-lifted at this stage.

The long-awaited diesel version of the B-series engine finally emerged, using the 1489 cc engine as its basis, but, naturally enough, with extensive redesigning having been carried out to cope with the extraordinary stresses suffered by such engines, not least that imposed by the 23:1 compression ratio. The J-series vans were the first recipients of the engine, and also the Austin Cambridge saloon, for export only.

1962

The diesel engine was fitted to the Austin Cambridge and also the Oxford Series VI for the home market, but it was not a successful diesel engine in any sense, and a noisy, smelly, underpowered (36.5 bhp) engine was most unsuited to the 'bread and butter' Farina range of cars.

In September, the MGB with the new 1800 engine was launched. The 1798 cc engine was grown from the 1200/1500 B-series unit, but only by siamesing numbers 1 and 2 and numbers 3 and 4 bores—in other words the water jackets were

No MG enthusiast worth his or her salt gives a care about tight maintenance, nor about the frequent jibes that Ford engines are so much quicker. Perhaps BL should have done more sooner to update the engine before being forced into a hole of their own digging, appropriately named the O-series, but any MGB owner knows that the B-series engine will outlive anything from Dagenham—and that performance is not that bad anyway!

removed from between these cylinders and the water jacket between numbers 2 and 3 was narrowed, which enabled the much larger bore to be fitted in. Even so, the bore centres had to be changed and the engine was widely redeveloped, its three main bearings being enlarged to help cope with the extra power.

1964

Once again MG had tested a new engine—but this time found it wanting! The three main bearings were found inadequate, and upon the insistence of Sid Enever at MG, who hated the amount of whip the 1800 crank was generating in his MGBs, the bottom end was redesigned to take five main bearings, which Eric Bareham described as being a rather difficult exercise because of the problem of squeezing the extra main bearings around the oil pump and distributor drive. The engine in its new form was used in the new Austin medium-sized car in the Issigonis idiom, the 1800, which should have replaced the Farina range—except that the Farina range stayed on! The 1800, it is generally felt, was much too large and lumbering for its class, but in fact it was a most comfortable car with far more room inside than even its ample external measurements would suggest, and it was a breakthrough in the sense that it was the first time the B-series engine had ever been mounted transversely.

Exports unlimited

Over the years many developments took place which did not fit within the pattern shown above. Engines were used for boating purposes by Messrs. Boats and Engines and later Newage Ltd,

In 1975, MGBs were fitted with rubber bumpers over strong body reinforcements and the ride was raised all to satisfy new US safety regulations. No one seems to want to say it, but this writer feels that the slightly re-styled car was a considerable improvement over the old one both in aesthetic and in sensible safety terms

OVERLEAF

Two-thirds of all MGBs built were exported to the USA which means that as a very rough guess (no figures are available) a little over half-a-million B-series engined cars found their way over the Atlantic, including the MGA and American versions of the Marina as well as a relative handful of other vehicles. In this shot, American enthusiasm for the MGB is demonstrated at an American MGB Association convention in New York State

and several small car builders such as Gilbern, Ginetta and Elva used the B-series engine for their rather sporting little cars, which gives some indication as to how tuneable the engine was and is. The engine was even used by two overseas makers, Hanomag in Germany and International Harvester in the United States, to power commercial vehicles. The Hanomag Tempo van was a front-wheel-drive van, coupling the BMC engine in-line to the German maker's own gearbox with trans-shafts (which was in fact the Vidal gearbox—Vidal having been taken over by Hanomag); the International Harvester panel van was less than an overwhelming success, however, and Eric Bareham had to visit the US to try to explain why the B-series engine was so short-lived in the IH van, coming to a conclusion that was not enthusiastically received by the International Harvester management—that too much was being asked of the engine in the sense that the vans were large, driven over long distances and inadequately cooled by the IH cooling system. Certainly, lack of longevity has never been a problem for the B-series engine in any other context! The uses for the B-series engine in the industrial context were too numerous to mention, powering industrial compressors, refrigeration systems and just about anything else that needed a steady, reliable, fairly portable power source in petrol or diesel form.

Two overseas developments were very interesting with regard to the B-series unit. The Indian company Hindustan Motors Ltd took its first steps in Anglo-Indian motoring co-operation in 1947 when Sir Miles Thomas, then head of the Nuffield group, negotiated with his opposite number, G. D. Birla, and his nephew B. M. Birla, on the building of British cars in India, the advantage to Nuffield being that they could then sidestep the Indian Government's opposition to car imports. A different grille and badge were designed for the Series M Morris, the components were manufactured in the UK and assembled in India and sold as the Hindustan 10. Next, the Morris Oxford Series MO (the one like an

Unfortunately, US emission regulations strangled the B-series engine to the extent that it was incapable of pushing the MGB much past 70 miles per hour! This shot shows the air injection pump fitted to the post-1975 MGB (Photo Steven E. Glochowsky)

overinflated split-screen Minor) was built there and known as the Hindustan 14, and then, later, the Morris Oxford Series II was reborn and built from scratch in India as the Hindustan Ambassador, complete with its Indian-built B-series engine. Over the years, the Ambassador has evolved steadily from the grille- and badge-changed Oxford as Hindustan's own modifications have been introduced, until by the early 1980s Mr T. Sinka, Hindustan's publicity manager, wrote to say that much of the Hindustan's trim was different to that of the old Morris, as well as some of the front panels, while Hindustan's own design of gearbox and clutch, prop shaft, rear axle and front brake drums and bearings were fitted. Although the standard 1498 cc engine in 50 bhp form was retained as an option, with its 7.2:1 compression ratio (but all Indian-built of course), an interesting Hindustan development with 'extra power to save you precious minutes in an emergency' as the catalogue put it, meant that Hindustan had done their own 'ultimate' B-series engine stretch to 1760 cc, which unlike the BMC stretch remained a three-bearing engine. Unfortunately, the car itself never used brakes larger than 8 in. drums, which must have given problems in hilly districts. However, as a functional, utterly reliable, easy-to-maintain car, the Oxford/Ambassador, complete with all-Indian modifications, is perfect for the job.

Another, this time slightly bizarre, development of the B-series, built for the Australian market, was the six-cylinder Blue Streak engine. This was designed and developed at Longbridge some time between 1953 and 1956, according to Stan Johnson. He remembers that the only problem lay with designing the crank, which was a four-main-bearing unit, but that otherwise the six-cylinder development of the B-series presented no real problems, being at first a B-series 1500 pure and simple with two extra 'pots', giving it a capacity of around 2250 cc, although it seems certain that, later on, the 1622 cc engine was six-cylinderized, too, and that this was the engine finally used in Australia, giving almost $2\frac{1}{2}$ litres. The engine was fitted to the 'Farina' Austin-type bodyshell and called the Austin Freeway and Wolseley 24/80 in more up-market form. Although designed at Longbridge, the so-called 'Blue Streak' engine was built in Australia in the plant built to make the Australian versions of the Wolseley 1500/Riley 1.5 and its longer-wheelbase Australian derivative. Datsun in Japan have also had their fingers in the B-series engine pie and probably quite extensively, too. Unfortunately, they seem a little coy about their involvement, probably being sensitive to the criticism that Japanese manufacturers are superb copiers but lousy innovators. Circumstantial evidence for Datsun's use of a B-series-type engine starts with the fact that Datsun bought the rights to produce the old A40 engine under licence, Stan Johnson remembering the sight of two Japanese gentlemen scuttling out of the factory clutching armfuls of drawings, 'an extraordinary sight right after the end of the Second World War,' and indeed he recalls that his first job at Austin started on 6 December 1945, working in the drawing office on the 1000/1200 cc engine and including the production of drawings for Datsun. From then on, the evidence becomes a bit apocryphal. David Garrett, much travelled chairman of the Morris Cowley, Oxford Club, has seen the Datsun J-type engine in many different parts of the world and in many different circumstances and he reckons that it is a 'dead ringer' for the B-series unit, to the extent that many of the parts are interchangeable! David has seen the J-series engine in the Datsun pick-up and believes it to have been used in the Bluebird, in both cases until the advent of the Datsun ohc engines. He remembers seeing a Datsun 1200 in Nairobi with what looked like a perfect B-series engine, but there was something wrong that he couldn't put his finger on. Then he suddenly realized that it was a mirror-image 'B-series' engine, with everything completely reversed!

5 BMC's sinking sixties

'The scope of the designers [was] greatly restricted by George Harriman's edict that BMC would not enter into head-on confrontation with the Ford Cortina. It is difficult to avoid the conclusion that this was the key error of judgement which, in a short time, left BMC's long-term future so weak that the Leyland takeover was inevitable. At one stroke it surrendered the centre of the market to Ford. . . .'—from *The Leyland Papers* by Graham Turner.

Shortly after the launch of the Mini in 1959, Leonard Lord took retirement and was elevated to the House of Lords. George Harriman took over control of the Corporation at a time when the design endeavours of the 1950s were coming to fruition and BMC's (or more accurately, the old Austin's) designers were continuing to come up with new ideas. The trouble was that Harriman seemed highly reluctant to prune back the old growth to allow the new to come through. By now an older man, and by all accounts a kindly, rather gentle soul, he seems to have been reluctant to bite the bullet. As a result, the BMC model range by 1967 was weighty to say the least. There were no fewer than five ranges of motor cars, encompassing no fewer than 28 models, not including the huge variety within each model range such as estates, automatics, and so on. Quite apart from the successful half a dozen sports cars, there was a large brood of Minis, which also formed a sensible and almost homogeneous group. But there reason ended. In spite of the introduction of the adventurously engineered 1800 in 1964, an answer to the critics of BMC's ultra-conventional pre-Issigonis approach, the huge range of Farina cars continued in production. In other words, two separate and distinct ranges of cars, both using the same engine and in competition with each other, were being built

simultaneously! Even worse, in the next class size down from the Cambridge–1800 size range were the A-series-engined Austin A40, the Morris Minor, the 1100 and 1300 ranges leaving the Minor-based, B-series-engined Wolseley 1500/Riley 1.5, as the only users of the now otherwise obsolete 1489 cc, B-series engine. In the 'flagship' class, where other makers were content with one model, BMC had three: the Vanden Plas Princess limousine, the C-series-engined Austin Westminster and the ill-conceived Austin 3-litre with MGC engine and rear-wheel drive.

This panoply of models, which must have numbered well over the hundred mark when badge-engineered derivatives and different body types were taken into account, represented a reckless frittering away of resources and of the high-volume principles upon which the two leading founders of the company had operated and upon which Leonard Lord had built. It made a lot of sense to base the model line-up on the A-, B-, C-series engines; it made a lot of sense to build the A-series and B-series units as 850 cc, 948 cc, 998 cc (although these two were illogically close together), 1098 cc, 1275 cc, 1489 cc, 1622 cc and 1798 cc; but it made no sense at all to plonk the engines into so many models of car, which meant, by definition, that they would be in competition with one another and so adversely affect each other's sales potential.

Sales potential, as an aspect of marketing, was another disaster for BMC in the 1960s. George Harriman is said to have planned for BMC production of the 1800 to reach 4000 per week, or around four times as many as the Farina. In practice, its largest-ever production run, averaged out over its best production year of 1971, reached the staggering total of 753 cars per week! The public gained a low opinion of the car: it was ugly, heavy to drive, switches and the handbrake were literally impossible to reach when strapped into a seat belt and the car was just too big and too heavy for its market slot. In 1970, *Motor* carried out a second-hand 'Buying' spot check on the car, commenting that, 'Since 1964 a number of modifications have been made to eliminate the car's faults; indeed so numerous have these been that a complete tally is outside the scope of this spot check.'

From B to E—and back . . .

Sadly, the B-series engine was showing its age by the mid-1960s, if indeed it had not done so before. In 1965, Eric Bareham was formally appointed assistant chief designer to Bill Appleby, whereupon Issigonis came across him at Longbridge, found that he was no mere administrator but a very fine draughtsman/designer in his own right and in Eric's own words, 'Issigonis exclaimed, "M'dear boy, you can draw!" and whipped me out from behind my desk to work with him on the E-series Maxi engine.' The engine began life as a 1300 cc and 1500 cc unit with a short-block, short-stroke 1150 cc engine developed as an option that was never taken up. With an alloy head and single-overhead camshaft the engine should have been a much more modern replacement for the venerable B-series unit and one that would slot into the original B-series size concept before the notion of the ever-expanding universe took the B-series engine sizes along with it, but with theoretically less weight and greater thermal efficiency. One would not expect people like Eric Bareham or Stan Johnson to be very proud of this Issigonis engine, however. For some reason, it turned out to be remarkably tall, with an old-fashioned long stroke—and it was disappointingly low on power because, although it produced 75 bhp at 5500 rpm to the 61 bhp at 5100 rpm of the Austin Cambridge, and although the maxi was around 20 per cent lighter than the Cambridge, it had higher gearing, accentuated by its 'overdrive' fifth gear, and more importantly, developed a great deal less torque than the Cambridge B-series 1622 cc unit. Torque is a more useful measure of power output for ordinary give-and-take driving because it is the characteristic that determines whether you have to change down early and whether or not there is sufficient low-down power to whisk you along without the uncomfortable feeling that the engine is labouring and having to be rowed along with the gear stick. The Maxi E-series 1485 cc

engine produced only 84 lb.ft at a high 3500 rpm (or, in other words, it was not pulling its maximum torque below 69 mph in fifth or, to be fair, a still high 55 mph in direct ratio fourth gear, while the good old 'Aunty' Cambridge pulled 90 lb ft at only 2100 rpm which represented only 37 mph. In other words, the B-series 1622 cc unit produced its greatest pulling power at high-road and by-road speeds, while the overhead camshaft E-series produced its maximum, which was lower anyway, just at the sort of speeds when it was least required! The larger and more powerful 1748 cc E-series, although never part of the original planning, came about purely because of the outraged cries from the motoring press and the public, who by 1969 and the time of the Maxi's launch, were starting to expect failure. But we go ahead of ourselves.

Before Eric Bareham went off to work on the E-series engine, he and Stan Johnson worked on a project that few people seem to know about but which later was to become a kind of political tennis ball, banged backwards and forwards between rival factions. At this early stage, there was no such antagonism, simply the prolific output of the Corporation at the time. Stan Johnson disclosed with some pride that, 'We made something like six 2-litre B-series engines in 1964–65. I was chief draughtsman at the time, but Eric was the boss, under Appleby. But I wouldn't want anything recorded against me—record it against Eric, because he was still in charge. 1 and 2; 3 and 4 cylinders were already siamesed at 1800. Now in order to get 2 litres we had to put the barrel up from 3.16 to 3.34 (but remember we were Imperial in those days) and we had to move numbers 2 and 3 barrels inwards towards one another and numbers 1 and 4 outwards, so we then got fully siamesed barrels with no water between any pair. We used an offset conrod, which allowed us to keep the main bearings exactly where they were before. I remember we credited the block with the part number 19E2934,' he said with the air of a proud father. 'And to this day,' he went on, 'those dimensions are the ones on the O-series. But that's another story. . . .'

While things were looking interesting and, superficially, even rosy at BMC in the early 1960s, at the top of the organization latent disaster was starting to form. Len Lord had never sought to reduce the number of marque names he inherited from the old Nuffield and Austin empire but

Some MGBs have been cannibalised and made into 'specials' like the GRP bodied car shown here. Even scrap MGBs command quite high prices, however, as interest in the cars is tremendously high and almost anything that has not been rolled up into a little ball in a smash can be restored

instead chose to make them work against each other, providing competitive edge for producers and dealers alike, and the public with the brand names they wanted. At the same time, he singularly failed either to make sense of the companies' internal accounting procedures ('Morris' engines would be sold to 'Austin', for instance, without any real check on costs at either end of the transaction, with the result that, quite literally, no one knew whether certain cars were making or losing money), and perhaps worst of all, he fell into exactly the same trap as his old adversaries, Austin and Nuffield, and failed to bring on thrusting, bright new managers. As a direct consequence, quality control, marketing, product planning all drifted into becalmed waters that left BMC a decade behind the opposition— people would put up with frequent returns for service problems, ugly cars and poor layout just after the war, but by the 1960s folk were becoming more discriminating.

This static management structure was epitomized by the position of George Harriman, who had worked with Leonard Lord before the war and was groomed by him to take over as chairman and managing director in 1961, thus effectively blocking the top positions for decades on end.

It is important to understand something of the industrial and economic context that gripped the motor industries in the 1960s. Harold Wilson's 'white heat of technology' was beckoning, expansion and growth were thought to be limitless and, apparently, painless while received wisdom had it that Big was Beautiful. In 1964, Volkswagen, Mercedes-Benz and Auto-Union (Audi) merged, followed two years later by a Renault-Peugeot collaboration deal. Also in 1964, George Harriman started to talk to the brash Leyland group, who had rapidly expanded, taking over Standard-Triumph on the way. Through the early 1960s with BMC's Issigonis revolution running alongside the still-profitable old-fashioned models whose development costs had long since been amortized, the Corporation were led into a fool's paradise. Profits rose while the company's standing with the public and the quality of its management and production engineering fell. Harriman, complacent and indecisive, continued to talk to Sir William Black at Leyland and his assistant, 'Super Salesman' Donald Stokes, and even Harold Wilson, the Prime Minister, and Tony Wedgwood-Benn (as he then was), Minister of Technology, were in active agreement that a merger between the two companies was highly desirable. The plan was that Black would stand down, Harriman would become chairman of the new mega-group, with Donald Stokes his deputy. At first, the strength of BMC compared to that of Leyland was seen as a technical stock-market stumbling block, but then doubts began to appear on the Leyland side. According to Graham Turner's *The Leyland Papers*, an independent assessment of the company in 1967 concluded that there was 'an enormous staff surplus' and 'a serious lack of foresight' on the part of BMC's senior management.

In 1966, Harriman perpetrated what can only be seen now as an amateurish blunder. He appointed Joe Edwards, who had been fired by Lord in 1956, as MD of the newly formed British Motor Holdings (BMC plus Jaguar, which itself included Henry Meadows, Coventry Climax, Daimler and Guy Motors, all acquired by Jaguar's William Lyons between 1960 and 1964). Edwards, naturally enough, attempted to protect his newly gained position, which would have been lost under the original BMC-Leyland merger plan, and for some time was a major obstacle to the long-drawn-out merger negotiations.

In the event, Edwards lost out anyway. By 1967, BMH's market share was down to less than 28 per cent, and Leyland's profits and stock market value rose higher than BMH's. By January 1968, the unthinkable was happening; the minnow was threatening to eat the bigger fish as Stokes threatened to buy out BMH, and so a Leyland-dominated merger was forced through with Leyland and Donald Stokes as undisputed top dogs, while the sick and dispirited George Harriman died within months of the takeover taking place. George Turnbull became the new British Leyland's managing director, from Standard-Triumph, and another Standard man, Harry Webster, became executive chief engineer.

Among senior men, only Filmer Paradise, sales director, and John Barber, financial executive, brought into BMC by Edwards from Ford, remained unscathed. (A former colleague remembers Paradise as a hugely likeable, no-nonsense American individual who would sit through plannings meetings, chewing thoughtfully on one of a vast range of cheroots he had lined up before him while some jumped-up individual over-rehearsed his prejudices and vocal cords. After politely letting him finish, Filmer would slowly take a last draw, let the smoke out and drawl, 'Horse-sheeit!' before getting on to the heart of the matter.)

In 1968, Bill Appleby retired and Harry Webster, acting on the advice of BMC man Charlie Griffin, appointed Eric Bareham as chief designer, but within a year had moved him into internal exile into one of Issigonis' East Works experimental 'cells', placing the brilliant ex-BRM designer Geoffrey Johnson in Bareham's position. An ex-colleague, now retired, claims that Webster had to make his mark and one of the easiest targets was the self-effacing Bareham, in spite of the fact that Bareham was a talented engineer of whom Issigonis said, after Bareham had rapidly designed him an efficient four-valve head for the A-series engine, 'I just didn't realize he had so much potential.'

Eric Bareham's ex-colleague claimed that the way in which he lost his job was absolutely unfair and also the wrong thing to have done, 'Because Engines were never run better than Eric would have run them, to say the least; O-series never did us any credit, did it . . . ?'

One of the last models released during Eric Bareham's brief period of tenure was the sporting 1800S, with a Daniel Richmond-designed big-valve head. The engine was not an MGB engine, and in fact developed more power than the 'B'. The Maxi also appeared during this time with its ohc engine and faults as already mentioned, plus a gearchange that was described by one tester in immortal terms as, 'like trying to stir a bag of marbles with a knitting needle'. By 1971, Leyland had their Cortina answer ready, the Marina, and were saved from a road-holding disaster only by the amazed protestations of the British magazine road testers, who, in an unprecedented move, got together to persuade the company to improve the front suspension set-up before launch, which they did. The Marina used the A-series 1275 cc engine or B-series 1800 cc unit as options, missing out the

Ford engine capacities altogether, the 2-litre still not seeing the light of day and the 1500 E-series engine remaining only in the Maxi's transverse application. By 1975, the stylish, but not often admired Princess appeared with wedge-shaped bodywork and fitted either with the good old B-series engine or the 2227 cc six-cylinder unit developed by adding two more pots to the Maxi 1500 engine. (This had itself first been fitted to the 1971 six-cylinder version of the 1800.) Once again, the B-series engine, now twenty-one years old, a quarter of the age of the motor car itself, was fitted to a new car, and a front-wheel-drive car at that. On the face of it, there was no sense at all in fitting the B-series engine to the transversely-driven 1800 Princess range, but as Longbridge engineer John Wheatley points out, 'We didn't want to fit the E-series to the 1800 or Princess because then the four-cylinder cars would have had a five-speed box, while the six-cylinder cars could only take a four-speed box, and that would have been impossible in model-planning terms. Also, there was plenty of capacity on B-series, with the new crank-making facility, but none on E-series, which was also used on the Allegro.'

In fact, when the Marina was launched, it had proved necessary to extend crank manufacturing capacity to cope. MGB and the 'Land-Crab' 1800 all but used up the existing capacity of 2500 forged cranks and so capacity was doubled by opening up a parallel cast-crank facility à la Dagenham, which

meant that the crank could be counterweighted to run more evenly. This additional facility, costing around £5 million in 1971, was to play a profound part in the management machinations to come. But in the meantime, why was capacity of the 1750 Maxi engine never stepped up so that it could be fitted to the Marina? John Wheatley says, 'The Marina actually was planned to take the 1750—in fact I believe it was fitted in Australia in place of the B-series, but here the problems which were considered insuperable at the time were: (1) The oil pump shaft ran in a bearing in the bottom of the 1750 gearbox casting. Where else, with no transmission case, would you have put it? (2) The flywheel was fitted on a taper, similar to a Mini, and to fit a conventional flywheel would have meant producing a new crank, which the UK operation was not prepared to do. So it was 'Carry on B-series!'

In spite of all the rational explanations, one can now only wonder at an engine policy where two separate and distinct engine types filling the same needs were allowed to continue. You can understand management inheriting a good old 'workhorse' engine that was really too old, but not being able to afford to replace it; you can understand their headaches when inheriting a young, badly designed engine not fulfilling acceptable design criteria in terms of performance. It's just a bit hard to understand what they did about it!

The last few MGBs were built as 'Limited Edition' cars and had unique body colourings and special alloy wheels. They were sold very quickly but some of the ordinary cars hung around dealers showrooms for quite some time

6 'I wouldn't have started from here!'

'*You have to remember that people genuinely do their best for the company and for themselves, given the circumstances and the resources they have available to them at the time. Perhaps we can be too harsh, and perhaps it's too easy to look back and view these things with hindsight.*'—Stan Johnson, executive engineer, Advanced Engine Design, at Longbridge in 1984.

Have you heard the one about the tourists who stopped their car to ask a local yokel the way to a big town some miles away? After scratching his head and looking around him for some time, he bent down to the window and said, 'If I was 'ee, I wouldn't start from 'ere at all!' Even if it was possible to go back in time to visit Stokes, Webster and the others back in 1971, what other advice would it be possible to give them? They were running a wallowing company with gargantuan problems and, pre-nationalization, were without the sort of funds that only a government can provide for a massive but centrally important company to get out of deep trouble. On top of everything, the union were responding to appalling management by being themselves impossible. In spite of the mythology of the gutter press, it was not always thus. In 1984, John Barker, Vehicle Building and Automotive Officer of the giant Transport and General Workers' Union and ex-chief shop steward at Longbridge, talked first of the respect he and the other shop floor workers had for Leonard Lord, a man accused of being an impossibly arrogant, harsh man, by Leyland-watchers like Jeff Daniels and Graham Turner. 'Lord was quiet, unassuming, very sharp and very acute; he knew his business,' said John Turner. 'He was a motorcar man, *not like many of those who followed him*' (my italics). An example of the poor way in which the workforce was treated was the imposition by

John Barber of the 'measured day' system, whereby men and women were paid for the time they worked rather than the 'piecework' system, where they were paid for what they produced. At Dagenham, Ford workers were used to measured day, knowing nothing else, but Birmingham workers by contrast, were used to piecework. John Barker describes how they would all muck in together to overcome line problems, even small design faults such as the holes in the Austin Westminster wings, where the chrome trims would fit, which allowed the trim to snap when fitted as recommended. The men would fetch pieces of rubber tube from the A40 line and make the trim fit properly, taking a typical Brummie's pride in getting the job done and keeping everybody's piecework rates ticking along nicely. Similarly, John Wheatley described how the B-series transfer machines became so old that the platens (the 'templates' for the drilling and cutting machinery) had been re-jigged so many times that they were like paper doilies, and the floor on which the machinery stood was slowly subsiding into the ancient catacombs of pipeworks and waterways beneath. 'It was only by the good grace of the blokes on the line that production didn't stop years earlier,' said John. 'They used to pack the machines up daily with cigarette papers to get everything lining up properly.'

So, by the time that Donald Stokes and his brash, abrasive new managers had got settled in, the problems of their successors, coupled with the additional problems of such a vast series of mergers—Rover had been added to Leyland too—were beginning to swallow all their fine plans. One of their major difficulties lay in finding a successor to B-series and in making sense out of the medium-sized engine range. To add to the complications was the existence of the excellent slant-four engine, yet another mid-range unit that Triumph had designed for Saab and that was available for use in Leyland cars by January 1975, when the TR7 was first made available for export only (a situation which prevailed for the next year and a half, much to the annoyance of UK consumers).

In mid-1972, a critical look was taken at the 'Austin' medium engine options open to BL. As well as the Eric Bareham/Stan Johnson 2-litre B-series engine, Bareham's successor Geoffrey Johnson had developed an aluminium head over-camshaft version of the engine with the camshaft acting only as a jackshaft to drive the distributor and oil pump, and by June 1972 this engine was undergoing its first running trials. Taking the 1973-model year 1800 MGB as a reference point, other engines produced the following power output figures:

B-series 1800 MGB	96 bhp gross	
B-series 2000 push-rod	106 bhp gross at MGB specification	
B-series 2000 ohc	112–115 bhp gross expected, although only 106 bhp obtained on first non-tuned run	
	1750 'E'	80 bhp gross in single carb form
	1750 'E' HL	93 bhp gross (twin carb)
	1500 'E'	74 bhp gross (single carb)

In addition, dry weights were 520 lb for the MGB engine, but only 385 lb for the 1750 E-series. Even the 2227 six-cylinder E-series weighed only 538 lb!

At first, the 2-litre ADO 73–20V engine was considered, but block changes would have been considerable, involving moving the bore centres around and also the addition of tappet chest modifications to add water flow around the bores. The cost of putting the engine into production was put at around £400,000, a considerable sum for a company with dire cash-flow problems. On the other hand, comparisons between the Cortina 2-litre and Marina 2-litre showed that the Marina's straight-line performance would have been better in every respect. (Quite what would have happened when the Marina had hit the twisty bits might have been another matter!) Then, the 2-litre ohc engine was considered as an alternative in the MGB with the surprising conclusion that

while 2-litre pushrod would cost around an additional 0.25 pence per unit over the existing cost of £81.26, the overhead camshaft engine would be £1.25 cheaper because of labour savings.

However, the situation was becoming extremely difficult because, as an internal memo pointed out, 'The current B-series facilities are in a critical position.' At the same time demand for the engine was expected to be high when fitted to: ADO 28 Marina in US and European forms and MGB and 'loose' sales, still including the Hanomag/Vidal Tempo Van sales. 4500 units were thought to be needed for 1974/75, rising to 6000 in each subsequent year.

Another problem was the production transfer-lines themselves. If B-series was to be modified to ohc form (which was also considered for the 1800 engine), new machinery would have to be purchased and fitted, which would have meant a heavy commitment to an already aged engine and a very large gap whilst no production took place. 'This would create severe disturbances to production and involve production losses extending well beyond the period of shutdown, and we do not see a feasible scheme for implementing these changes,' according to the company's financial analysts. In addition, the new facilities 'would create problems with machining the 1500 and 1800 cc diesel blocks'.

The following is intended as a full list of all cars and LCVs (Light Commercial Vehicles) made by the company and fitted with B-series engine.

The model name is given but remember that 'Mk I' nomenclature is virtually always apocryphal for the simple reason that a 'Mk I' cannot be named as such until a 'Mk II' has come along by which time, granting the title 'Mk I' is retrospective and therefore could never have been used in the contemporary literature or on a car's badging. It is, however, a useful label for the enthusiast to use. The maker's 'Type number' is also given, this usually forming the chassis number prefix. The 'Dates produced' quoted are those 'officially' quoted and there will be cars from every type that were first registered well after production ceased; the last MGBs some of which were still on sale two years after production ended being a case in point.

Austin

Model	Type number	Dates produced
A40 Cambridge	GS4	Oct. 54–57
A40 Cambridge Countryman	GP5	Oct. 54–57
A50 Cambridge	HS5	Oct. 54–57
(Manumatic A50)		Oct. 56–57
A55 Mk I Cambridge	HS6	Feb. 57–58
(Manumatic A55 Mk I)		Feb. 57–58
A55 Mk II Cambridge	HS8	Jan. 59–61
A55 Mk II Countryman	HW8	May-built, announced Sept. 60–61
A60 Cambridge	HS9	Oct. 61–64
(Cambridge auto)	HS9	Oct. 61–64
A60 Cambridge Countryman	HW9	Oct. 61–Feb. 69
(A60 Cambridge auto)	HW9	Oct. 61–Feb. 69
A60 diesel	AD/HS9	Oct. 61–Feb. 69 (Aug. 62–UK)
1800 Mk I	A/HS10	Oct. 64–May. 68
1800 Mk II	A/HSA/D	May. 68–Mar. 72
1800 Mk IIS		July 69–Mar. 72
1800 Mk III	A/H4SE	Mar. 72–Feb. 75
18–22	AM4SGD AM4SGS (HL) (but also 2200)	Mar. 75–Sept. 75

MG

Model	Type number	Dates produced
Magnette ZA	KB[1]	Oct. 53–Oct. 56
Magnette ZB	KB[1]	Oct. 56–Feb. 59
Magnette ZB Varitone	KB[1]	Oct. 56–Feb. 59
Magnette ZB Manumatic	KB[1]	Oct. 56–Feb. 59
Magnette ZB Varitone Manumatic	KB[12]	Oct. 56–Feb. 59
Magnette Mk III	GHS1	Feb. 59–Oct. 61
Magnette Mk IV	GHS2	Aug. 61–April 68
Magnette Mk IV auto	GHS2	Aug. 61–April 68

[1]Third letter indicates original colour of car
[2]Fourth letter indicates originally two-tone paint

As soon as it was known that a substantial part of the cylinder block manufacturing facility would have to be replaced, a new engine was proposed, based on the work carried out on the B-series 2-litre and ohc, but deleting the jackshaft/camshaft and getting rid of the old tappet chest area altogether. However, two important points were made by senior management which everyone at BL concedes privately was a disastrous error of judgement. Because the new engine had to be compatible with the existing transverse transmission case (no money or time was available to redesign it) and because the new cast-crank facility had been installed for B-series, *the existing B-series crank had to be used!* The new O-series engine, as it was to be called, thus shared its leading crank dimensions with 1800 B-series (1969), 1200/1500 B-series (1954), A40 (1947) and even Austin 10/4 (1932). So many constraints were built into the engine by continuation of this crank, that the reverberations if not the recriminations are still felt at Longbridge today. But by September 1972 it was reported internally that, 'block and head designs (of "O"-series) are frozen and drawings of major components are to be released'. In fact Geoffrey Johnson has pointed out that the O-series was then nowhere near the final design stage but the general layout was 'frozen' so that advantage would be taken of the then current recession by buying in the production machine tools at a cheap rate. Buying the machinery before the engine was designed gave Geoffrey Johnson some of the biggest headaches of his career in trying to make a new engine fit pre-advised facilities: and when you realize that he had previously coped with the design for a 16-cylinder, 64-valve engine for BRM, you realize that the problems wrought by such a bizarre management decision were, in perspective, intense indeed! Harry Webster decided that the two engine sizes to be used were 2 litre and 1.7 litre, because the same cylinder head could be used on both but not on 2/1.6-litre engines. The larger engine was to be the 'base' engine, with 1.7 using, unusually for the company, the same bore but a shorter-stroke crankshaft. It has since been pointed out that 2 litres was even then a shrinking market area and that 1.7 was still larger than the 'ideal' 1.6 Ford size, but it is easy to be wise with hindsight. But perhaps some foresight or at least determination on the part of those at the top would have prevented the privately enacted fiasco over the introduction of O-series and the closing down of its successor, the B-series engine.

One should not really mock, but the planning procedure was nothing short of farcical. By September 1972, it was decided the O-series had to be fitted to MGB as a 'critical' matter in order to meet impending US emission restrictions. In October it was decided to delete MGB. In November, MGB was reinstated at a planned level of 600 per week. In December, TR7 launch was planned and MGB planned level reduced to 450 per week.

In 1973, things slowed down a little and a programme was set in motion to 'Federalize' O-series for MGB. The forecast level was 1000 per *year*! (The MGB never sold anywhere near that badly, but the planners were convinced at the time that TR7 would knock MGB for six.)

In 1974, it was decided to fit O-series to Marina

first, then MGB later, while B-series was to continue for a further year, to 1971. By December, the US Marina was cancelled.

By January 1977, B-series had been 'Federalized' after all and it was decided to fit O-series to the MGB in 1980, and an emission control programme was restarted.

In September 1979, MGB was cancelled, but in 1980 it was decided to fit O-series to the TR7 from the 1982-model year. The car was of course discontinued in October 1981. With the MGB, the petrol B-series engine passed out of production, the Marina having given up its B-series engine to be the second recipient of the O-series engine in September 1978, the Princess

The very last MGB and thus the last BL car to be fitted with a B-series engine rolled down the track at Abingdon on 22 October 1980, a fact marked patriotically by those who built it. This snap-shot was taken by then-MG publicity manager Peter laidler, a true MG enthusiast

having used it in transverse form from July of the same year.

Federalizing the B-series
While all the doubt and confusion raged over the O-series engine, the B-series unit *had* to be pushed through US Federal emission specifications. At first it was intended to Federalize both MGB and Marina engines, but as the previous paragraphs

show, North American Specification Marinas were cancelled at the last moment. The biggest problem in Federalizing the B-series was in preventing the valve seats from rapidly deteriorating, since the lead which normally builds up a protective layer on the surface of the valve face and valve seat would be removed from US petrol. With the B-series engine, the problem was particularly acute, because it was not possible to machine out the valve seats and insert very hard seats as was done on the Triumph TR7 engine, for example. The valves bore directly on to the surface of the casting and the valve seats were so close together that inserts would have broken into each other. A solution was found by the complex process of adding 1 per cent of tin to the molten iron and then, because the material in direct contact with the mould takes on an unsuitable molecular structure with tin in the iron, excess material had to be cast in place and the outer skin machined off. Then the iron could be induction hardened around the valve seats, itself a difficult operation and one that was only carried out on models bound for the US. In addition, it was found that smaller valves would have less tendency to burn out and also allowed an increase in the size of the water passages in this critical area. Because oil passing through the engine could contaminate the exhaust catalyst, BL took the opportunity to cut down on oil consumption, a problem that had niggled at all pre-1974 cars, with an improved piston and ring pack. Another long-standing problem, the head gaskets, were becoming increasingly prone to failure due to problems experienced by the suppliers, who were trying to cut down on the amount of asbestos used. They were upgraded, and also the diesel 1800 head gaskets, which were a terrible problem with the extremely high compression ratios used, were upgraded at the same time.

The camshaft was also changed for US cars only, and the valve stems tuftrided for all cars to cut down on wear and contribute to low oil usage. Cylinder head studs were upgraded in specification and additional water flow through the head ensured by enlarging the passages in the top face of the block. Because of a change in the oil feed hole to the rocker shaft, head gaskets were modified to fit both early and late cars, but the company pointed out that the early-type gasket should *not* be fitted to 1975-on cars. The total cost of the changes required to harden the valve seats alone was £173,000, with operating costs of

£9000 pa in 1973, but as an internal memo pointed out, 'The "B"-series engine powers around 90 per cent of Austin Morris exports to the US, representing some 64,000 units a year. Exclusion from this market in 1975 would result in an economic profit loss of £12m.' The show *had* to go on!

The diesel engines

The 1961 1500 cc diesel engine was endowed with all the usual features of diesel units of the time: it was smelly, noisy, not all that easy to start in cold weather and, at 37 bhp, not exactly powerful! Nevertheless, its typical low-speed torque and rugged reliability made it a firm choice for many industrial applications, where the noise was unimportant, and it provided the diesel power source for the J-series vans, while firms like Petters have continued to use the unit for refrigeration plant right up to the present time.

In 1969, work began on 'dieselizing' the 1800, which was already well under development for use in the MGB, ready for introduction in April 1974. The 1500 diesel had fitted quite well into Len Lord's concept of a 'universal' B-series engine, but the 1800 was not quite so accommodating. While the 1500 could be built using major components which were common to both engines, the 1800 diesel proved to require all sorts of modifications. For instance, the injector pump on the 1500 was run off a skew gear on the camshaft, similar to that used on the petrol engines, which, although it had in the past been subject to excessive wear, at least shared parts with the petrol engine. Wear was found to be even worse on the 1800 engine and so a chain drive had to be run to the pump from the front of the camshaft—a fairly expensive modification. Although the same crank was used as the petrol engine, there were actually problems with crank breakage, which were overcome by paying close attention to the radii on the bearing fillets, and also the bearing caps, which were found to be weak, were beefed up for both diesel and petrol engines.

Barry Poole, a principal engineer at Freight-Rover today, and someone who was closely involved in development of the 1.8 diesel, explained that the problems in design and development actually went much further and led to BL having to redesign the block and the head, so losing the advantages of shared components. The head was at first actually a reworked 1500 head casting, but later a special casting was developed with extended waterways into the areas around the valves, where cracking was found to take place. The valve seats wore badly on early 1800 units under test, and altering the cam forms, induction hardening the seats and several other possible solutions all failed to provide an answer, and so special inserts made of Brico Alloy 52 were fitted. These cured the wear problem, but caused some highly embarrassing and very expensive difficulties when some early production models actually shed their inserts, causing in most cases a partially or sometimes a completely wrecked engine.

The 1800 diesel was actually introduced into the new BL van, the Sherpa, in September 1974, just six months behind schedule. Fitted to it was a cost-reduced MGB gearbox, giving a sturdy dependable power and transmission pack, especially after the engine's teething troubles were sorted out. Traditionally, British manufacturers, discouraged by successive governments' insistence on taxing diesel fuel heavily, so giving little price incentive for motorists to switch to the cheaper, less polluting fuel, have been well behind continental Europeans in diesel development. By 1974, BL were starting to look critically at what

their diesel engines had to offer and commissioned an engineer to compare the two B-series diesel engines and also the 2.52-litre BL diesel with the Opel 2.1-litre. Quite apart from comparisons of materials and specialized treatments to various parts of the engine, performance was also put under the microscope. Bhp was shown to be well down on the BL engines, while the Peugeot's torque was only in the same range as the British engines because Peugeot had deliberately kept the figure down in order to control smoke emissions at altitudes above 1500 metres. There had been complaints regarding BL diesel engines run at high altitudes, but while Peugeot could report that their injection nozzle had been modified to prevent loud knocking at high altitude and its position modified to cut down on smoking, the BL report disturbingly pointed out

At the end of it all, Eric Bareham, pictured here by the author in 1984, retired to his home comforts and his beloved steam engine. Although bemused that folk should take such a keen interest in what was to him, something workaday. Eric's records and reminiscences were freely given by this very likeable and rather shy and gentle man: the man behind the B-series

that, 'No high-altitude testing has been carried out. No variations on nozzle angular positions or depths tested,' and indeed it was not possible to vary the nozzle adjustment in the B-series diesels. Indeed, the whole emphasis on testing seems to have been more thorough at the French company. Their diesel had been tested for 1500 hours at full load and 500 hours at part load, while some had been run for no less than 5000 hours to assess a revised crank. The B-series diesels had been run for a relatively miserable 250 hours at maximum torque, 250 hours at maximum power and 250 hours under the highly stressful condition of 5 per cent overfuelled and 10 per cent overspeed. While in general the report painted a bleak picture of low-powered, under-developed diesel B-series engines, with a lack of co-operation from gasket and pump manufacturers adding to development problems, the whole point of the report was to look forwards rather than back, identify weaknesses and attempt to put them right.

The outcome was the diesel engines known at Freight-Rover, the 'commercial' arm of the company, as the Phase II engines, quietly introduced in 1977–78. But even before the redeveloped engines appeared on the scene, BL were thinking very seriously about fitting diesel engines to their saloon cars for the British market. In 1972, the 1.5L diesel engine had been offered in the Marina for the Far East market, but as BL pointed out at the time, 'Whilst the 37 gross bhp from the 1.5L engine is adequate for the Singapore and Malaysian market, the overall road performance of this vehicle in European market terms is quite unacceptable, with poor acceleration and gradeability [sic] and a top speed of only 65 mph. There is a very real danger that the poor performance of the 1.5L-engined vehicle could so damage the diesel car image that future sales of an improved model could be severely prejudiced. . . .'

The 1.8L diesel engine was found to develop 52 gross bhp, which gave performance very close to that of the 1.3-litre petrol-engined Marina, which was of course perfectly acceptable for the UK market. Unfortunately, there was a snag. The ex-Triumph Herald gearbox fitted to the Marina was not considered capable of coping with the cyclic torque variations created by the 1.8 diesel. In non engineering terms, the problem was that a diesel engine—any diesel engine—produces a great deal of torque even at very low revs. While a petrol engine at very low revs produces relatively little

torque, so that within each revolution of the engine the 'pulses' of power coming from the cylinders are fairly low, a diesel engine produces much larger 'pulses' of power, putting sudden, sharp loadings on the drive train, especially when attempting, for instance, a low-revving hill start. George Jones, who was responsible for giving the engineering sign-off for the gearbox, resolutely refused to do so and this killed the project, even though the idea was tinkered with for some time after, and there is even said to be a T-registration Diesel Marina haunting Longbridge at the time of writing. Barry Poole, a principal engineer at Longbridge, who worked on 1.8L diesel development, now reckons that killing Marina diesel for the UK market was an engineering mistake, 'although there were strong "social" reasons, as we called them, for not fitting the engine for the UK market,' he says. 'There were problems such as bad vibration at idle speeds, blue smoke on a cold start (CAV just couldn't be persuaded to produce the pump we wanted), and in any case the engine was on the bone, size-wise, for the weight of the vehicle. In any case, this was before the engine redesign had been completed and there were fears of expensive service problems.'

None of this stopped BL from exporting 1.8L Marina diesel as well as the 1.5 diesel, to markets such as Portugal, Malaysia, Singapore and Malta. Nor did it stop them from going into pilot production of a Princess 1.8L diesel in the late 1970s. Indeed, what must have been the only transverse-engined diesel (almost) in production was by all accounts a highly successful motor car, apart from the 'social' reasons which, again, BL marketing people believed would stop the car in its tracks in spite of the fact that diesel-engined cars were becoming increasingly popular in continental Europe.' Around fifty of the cars were built and it would seem that many were sold to taxi drivers in the Oxford area, because Barry Poole is still telephoned now and again by a taxi driver from that area who wouldn't dream of parting with his Princess diesel, but wants to know if special bits and pieces like throttle cables are still available.

Another query which Barry used to process very frequently around the time of 1977 to 1980 was from folk who wanted to fit a diesel engine into their Marina. Just to be helpful, he produced his own 'unofficial' parts list of mainly Sherpa bits and pieces, which enabled the engine to drop straight in, although he says that a standard clutch plate is destroyed by the diesel's high torque as the centre comes out within the 30,000 to 40,000 miles mark.

Alternatives are to cut down a Transit clutch, or drill the rivets out of the standard clutch and replace them with hardened rivets. The rest of the clutch flywheel assembly has to consist of a 'petrol' clutch, pressure plate and flywheel, but fitted with a Sherpa Automatic ring gear. The diesel fittings, ex-Sherpa, are 'easy to fit for a diesel engineer, but impossible if you don't know the first thing about diesels,' according to Barry.

With the diesel engine still in production at the time of writing and being used by Sherpa, Newton tractors and Petters for refrigeration plant, the B-series engine with its original-type forged crank is still being made at the time of writing, although it is hanging on by the skin of its teeth. It is an open secret that BL are planning to take it out of production by the mid-1980s and that Perkins, the well-known diesel engine manufacturers, are wrestling with O-series so that it can be dieselized. (After all, O-series was originally designed, it now seems, for transverse usage only, once MGB and Marina applications were discarded – although only temporarily in the latter case. The gearcase gave it additional stiffness, so when it became in-line, block flexing was a problem that had to be cured for the petrol engine, so there is clearly an inherent problem there to be overcome.)

However, in the current spirit of things at BL, there will be no chance of an inadequate engine appearing on the market, but it does seem that the B-series engine is shortly doomed for extinction. Or is it? B-series petrol is still being built in quantity by the Hindustan Motor Co. in India, while there is a strong possibility that B-series diesel could be built in Pakistan and/or Portugal, so the engine that Eric Bareham and his colleagues designed to do a robust unsophisticated job of work in the postwar British market is taking on an honourable existence, fulfilling exactly the same criteria in countries where its qualities are now most appreciated—a fitting purpose for a fine engine!

When the pre-Farina Morris Oxford ceased production, the design was quickly snapped up by the Hindustan Motor Company and produced as the Ambassador. Thirty years on the car is still going strong, although production should cease in the mid-to-late Eighties, making the B-series engined car by far the commonest car on Indian roads

PART TWO

B-series data file

1 BMC/BMH/BL cars and LCVs with B-series engine

MG

Model	Code	Dates
MGA Roadster 1500	GHN	Oct. 55–July 59
MGA FHC 1500	GHD	Oct. 56–July 59
MGA Roadster 1600	GHN	July 59–June 61
MGA FHC 1600	GHD	
MGA Mk II Roadster	GHN2	June 61–June 62
MGA Mk II FHC	GHD2	
MGA Twin Cam Roadster		July 58–June 60
MGA Twin Cam FHC		
MGA Roadster 'De Luxe'	GH	June 60–unknown
MGA FHC 'De Luxe'	GH	June 60–unknown
MGB Roadster (3 main bearing)	GHN3	July 62–Sept. 64
MGB (5 main bearing)	GHN3	Sept. 64–Oct. 67
MGB GT	GHD3	Oct. 65–Oct. 67
MGB Roadster Mk II	GHN4	Oct. 67–Oct. 69
MGB GT Mk II	GHD4	Oct. 67–Oct. 69
MGB Roadster	GHN5	Oct. 69–Oct. 71
MGB GT	GHD5	
MGB Roadster Mk III	GHN5	Oct. 71–Oct. 74
MGB GT	GHD5	
MGB Roadster (rubber bumper)	GHN5	Oct. 74–Jan. 81
MGB GT (rubber bumper)	GHD5	Oct. 74–Jan. 81
MGB GT Jubilee	GHD5	May 75
MGB GT Limited Edition	GHN5/ GHD5	Jan. 81

Morris

Model	Code	Dates
Cowley	EA¹	July 54–56
Cowley 1500	EA¹	Oct. 56–59
Oxford SII	DA¹	May 54–56
Oxford SII Traveller	DL¹	Oct. 54–56
Cowley & Oxford S III	DA¹/EA¹	Oct. 56–59
Cowley & Oxford S III Traveller	DL¹/EL¹	Oct. 56–57
Cowley & Oxford S IV Traveller (all metal)	DL¹	Aug. 57–April 60
Cowley & Oxford S V	M/HS5	Mar. 59–61
Cowley & Oxford S V Traveller	M/HWS	Sept. 60–61
Cowley & Oxford S VI	M/HS6	Oct. 61–64
Cowley & Oxford S VI Traveller	M/HW6	Oct. 61–64
Cowley & Oxford S VI Traveller (auto)	M/HW6	Oct. 61–64
Oxford diesel	MD/HS6	Mar. 62–Jan. 69
Oxford Traveller diesel	MD/HW6	Sept. 64–Jan. 69
1800 Mk I	M/HS7	Mar. 66–Mar. 68
1800 Mk II	M/HS8/D	Mar. 68–Mar. 72
1800S	M/HS8/D	Sept. 68–Mar. 72
1800 Mk III	M/H4SE	Mar. 72–Feb. 75
18–22	MM4SGD	
	MM4SGS (HL, also 2200)	Mar. 75–Sept. 75
Marina 1.8 sal. 4 door	MH4S9	Apr. 71–unknown
	Sal 4 dr.	
Marina Super de-luxe 4 door	MH4S9S	Apr. 71–Sept. 75
Marina sal. TC	MH4S9T	Apr. 71–Sept. 75
Marina Coupé 2 door	MH2S9	Apr. 71–Aug. 73
Marina Coupé Super Deluxe 2 door.	MH2S9S	Apr. 71–Oct. 75
Marina Coupé TC	MH2S9T	Apr. 71–Sept. 75
(Auto option all but basic saloon and coupé)		
Marina Estate	MH5W9	Oct. 72–Oct. 75
Marina TC 'Jubilee'	MH2S9	Sept. 73 only
Marina sal. GT 2 door.		Sept. 75–Oct. 75
Marina sal. HL		Sept. 75–Oct. 75
Marina 2 1.8 sal. Super 2 door	MM2SKS	Oct. 75–Sept. 78
Marina sal. Super 4 door	MM4SKS	Oct. 75–Sept. 78
Marina sal. Special 2 door	MM2SKN	Oct. 75–Sept. 78
Marina sal. Special 4 door	MM4SKN	Oct. 75–Sept. 78
Marina GT 2 door	MM2DK	Oct. 75–Sept. 78
Marina HL 4 door	MM4SKJ	Oct. 75–Sept. 78
Marina est. Super 4 door	MM5WKS	Oct. 75–Sept. 78
(auto option on 4 door saloons and Estates only)		

Marina 1700L introduced with 1700 O-series engine Sept. 1978.

Princess

Model	Code	Dates
1800	PM4SGD	Sept. 75–July 78
1800HL	PM4SGS	

(superseded Austin/Morris 18-22 and also Wolseley 22 ranges)

Princess 2 range introduced with 1700 and 2000 O-series engines, July 1978.

Riley

One-Point-Five	R/HS1	Nov. 57–Oct. 61
	R/HS2	Oct. 61–Apr. 65
4/Sixty-Eight	R/HS1	Apr. 59–Oct. 61
4/Seventy-Two (also automatic)	R/HS3	Sept. 61–Oct. 69

Wolseley

Fifteen-Fifty		June 56–59
Fifteen-Fifty Manumatic		Oct. 56–59
Fifteen Hundred	W/HS1	Apr. 57–Oct. 61
Fifteen Hundred 'Fleet Model'	W/HS1	Jan. 59–Oct. 61
Fifteen Hundred	W/HS3	Oct. 61–Apr. 65
Fifteen Hundred 'Fleet Model'	W/HS3	Oct. 61–Apr. 65
Fifteen-Sixty	W/HS1	Dec. 58–Oct. 61
Sixteen-Sixty	W/HS3	Oct. 61–Apr. 71
Sixteen-Sixty (automatic option)		Oct. 61–Apr. 71
18/85 Mk I	W/HS4	Mar. 67–July 69
18/85 Mk II	W/HS5	May 69–Mar. 72
18/85 Mk IIS	W/HS5D	Sept. 69–Mar. 72

(automatic option all models)
(Replaced by Wolseley 6 with 2227 cc six-cylinder E-series engine)

Nash Metropolitan

A40 (probably Somerset engine)	NK1	Aug. 53–July 54
A40 Series II (B-series)	NK1	Aug. 54–July 55
A50 Ser. III	NK1	Aug. 55–Jan. 59
A50 Ser. IV	NK1	Jan. 59–61
Austin Metropolitan '1500' 'Hard Top'	HE6	Dec. 56–Jan. 59
Austin Metropolitan '1500' 'Convertible'	HD6	Dec. 56–Jan. 59
Austin Metropolitan '1500' 'Hard Top' (reintroduced)	AHP7	1960–61 (exact dates unkown)
Austin Metropolitan '1500' 'Convertible' (reintroduced)	AHJ7	

Model	Part no.	Engine prefix	Change points	Remarks
A50 Cambridge (HSS)	8G 203 R	1 H	101 to 22737 and 23000 to 24203	
	48G 346 R	1H	22738 to 22999 and 24204 on	
A55 Cambridge (HS6)	48G 359 R	15		HC. Saloons and Countryman
	48G 346 R	15		LC. Vans, etc.
A55 Mk II Cambridge	48G 416 R	15 AMW		HC
	48G 347 R	15 AMW		LC
A60 Cambridge	48G 233 R	16 AMW		HC. Standard
	48G 234 R	16 AMW		LC. Standard
	48G 269 R	16 AMW		HC. Auto
	48G 286 R			1.5-litre diesel. Engine codings: 15X/U/D ⎰DPA Mk I 15X/N/D ⎱pump 15XA/U/D ⎰DPA MkI 15XA/N/D ⎰pump and C40L ⎱dynamo
	48G 338 R			1.5-litre diesel. Engine codings: 15XD/U/D ⎰DPA Mk II 15XB/N/D ⎰pump and M45G ⎱starter
½-ton Van (HV6 facelift)	48G 297 R	15AC		HC
	48G 298 R	15AC		LC
	48G 313 R	16AC		LC
1800	48G 375 R	18AMW		HC
Metropolitan (HD6, HE6)	48G 346 R	15A		
Morris				
Oxford Series II	48G 345 R	BP15M	From (E) 17685	
	SRH 5 R	BP15M	Tp (E) 17684	
Oxford Series III	48G 360 R	15M	From (C) 248401 to 300634	HC
	48G 349 R	15M	From (C) 248401 to 300634	LC
Oxford Traveller Series IV	48G 360 R	15M	To (C) 306517	HC
	48G 349 R	15M	To (C) 306517	LC
Oxford Series V	48G 416 R	15AMW		HC
	48G 347 R	15AMW		LC

Model	Part no.	Engine prefix	Change points	Remarks
Oxford Series VI	48G 233 R	16AMW		HC. Standard
	48G 234 R	16AMW		LC. Standard
	48G 269 R	16AMW		HC. Automatic
	48G 286 R			1.5-litre diesel. Engine codings:
				15X/U/D ⎰DPA Mk I
				15X/N/D ⎱pump
				15XA/U/D ⎰DPA Mk I
				15XA/N/D ⎱pump and C40L dynamo
	48G 338 R			1.5 diesel. Engine codings:
				15XD/U/D ⎰DPA Mk II
				15XD/N/D ⎱pump and M45G starter

BMC commercials with B-series engines

Austin commercials

10 cwt

'J' type van Ser. 101 (1.5 litre petrol)	Mar. 58–Jan. 61

10/12 cwt

Van, Pick-up (petrol) 1.5 litre	1960–62
JH M10 designation (petrol)	1962–Oct. 63
Van, Pick-up (1.5 litre diesel)	1961–68
180 J4 or 200 J4 designation (1.5 diesel)	1968–74
10/12 cwt J4 M10 Van (1622 cc petrol)	Oct. 63–Jan. 68
180 J4/200 J4 designation (1622 cc petrol)	Jan. 68–71
J4 M10 Van (petrol or diesel, auto option)	April 64–Jan. 68
180 J4/200 J4 designation (petrol or diesel, auto option)	Jan. 68–71

15 cwt

'152' Omnivan (1.5 litre petrol)	April 56–61
'152' Omnitruck (1.5 litre petrol)	Aug. 56–61
'152' Omnitruck (10 seats) (1.5 litre petrol)	July 56–61

'152' Omnicoach (13 seats) (1.5 litre petrol)	July 56–61

16/18 cwt

'152' Omnivan, Omnitruck and Omnicoach (1.5 litre petrol)	1961–Jan. 62
Redesignated J2 M16 (1.5 litre petrol)	Jan. 62–Oct. 63
152 Omnivan, Omnitruck and Omnicoach (1.5 litre diesel)	1961–May 67
16/18 cwt J2 M16	
'152' Omnivan, Omnitruck and Omnicoach (1622 cc petrol)	Oct. 63–May 67
250 JU Van, Pick-up and Bus (1622 cc petrol)	Jan. 67–
250 JU Van, Pick-up and Bus (1.5 litre diesel)	Jan. 67–

Morris Commercial

½-ton *Van* Series III Van (1489 cc petrol) Truck and Cab	1956–60
½-ton *Van and Pick-up* (1489 cc petrol)	Sept. 62–Sept. 63
(1622 cc petrol)	Sept. 63–

2 B-series engine prefixes and change points

This is an incomplete list of B-series engines (it is all that is at present available) showing the parts list 'part no.' and the 'engine prefix', shown on the engine number plate affixed to the engine, and the chassis number change points, where available. This information should help in identifying a 'scrapyard' engine: the part number may well be cast into the side of the block, the engine prefix will be on the engine number (but see note below) and the chassis number change point is sometimes given as a 'car number' change point. The exact location of a car's 'car number' will be stated in the workshop manual.

Note Engine numbers are often changed when a car is reconditioned. BMC/BL had their own system of engine numbers for reconditioned units but these were not readily available to the author. Non-BMC reconditioners sometimes remove the engine number and stamp their own in its place, while the unscrupulous have been known to remove or eradicate an engine number to disguise the fact that the 'wrong' engine has been used, e.g. a Cambridge engine having been placed in an MGA.

N.B. (E) indicates engine number, (C) indicates car number, HC—high compression, LC—low compression

Model	Part no.	Engine prefix	Change points	Remarks
Cowley Series I	8G 119 R	12M		
	SRG 20 R	12M		
Cowley Series II	48G 360 R	15M	From (C) 18001 to 22633	HC
	48G 349 R	15M	From (C) 18001 to 22633	LC
½-ton Van Series III	48G 349 R	15M	From (C) 44201 to 60377	LC
½-ton Van MV4	48G 297 R	15AC		HC
	48G 298 R	15AC		LC
	48G 313 R			LC
Wolseley 1500	48G 354 R	15WA	To (E) 32301	LC
	48G 355 R	15WC	From (E) 101	LC
	48G 304 R	15WD	From (E) 101	HC
	48G 305 R	15WD	From (E) 101	LC
15/50	48G 351 R	BP15W	To (E) 1420	
	48G 415 R	BP15HW	From (E) 101	HC
	48G 351 R	BP15LW	From (E) 101	LC
15/60	48G 416 R	15AMW		HC
	48G 347 R	15AMW		LC
16/60	48G 233 R	16AMW		HC. Standard
	48G 234 R	16AMW		LC. Standard
	48G 269 R	16AMW		HC. Auto
MG Magnette ZA	SRH 4 R	BP15GA	To (E) 3271	
	8G 205 R	BP15GA	From (E) 3272 to 9424 (plus 9501 to 9573)	
	48G 350 R	BP15GA	From (E) 9425 to 16985 (less 9501 to 9573)	
	48G 351 R	BP15GA	From (E) 16986	

Model	Part no.	Engine prefix	Change points	Remarks
Magnette ZB	48G 356 R	BP15GC		Standard
MG Magnette Mk III	48G 357 R	15GE		Standard. HC
Magnette Mark IV	48G 244 R	16GE		Standard. HC
	48G 274 R	16GE		Automatic. HC
MGA	48G 362 R	BP15GB	To (E) 51767	
	48G 361 R	BP15GD	From (E) 101	
MGA 1600	48G 157 R	16GA		HC
MGA 1600 Mk II	48G 214 R	16GC		1622 cc HC
MGB	48G 279 R	18G		HC
	48G 343 R	18GA		HC. Closed-circuit breathing
MGB, MGB GT	48G 392 R	18GB		HC. Closed-circuit breathing
Riley				
One-Point-Five	48G 364 R	15R		HC
	48G 363 R	15RB		HC
	48G 308 R	15RD		HC
4/Sixty-Eight	48G 363 R	15RA		HC
4/Seventy-Two	48G 248 R	16RA		HC. Standard
	48G 272 R	16RA		HC. Auto

B-series engines

Model	Part no.	Engine prefix	Change points	Remarks
JR Van	AAK1163R	VS15C		SV
JB, A101	48G 350 R	BP15LJB	To (C) 42991	Was 48G 155 R
	48G 353 R	15JD	From (C) 42992	Was 48G 173 R
JS, A152	48G 350 R	BP15J		1500 cc LC. Was 48G 156 R and 48G 164 R
	48G 352 R	15JC	From (E) 15JC101, also from BP15LJ36342	
	48G 327 R	16JC		1622 cc LC
J4, 10/12 cwt	48G 181 R	15JE		1500 cc LC
	48G 331 R	16JE		1622 cc LC

1.5-litre diesel engines

Model	Part no.	Engine prefix	Change points	Remarks
JB Van GPO	48G 228 R			Engine coding 15YA/U/D DPA Mark I pump
JO2, A152	48G 256 R			Engine coding 15Y/U/D DPA Mk I pump, 15JA/U/D DPA Mk I pump. C40L dynamo
	48G 339 R			Engine coding 15JF/U/D DPA Mk II pump M45G starter
	48G 334 R			Auto engine coding 15Y/A/D DPA Mk I pump 15JA/A/D C40L dynamo
	48G 372 R			Auto engine coding 15JF/A/D DPA Mk II pump M45G starter
JO4, 10/12 cwt	48G 260 R			Engine coding 15Z/U/D DPA Mk I pump 15ZA/U/D DPA Mk I pump C40L dynamo
	48G 340 R			Engine coding 15ZB/U/D DPA Mk II pump M45G starter
	48G 335 R			Auto engine coding 15ZA/A/D DPA Mk I pump C40L dynamo
	48G 373 R			Auto engine coding 15ZB/A/D DPA Mk II pump M45G starter

3 Parts interchangeability

When an engine has had a production life of over a quarter of a century, it's inevitable that it will have evolved in almost every way. As a result, although you can look at a 1980 MGB engine and a 1953 MG Magnette engine and know that they are both B-series, you can't actually swap many, if any, of the parts over!

Unfortunately, it would be an impossible task to detail just which parts could be used on which engines. Unlike the A-series engine, which has always been raced and tuned, the B-series engine has never developed a body of adherents to whom one can turn to find the sort of practical information to pass on as empirical fact in a book of this sort. So, in a sense, if you're stuck for engine parts, you're on your own, but as someone who, many years ago, fitted an MGA engine into an MGB (*not* recommended!) when funds were tight and nothing else was available, and then fitted a Cambridge crank to replace the broken one in the MGA engine, this writer can offer a few pointers to what can be swapped with what.

The first place to look is in the BMC/BL parts list where you can be virtually certain that if the parts used in two different engines are identical, they will be given the same part number. If what you need is a service part such as an oil filter, use the manufacturer's applications lists available at motor factories where you may even find that the parts you require were used by a whole lot of different manufacturers.

However, you may wish to use a part which has been modified or up-dated in place of the original in which case comparing parts numbers will be of no use. Then you will have to use a little detective work. An example is the timing chain cover which on earlier cars has a felt oil seal which is almost guaranteed to leak, especially after some use, and the timing chain cover on later cars with a more

modern, efficient type of oil seal. If you rebuild an early engine, it would be foolish not to try to update this part of the engine—unseen to the naked eye but giving a cleaner engine and a cleaner garage floor. But do *all* later timing chain covers fit *all* earlier engines? The only way of telling is by comparing one part with another before you buy, whether at autojumble or scrap yard. Take your existing component with you—even if it's a broken crank or burned piston—and make comparisons visually and by measuring them. Also, think not only in terms of the part itself but the part that the part bolts on to! If you can't get hold of the oil filter you need, perhaps you could buy a 'scrapyard' oil filter can and mounting—complete with studs from the block if necessary—and fit the lot to your engine. If you want to fit later-type pistons (although at the time of writing, earlier ones are freely available) you may be able to do so by fitting later-type con-rods as well. There's no way to make definitive statements about what will fit what: you will just have to 'suck it and see'—try out second-hand bits and see if they fit.

Actually, one of the best sources of information about which later parts can be used on earlier engines, can be a well-established engine reconditioner (see 'Suppliers' section of this book) who will be well versed in finding 'foreign' parts for engines. Some combinations are non-starters of course. If anyone can work out how to fit a five-main bearing crank to a three-main engine, they'll be doing well. Others are not impossible, just darned difficult! The fiasco of putting an MGA engine into an MGB came about because I had an early three main-bearing MGB and couldn't find a replacement for my engine which was worn to the point of being scrap. The spigot shaft bushes in three-main and five-main engines are very different in diameter but what I hadn't then worked out was that I could have had a special thick bush turned to suit the large five-main crank spigot with a small internal diameter to suit the three-main engine's gearbox. In the same way, a five-main MGB engine can be fitted to any earlier car (although whether it would be safe to do so is another matter) as long as an early clutch, backplate and flywheel were used, partly to suit the splines on the gearbox, 'five-main bearing' gearboxes having fewer, thicker splines. (See 'Engine tuning' for more details.)

If you are swapping B-series engines about between cars, fitting, say a Riley 1.5 unit into an A55 Cambridge, another component to be changed will be the front plate. It seems that all front plates (complete with engine mounts) are interchangeable between engines of the same size and they may easily be interchangeable between different engine sizes, too.

There is quite a lot of interchangeability between cylinder heads, particularly between those on sub-1800 engines and between 1800

engines themselves. Watch out for valve size problems on 1800s (see 'Modifications' chapter for details) and for combustion chamber sizes. A 1500 head on a 1622 cc engine would give a sporty compression ratio but weedy valves while a 1622 head on a 1500 would give a positively medieval compression ratio. A swap in either of these directions could be made possible through machining but the supply of second-hand and new-old stock components won't dry up for many, many years to come, there having been so very many of the engines built.

Finally, if you want to carry out a component transplant and you don't know whether it can be done, join the one-make club that is relevant to your car and simply ask around the members, the technical adviser (most clubs have one) and the club's specialist suppliers and those suppliers who advertise through the pages of the club magazine. You can be sure of one thing, whatever you want to try, someone, somewhere is sure to have tried it before you!

4 Engine data

The following information will be useful in a number of ways, allowing you to check standard specifications, helping you to identify an engine which has otherwise lost its identifying marks, helping you to choose uprated parts or interchangeable parts when rebuilding your engine and giving basic information such as torque wrench settings to be used in conjunction with the section of this book showing you how to overhaul your engine. The data given is factory sourced, edited slightly here and there for consistency only.

Some data on some of the latest engines such as those used in the Princess or 1800 and some commercials/diesels has not been included here on the basis that they are not yet 'enthusiasts' cars'. The only other car to use the 1798 cc engine, the MGB, would not benefit from using parts from these cars since they would lower its specification other than in the case of the 1800S for which advice is given under 'Tuning'.

Austin A40 and A50 Cambridge, Morris Cowley, Cowley 1500 and Oxford Series II engines 1954–56

1200 cc A40 GS5

GENERAL

Number of cylinders	4
Bore	2.578 in. (65.48 mm.)
Stroke	3.5 in. (89 mm.)
Capacity	73.17 cu. in. (1,200 cc.)
B.H.P.	42 at 4,500 r.p.m. (42.58 C.V.)
Torque	58 lbs.ft. at 2,400 r.p.m. (8.019 kg.m.)
B.M.E.P. (Max.)	122 at 2,400 r.p.m. (8.577 kg./cm.)
R.A.C. rating	10.6 h.p.
Firing order	1, 3, 4, 2
Valve position	Overhead; tappet, pushrod, and rocker operated
Compression ratio	7.2 to 1

TORQUE WRENCH SETTINGS

Cylinder head nuts	45 lbs./ft. (6.22 kg.m.)
Main bearing stud nuts	77–80 lbs.ft. (10.65–11.06 kg.m.)
Connecting rod big ends setscrews	35 lbs./ft. (4.84 kg.m.)
Connecting rod small end clamping screw	26 lbs./ft. (3.6 kg.m.)
Front cover setscrews	8–10 lbs./ft. (1.12–1.38 kg.m.)
Front mounting plate setscrews	12–14 lbs./ft. (1.66–1.94 kg.m.)
Rear mounting plate setscrews	20 ($\frac{5}{16}$"); 30 ($\frac{3}{8}$") lbs./ft. (2.76; 4.15 kg.m.)
Flywheel/crankshaft bolts	35 lbs./ft. (4.84 kg.m.)
Engine support bracket bolts to front plate	18 ($\frac{5}{16}$"); 30 ($\frac{3}{8}$") lbs./ft. (2.45; 4.148 kg.m.)
Camshaft gear to camshaft hub	95 lbs./ft. (13.13 kg.m.)

CYLINDER LINERS

Diameter of bore to receive liner	2.719–2.719$\frac{1}{2}$-in. (69.063–69.075 mm.)
Outside diameter of liner	2.721–2.721$\frac{3}{4}$-in. (69.1134–69.1325 mm.)
Finished bore of liner	2.577–2.578$\frac{1}{2}$-in. (65.456–65.494 mm.)

PISTONS

Material	Aluminium alloy
Piston clearance at skirt (measured at right angles to the gudgeon pin)	.0006–.0012-in. (.015–.030 mm.)

PISTON RINGS AND GROOVES

Compression groove width	.0796–.0806-in. (2.022 2.047 mm.)
Oil control groove width	.1578–.1588-in. (4.008–4.034 mm.)
Compression ring grooves:	

1st groove	Plain
2nd and 3rd grooves	Taper
Oil control ring groove	
4th groove	Slotted scraper
Ring width:	
Compression	.0771–.0781-in. (1.958–1.984 mm.)
Oil control	.1552–.0562-in. (3.942–3.967 mm.)
Clearance in groove:	
Compression	.0015–.0035-in. (.038–.089 mm.)
Oil control	.0016–.0036-in. (.041–.091 mm.)
Ring gap	.008–.012-in. (.203–.305 mm.)
Oversize pistons and rings available	.010-in. (.254 mm.), .020-in. (.508 mm.), .030-in. (.762 mm.) and .040-in. (1.016 mm.)

GUDGEON PIN

Type	Floating in piston
Fit	Thumb fit at 70°F. (21.1°C.)
Length	2.271$\frac{1}{4}$-in. (57.6898–57.9438 mm.)
Diameter	.6869–.6871-in. (17.447–17.452 mm.)

CRANKSHAFT

Material	Steel forging
Diameter of main journals	2.000$\frac{1}{2}$–2.001-in. (50.813–50.825 mm.)
Diameter of crankpin	1.8759–1.8764-in. (46.648–47.661 mm.)
Crankshaft end float	.002–.003-in. (.051–.076 mm.)
Main journal clearance	.000$\frac{1}{2}$–.002-in. (.0127–.0508 mm.)
Main journal regrinding sizes:	
1st undersize	.010-in. (.254 mm.)
Journal diameter	1.990$\frac{1}{2}$–1.991-in. (50.559–50.571 mm.)
2nd undersize	.020-in. (.508 mm.)
Journal diameter	1.980$\frac{1}{2}$–1.981-in. (50.305–50.317 mm.)
3rd undersize	.030-in. (.762 mm.)
Journal diameter	1.970$\frac{1}{2}$–1.971-in. (50.051–50.063 mm.)
4th undersize	.040-in. (1.016 mm.)
Journal diameter	1.960$\frac{1}{2}$–1.961-in. (49.797–49.809 mm.)
Crankpin regrinding sizes:	
1st undersize	.010-in. (.254 mm.)
Crankpin diameter	1.8659–1.8664-in. (47.394–47.407 mm.)
2nd undersize	.020-in. (.508 mm.)
Crankpin diameter	1.8559–1.8564-in. (47.140–47.153 mm.)
3rd undersize	.030-in (.762 mm.)
Crankpin diameter	1.8459–1.8464-in. (46.886–46.899 mm.)
4th undersize	.040-in. (1.016 mm.)

Crankpin diameter	1.8359–1.8364-in. (46.632–46.645 mm.)
End float taken on	Washer at centre bearing

CONNECTING RODS

Material	Steel forging
Length, centre to centre	6.498–6.502-in. (165.049–165.151 mm.)
Big end housing diameter	2.0210–2.0215-in. (51.333–51.346 mm.)
Connecting rod side clearance	.008–.012-in. (.203–.305 mm.)
Big end bearing clearance	.001–.0016-in. (.025–.040 mm.)

MAIN BEARINGS

Type	Thinwall, steel backed white metal
Number	3
Overall length	1.37–1.38-in. (34.798–35.052 mm.)
Outside diameter	2.1465-in. (54.521 mm.)
Thickness	.072–.072$\frac{1}{4}$-in. (1.8288–1.8352 mm.)
Housing diameter	2.146–2.146$\frac{1}{2}$-in. (54.508–54.521 mm.)

BIG-END BEARINGS

Type	Thinwall, steel backed white metal
Overall length	.995–1.005-in. (25.273–25.527 mm.)
Thickness	.072–.072$\frac{1}{2}$-in. (1.8288–1.8352 mm.)
Outside diameter	2.015-in. (51.346 mm.)
Material	Steel forging
Journal diameters:	
Front	1.788$\frac{3}{4}$–1.789$\frac{1}{4}$-in. (45.4343–45.4470 mm.)
Centre	1.728$\frac{3}{4}$–1.729$\frac{1}{4}$-in. (43.9103–43.9230 mm.)
Rear	1.622$\frac{1}{4}$–1.623$\frac{1}{4}$-in. (51.2179–51.2306 mm.)
End float	.003–.007-in. (.076–.178 mm.)
End thrust taken on	Locating plate
Drive	Duplex roller chain
Chain pitch	.375-in. (9.525 mm.)
Number of pitches	52

CAMSHAFT BEARINGS

Type	Thinwall, steel backed white metal
Number	3
Front bearings:	
Outside diameter (before fitting)	1.920-in. (48.768 mm.)
Housing diameter	1.915-in. (48.641 mm.)
Inside diameter (reamed in position)	1.790$\frac{1}{4}$–1.790$\frac{3}{4}$-in. (45.472–45.485 mm.)
Clearance	.001–.002-in. (.025–.051 mm.)
Length	1$\frac{15}{32}$-in. (37.306 mm.)
Centre bearing:	
Outside diameter (before fitting)	1.860-in. (47.244 mm.)
Housing diameter	1.855-in. (47.117 mm.)

Inside diameter (reamed in position)	1.730$\frac{1}{4}$–1.730$\frac{3}{4}$-in. (43.948–43.96 mm.)
Clearance	.001–.002-in. (.025–.051 mm.)
Length	$1\frac{1}{8}$-in. (28.575 mm.)
Rear bearing:	
Outside diameter (before fitting)	1.754-in. (44.552 mm.)
Housing diameter	1.749-in. (44.425 mm.)
Inside diameter (reamed in position)	1.629$\frac{1}{4}$–1.624$\frac{3}{4}$-in. (41.256–41.269 mm.)
Clearance	.001–.002-in. (.025–.051 mm.)
Length	$\frac{13}{16}$-in. (20.648 mm.)

VALVES

Material:	
Inlet	Silico Chrome Steel
Exhaust	XB Steel
Timing:	
Inlet opens	5° B.T.D.C.
Inlet closes	45° A.B.D.C.
Exhaust opens	40° B.B.D.C.
Exhaust closes	10° A.T.D.C.
Valve clearance for setting timing	.020-in.
Head diameter:	
inlet	1.370–1.375-in. (34.798–34.935 mm.)
Exhaust	1.182–1.187-in. (30.023–30.150 mm.)
Seat angle:	
Inlet and exhaust	45°
Seat width:	
Inlet (approx.)	$\frac{1}{16}$-in. (1.588 mm.)
Exhaust (approx.)	$\frac{1}{8}$-in. (3.175 mm.)
Stem clearance:	
Inlet	.0015$\frac{1}{2}$–.0025$\frac{1}{2}$-in. (.0394–.0648 mm.)
Exhaust	.0010$\frac{1}{2}$–.0020$\frac{1}{2}$-in. (.0267–.0521 mm.)
Stem diameter:	
Inlet and exhaust	.341$\frac{3}{4}$–.342$\frac{1}{4}$-in. (8.6805–8.6932 mm.)
Lift	.325-in. (8.19 mm.)
Length (overall):	
Inlet	$4\frac{5}{16}$-in. (109.54 mm.)
Exhaust	$4\frac{9}{32}$-in. (108. 74 mm.)
Working clearance	.015-in. (.381 mm.)

VALVE GUIDES

Length:	
Inlet	$1\frac{7}{8}$-in. (47.63 mm.)
Exhaust	$2\frac{9}{32}$-in. (57.94 mm.)
Outside diameter:	
Inlet and exhaust	.5635–.5640-in. (14.313–14.440 mm.)
Inside diameter:	
Inlet and exhaust	.3438–.3443-in. (8.733–8.860 mm.)
Height above spot face	$\frac{39}{64}$–$\frac{5}{8}$-in. (15.5–15.9 mm.)

VALVE SPRINGS

Free length	$2\frac{1}{64}$-in. (51.197 mm.)
Fitted length and load	$1\frac{17}{32}$-in. at 77.5 ± 2 lb. (38.894 at 31.15 ± .91 kg.)
Number of working coils	$4\frac{1}{2}$ (114.3 mm.)
Diameter of coil wire	.168-in. (4.267 mm.)
Core diameter	.993–1.007-in. (25.222–25.578 mm.)

TAPPETS

Type	Barrel, chrome base
Diameter	.811$\frac{1}{4}$–.811$\frac{3}{4}$-in. (20.606–20.619 mm.)
Length	2.293–2.303-in. (58.242–58.496 mm.)

ROCKER MECHANISM

Pushrods:	
Overall length	8.812$\frac{1}{2}$–8.843$\frac{3}{4}$-in. (223.838–224.631 mm.)
Stem diameter	.281$\frac{1}{4}$–.285$\frac{1}{4}$-in. (7.144–7.245 mm.)
Rocker shaft:	
Length	$14\frac{1}{32}$-in. (355.63 mm.)
Outside diameter	.624–.625-in. (15.850–15.875 mm.)
Rocker arm bush:	
Type	Thinwall, steel backed white metal
Outside diameter (before fitting)	.751–.752-in. (19.075–19.301 mm.)
Inside diameter (reamed in position)	.625$\frac{1}{2}$–.626-in. (15.888–15.901 mm.)
Thickness before reaming	.065$\frac{1}{2}$–.068-in. (1.664–1.727 mm.)
Clearance	.000$\frac{1}{2}$–.002-in. (.013–.051 mm.)
Rocker arm:	
Bore	.748$\frac{1}{2}$–.749$\frac{1}{2}$-in. (19.012–19.037 mm.)
Ratio	$\frac{63}{64}$: $1\frac{13}{32}$ (25.003: 35.719)

FLYWHEEL

Material	High tensile cast iron
Diameter	$11\frac{5}{8}$-in. (295.28 mm.)
Starter ring:	
Number of teeth	120
Diameter over teeth	12.041–12.046-in. (305.841–305.968 mm.)

LUBRICATION

Type of system	Forced feed
Type of pump	Rotor (co-axial)
Oil pressure:	
Running	60 lb./in.^{2} (4.218 kg./cm.^{2})
Idling	15 lb./in.^{2} (1.055 kg./cm.^{2})
External filter:	
Type	By-pass
Maker	A.C. or Purolator
Capacity	1 pint (1.78 litres)
Sump capacity	7 pints (3.978 litres: 8.4 U.S. pints)

A50–HS5 1500 CC ENGINE

Number of Cylinders	4
Bore	2.875 in.
Stroke	3.5 in. (89 mm.)
Capacity	1,500 cc
B.H.P.	50 at 4,400 r.p.m.

Maximum Torque	70 lb./ft. at 2,100 r.p.m.
Compression Ratio	7.2 to 1
Firing order	1–3–4–2
Valves	Overhead push-rod operation
Valve Timing:	
Inlet opens	5° B.T.D.C.
Inlet closes	45° A.B.D.C.
Exhaust opens	40° B.B.D.C.
Exhaust closes	10° A.T.D.C.

Morris engines (where different) and additional information

ENGINE

Compression ratio (to Engine No. BP15M 21644)	7.43:1
Later engine types BP15M and BP15ML	7.2:1
Engine type BP15MH	8.3:1
Connecting rod bearings	
Engine type BP15M	Steel-backed, white-metal or lead-tin-lined
Engine types BP15ML and BP15MH	Steel-backed, lead-indium or lead-tin-lined
Piston type	Aluminium alloy, concave crown, split skirt
Piston clearance, top of skirt	.0016 to .0024 in. (.041 to .06 mm.)
Piston clearance, bottom of skirt	.0008 to .0014 in. (.02 to .036 mm.)
Piston rings, compression	1 plain, 2 taper
Piston rings, oil control	1 slotted
Piston ring gap	.008 to .013 in. (.20 to .33 mm.)
Gudgeon pin type	Clamped in connecting rod
Gudgeon pin fit in piston	Double thumb press, .0001 in. (.002 mm.) tight to .0003 in. (.007 mm.) slack
Valve lift	.312 in. (7.94 mm.)
Valve rocker clearance	Running: .015 in. (.38 mm.) hot. For timing: .026 in. (.66 mm.)
Valve spring free length	$2\frac{1}{64}$ in. (51.2 mm.). Fitted: $1\frac{17}{32}$ in. (38.9 mm.)
Valve spring pressure	Shut: $77\frac{1}{2}$ lb. (35.15 kg.). Open: 130 lb. (58.9 kg.)
Carburettor type	S.U. semi-downdraught, $1\frac{1}{4}$ in.
Carburettor needle	Standard, M8; BP15ML, EB; BP15MH, M
Oil pressure relief valve operates	50 lb./sq. in. (3.5 kg./cm.²)
Oil pressure (normal running)	50 lb./sq. in. (3.5 kg./cm.²)
Oil pressure (idling)	15 lb./sq. in. (1.05 kg./cm.²)
Oil filter (external)	By-pass (Part No. 17H403). Later models full-flow (Element, Tecalemit or Purolator, B.M.C. Part No. 8G683.)

CLUTCH AND GEARBOX

Clutch	*Oxford and Cowley 1500:* Borg & Beck. 8 in. (20.32 cm.) *Cowley:* $7\frac{1}{4}$ in. (18.4 cm.)
Synchromesh	Second, third and top
Ratios:	
Top	1.0:1
Third	1.4904:1
Second	2.403:1
First	3.945:1
Reverse	5.159:1
Overall ratios *Oxford and Cowley 1500*	
Top	4.875:1
Third	7.266:1
Second	11.715:1
First	19.23:1
Reverse	25.15:1
Speedometer drive gear to pinion ratio	3:8
Commencing Gearbox No. 1601	5:12
Overall ratios *Oxford (Special) and Cowley*	
Top	5.125:1
Third	7.64:1
Second	12.32:1
First	20.22:1
Reverse	26.44:1
Speedometer drive gear to pinion ratio	5:13

ELECTRICAL

Distributor type	Lucas DM2
Distributor rotation	Anti-clockwise, viewed from top
Automatic advance (centrifugal)	*Oxford II:* 16° at distributor; *Cowley:* 9° to 11° at distributor
Automatic advance (vacuum)	*Oxford II:* 9° at distributor. *Cowley:* 12° at distributor
Automatic advance (centrifugal) later models	*Oxford II:* 16° to 18° at distributor. *Cowley:* 6° to 8° at distributor
Ignition timing	4° B.T.D.C. = $\frac{3}{16}$ in. (4.8 mm.) on crankshaft pulley *Oxford III and Cowley 1500 (BP15MH)*
Automatic advance (vacuum)	12° at distributor
Automatic advance (centrifugal)	11° to 13° at distributor
Ignition timing	5° B.T.D.C. = $\frac{15}{64}$ in. (5.9 mm.) on crankshaft pulley *Oxford III, Cowley 1500, and Van (BP15ML)*
Automatic advance (vacuum)	8° at distributor
Automatic advance (centrifugal)	16° to 18° at distributor
Ignition timing	6° B.T.D.C. = $\frac{9}{32}$ in. (7.14 mm.) on crankshaft pulley
Contact breaker gap	.014 to .016 in. (.36 to .40 mm.)

Sparking plug	Champion N8 (was code N8B) 14 mm., $\frac{3}{4}$ in. reach
Sparking plug gap	.025 in. (.64 mm.)
Charging system	C.V.C.
Dynamo	Lucas C39PV2. Lucas Service No. 22258D
Dynamo speed	1.37 × engine speed
Starter	Lucas M35G. Lucas Service No. 25022F
Drive ratio	13.33:1 (Teeth: 9/120)
Battery	Lucas GTW 9A2, 12-volt. Lucas service No. 401157F
Battery (some Cowley models)	Lucas GTW 7A, 2-volt. Lucas Service No. 4011517
Battery capacity	At 10-hr. rate, 51 amp.-hr. At 20-hr. rate, 58 amp.-hr.
Battery capacity (some Cowley models)	At 10-hr. rate, 37 amp.-hr.
Battery earth	Positive

FUEL SYSTEM

Carburettor	S.U. H.2 semi-downdraught
Choke size	$1\frac{1}{4}$ in. (3.175 cm.)
Needle: H.C.	M (standard) AH2 (rich) CF (weak)
L.C.	EB (standard) HA (rich) GG (weak)
Piston Spring: H.C.	8 oz. (227 gm.). Yellow
L.C.	12 oz. (340 gm.). Green
Air cleaner	A.C. oil bath type
Fuel pump	S.U. H.P.

TORQUE SPANNER DATA

Cylinder head	40 to 45 lb. ft. (5.53 to 6.22 kg. m.)
Connecting rod and flywheel	35 lb. ft. (4.84 kg. m.)
Gudgeon pin clamp	23 to 25 lb. ft. (3.18 to 3.46 kg. m.)
Main bearing	70 lb. ft. (9.68 kg. m.)
Rocker shaft bracket nuts:	
inner nut	25 lb. ft. (3.46 kg. m.)
outer nut	40 lb. ft. (5.53 kg. m.)
Pinion bearing nut	135 to 140 lb. ft. (18.69 to 19.35 kg. m.)
Differential bearing cap nuts	60 to 65 lb. ft. (8.30 to 8.99 kg. m.)
Crown wheel bolts	55 to 60 lb. ft. (7.60 to 8.30 kg. m.)
Pinion bearing pre-load	13 to 15 lb. ft. (.15 to .173 kg. m.)
Clutch to flywheel	25 lb. ft. (3.46 kg. m.)

Half-ton van and pick-up (Series III)

The general data for the Half-ton van and pick-up (Series III) are the same as for the Oxford (Series III) and Cowley 1500 with the exception of the following:

ENGINE

Type	BP15ML

FUEL SYSTEM

Carburettor needle	Standard: EB

Carburettor piston spring	Green

CLUTCH AND GEARBOX

Overall ratios:	
Top	5.125:1
Third	7.64:1
Second	12.32:1
First	20.22:1
Reverse	26.44:1
Speedometer drive to pinion ratio	3.11:1

Wolseley Fifteen-Fifty engine 1956–59

ENGINE

Type	BP15W Later models BP15W/L and BP15W/H (revised code: 15W)
Number of cylinders	4
Bore	2.875 in. (73.025 mm.)
Stroke	3.5 in. (89 mm.)
Capacity	90.88 cu. in. (1489 c.c.)
Firing order	1,3,4,2
Compression ratio	7.15:1 or 8.2:1
Capacity of combustion chamber (valves fitted)	38.2 to 39.2 c.c. (2.3 to 2.4 cu. in.)
Valve operation	Overhead by push-rod
Torque	78 lb. ft. (10.79 kg. m.) at 2,400 r.p.m.
Cooling system	Thermo-siphon, pump- and fan-assisted
Oversize bore:	
1st	.010 in. (.254 mm.)
Max.	.040 in. (1.016 mm.)

CRANKSHAFT

Main journal diameter	2 in. (50.8 mm.)
Minimum regrind diameter	1.937 in. (49.212 mm.)
Crankpin journal diameter	1.8759 to 1.8764 in. (47.648 to 47.665 mm.)
Crankpin minimum regrind diameter	1.812 in. (46.036 mm.)

MAIN BEARINGS

Number and type	Three. Shell type
Material	Steel-backed. White metal
Length	1.375 in. (34.925 mm.)
End-clearance	.002 to .003 in. (.051 to .076 mm.)
End-thrust	Taken by thrust washers at centre main bearing
Running clearance	.0005 to .002 in. (.013 to .051 mm.)

CONNECTING RODS

Length between centres	6.5 in. (165.1 mm.)

Big-end bearings

Material	Steel-backed. White metal
Material BP15W/L and BP15W/H	Steel-backed. Lead-indium
Bearing side-clearance	.008 to .012 in. (.203 to .305 mm.)

Bearing diametrical clearance	.0001 to .0016 in. (.002 to .04 mm.)

PISTONS

Type	Aluminium alloy
Clearances:	
Bottom of skirt	.0008 to .0014 in. (.0203 to .0356 mm.)
Top of skirt	.0016 to .0024 in. (.0408 to .061 mm.)
Oversizes	+.010 in., +.020 in., +.030 in., +.040 in. (+.254 mm.), (+.508 mm.), (+.762 mm.), (+1.106 mm.)

PISTON RINGS

Compression:	
Plain	Top ring
Tapered	Second and third rings
Width	.0771 to .0781 in. (1.96 to 1.98 mm.)
Thickness	.111 to .118 in. (2.81 to 3.0 mm.)
From Engine Nos. 15W/U/H10737, 15W/MU/H9810, 15W/U/L10408, and 15W/MU/L4331)	.119 to .126 in. (3.02 to 3.2 mm.)
Clearance in groove	.0015 to .0035 in. (.038 to .089 mm.)
Fitted gap	.008 to .013 in. (.20 to .33 mm.)
Oil control type	Slotted scraper
Width	.1552 to .1562 in. (3.94 to 3.99 mm.)
Thickness	.111 to .118 in. (2.81 to 3.0 mm.)
From Engine Nos. 15W/U/H10737, 15W/MU/H9810, 15W/U/L10408, and 15W/MU/L4331	.119 to .126 in. (3.02 to 3.2 mm.)
Clearance in groove	.0016 to .0036 in. (.40 to .091 mm.)
Fitted gap	.008 to .013 in. (.20 to .33 mm.)

GUDGEON PIN

Type	Clamped
Fit	.0001 to .00035 in. (.0025 to .009 mm.). Hand push fit at 68°F. (20°C.)
Diameter	.6869 to .6871 in. (17.447 to 17.4523 mm.)

VALVES AND VALVE GEAR

Valves

Seat angle	
Inlet	45°
Exhaust	45°
Head diameter:	
Inlet	$1\frac{3}{8}$ in. (34.9 mm.)
Exhaust	$1\frac{3}{16}$ in. (30.1 mm.)
Stem diameter:	
Inlet	$\frac{11}{32}$ in. (8.73 mm.)
Exhaust	$\frac{11}{32}$ in. (8.73 mm.)

Valve lift	.322 in. (8.18 mm.)
Valve rocker clearance:	
Running	.015 in. (.38 mm.) (hot)
Timing	.026 in. (.66 mm.)
Timing markings	Dimples on timing wheels
Chain pitch and number of pitches	$\frac{3}{8}$ in. (9.52 mm.), 52 pitches
Inlet valve:	
Opens	5° B.T.D.C.
Closes	45° A.B.D.C.
Exhaust valve:	
Opens	40° B.B.D.C.
Closes	10° A.T.D.C.
(with .021 in. (.53 mm.) valve rocker clearance (for checking purposes only))	

Valve guides

Length:	
Inlet	$1\frac{7}{8}$ in. (47.63 mm.)
Exhaust	$2\frac{9}{32}$ in. (57.94 mm.)
Diameter:	
Inlet: Outside	.5635 in. (14.31 mm.)
Inside	.3438 in. (8.73 mm.)
Exhaust: Outside	.5635 in. (14.31 mm.)
Inside	.406 in. (10.32 mm.)
Fitted height above head	.625 in. (15.87 mm.)

Valve springs

Free length	$2\frac{1}{32}$ in. (51.59 mm.)
Fitted length	$1\frac{17}{32}$ in. (38.9 mm.)
Number of working coils	$4\frac{1}{2}$
Pressure:	
Valve open	131 lb. (59.4 kg.)
Valve closed	79 lb. (35.8 kg.)

TAPPETS

Type	Flat base. Barrel type
Diameter:	
Body	$\frac{13}{16}$ in. (20.64 mm.)
Working face	$\frac{9}{16}$ in. (14.29 mm.)
Length	2.293 to 2.303 in. (58.25 to 58.5 mm.)

CAMSHAFT

End-float	.003 to .007 in. (.076 to .178 mm.)
Bearing: number and type	3. Thinwall steel-backed white metal
Clearance	.001 to .002 in. (.03 to .05 mm.)

ENGINE LUBRICATION SYSTEM

Oil pump

Type	Eccentric rotor
Pressure release valve operates	50 lb./sq. in. (3.5 kg./cm.^{2})

Oil filter

Type (external)	By-pass (element Part No. 17H403). Later models full-flow (Tecalemit or Purolator from Engine No. 4209—element Part No. 8G683)
Capacity	$\frac{1}{2}$ pint (.28 litre)

Oil pressure

Normal running	40 to 50 lb./sq. in. (2.8 to 3.5 kg./cm.²)
Idling	15 lb./sq. in. (1.05 kg./cm.²)

FUEL SYSTEM
Carburettor

Make and type	S.U. H2 semi-downdraught
Diameter	1¼ in. (31.75 mm.)
Needle (BP15W and BP 15W/L)	Standard EB; Weak GG; Rich HA
Needle (BP15W/H)	Standard M; Weak CF; Rich AH2
Jet	.090 in. (2.29 mm.)
[Up to Engine Nos. 8538 (H) and 7301 (L)]	

Fuel pump

Make and type	S.U. electric—high pressure
Delivery test	80 pints/hr. (45.4 litres/hr.)
Suction lift	33 in. (83.8 cm.)
Output lift	48 in. (121.9 cm.)
[Up to Engine Nos. 8538 (H) and 7301 (L).]	

Carburettor

Make and type	S.U. HS2 semi-downdraught
Diameter	1¼ in. (31.75 mm.)
Needle (high compression)	Standard M
Needle (low compression)	Standard EB
Jet	.090 in. (2.29 mm.)
[From Engine Nos. 8539 (H) and 7302 (L).]	

Fuel pump

Make and type	S.U. electric—PD type
Delivery test	45 pints/hr. (25.54 litres/hr.)
Suction lift	18 in. (45.7 cm.)
Output lift	48 in. (121.9 cm.)
[From Engine Nos. 8539 (H) and 7302 (L).]	

Austin A55 Mk II, 'Farina' Cambridge, Morris Oxford Series V, Wolseley Fifteen-Sixty engines 1958–69
(data not shown is unchanged from earlier engines)

ENGINE

Type	15AA
Number of cylinders	4
Bore	2.875 in. (73.025 mm.)
Stroke	3.5 in. (88.9 mm.)
Capacity	90.88 cu. in. (1489 c.c.)
Firing order	1, 3, 4, 2
Compression ratio	8.3:1 or 7.2:1
Capacity of combustion chamber (valves fitted)	2.4 cu. in. (39.2 c.c.)

Valve operation B.M.E.P.	Overhead by P.:
High-compression engine	137 lb./sq. in. (9.64 kg./cm.²) at 2,100 r.p.m.
Low-compression engine	127 lb./sq. in. (8.93 kg./cm.²) at 2,000 r.p.m.

Torque:	
High-compression engine	82.5 lb. ft. (11.41 kg. m.) at 2,100 r.p.m.
Low-compression engine	77 lb. ft. (10.65 kg. m.) at 2,000 r.p.m.
Oversize bore:	
1st	.010 in. (.254 mm.)
Max.	.040 in. (1.016 mm.)

CRANKSHAFT

Main journal diameter	2.0005 to 2.001 in. (50.813 to 50.825 mm.)
Minimum regrind diameter	1.96 in. (49.78 mm.)
Crankpin journal diameter	1.8759 to 1.8764 in. (47.648 to 47.661 mm.)
Crankpin minimum regrind diameter	1.835 in. (46.61 mm.)

Main bearings

Number and type	3 shell-type
Material:	
Bottom half	Steel-backed white metal
Top half	Steel-backed white metal
Length	1.375 in. (34.925 mm.)
End-clearance	.002 to .003 in. (.051 to .076 mm.)
End-thrust	Taken by thrust washers at centre main bearing
Running clearance	.0005 to .002 in. (.0127 to .0508 mm.)

CONNECTING RODS

Length between centres	6.5 in. (165.1 mm.)

Big-end bearings

Material:	
Bottom half	Steel-backed lead-bronze, lead-indium-plated
Top half	Steel-backed lead-bronze, lead-indium-plated
Bearing side-clearance	.008 to .012 in. (.203 to .305 mm.)
Bearing diametrical clearance	.001 to .0025 in. (.0254 to .063 mm.)

PISTONS

Type	Aluminium alloy. Split Skirt. Anodised
Clearances:	
Bottom of skirt	.0006 to .0014 in. (.0152 to .0355 mm.)
Top of skirt	.0022 to .0034 in. (.0559 to .0863 mm.)
Oversizes	+.010 in., +.020 in., +.030 in., +.040 in. (+.254 mm., +.508 mm., +.762 mm., +1.02 mm.)

PISTON RINGS

Compression:	
Plain	Top ring
Tapered	Second and third rings
Width (plain)	.0771 to .0781 in. (1.95 to 1.98 mm.)
Thickness	.119 to .126 in. (3.02 to 3.20 mm.)

Fitted gap	.008 to .013 in. (.20 to .33 mm.)
Clearance in groove	.0015 to .0035 in. (.038 to .089 mm.)
Oil control type	Slotted scraper
Width	.1552 to .1562 in. (3.94 to 3.99 mm.)
Thickness	.119 to .126 in. (3.02 to 3.20 mm.)
Fitted gap	.008 to .013 in. (.20 to .33 mm.)
Clearance in groove	.0016 to .0036 in. (.040 to .091 mm.)

GUDGEON PIN

Type	Clamped
Fit in piston	.0001 to .00035 in. (.0025 to .009 mm.)
Fit in connecting rod	.0001 to .0006 in. (.0025 to .0150 mm.)
Diameter (outer)	.6869 to .6871 in. (17.447 to 17.452 mm.)

VALVES AND VALVE GEAR
Valves

Seat angle:	
Inlet	$45°$
Exhaust	$45°$
Head diameter:	
Inlet	1.370 to 1.375 in. (34.89 to 34.92 mm.)
Exhaust	1.182 to 1.187 in. (30.02 to 30.16 mm.)
Stem diameter:	
Inlet	.3422 to .3427 in. (8.691 to 8.704 mm.)
Exhaust	.34175 to .34225 in. (8.680 to 8.693 mm.)
Valve lift	.312 in. (7.925 mm.)
Valve stem to guide clearance:	
Inlet	.0015 to .0025 in. (.038 to .063 mm.)
Exhaust	.002 to .003 in. (.051 to .076 mm.)
Valve rocker clearance:	
Running	.015 in. (.38 mm.) (hot)
Timing	.021 in. (.53 mm.)
Timing markings	Dimples on timing wheels
Chain pitch and number of pitches	$\frac{3}{8}$ in. (9.52 mm.), 52 pitches
Inlet valve:	
Opens	$5°$ B.T.D.C.
Closes	$45°$ A.B.D.C.
Exhaust valve:	
Opens	$40°$ B.B.D.C.
Closes	$10°$ A.T.D.C.

[with .021 in. (.53 mm.) rocker clearance (for checking purposes only)]

VALVE GUIDES

Length:	
Inlet	$1\frac{7}{8}$ in. (47.63 mm.)
Exhaust	$2\frac{13}{64}$ in. (55.95 mm.)
Diameter—inlet and exhaust:	
Outside	.5635 to .5640 in. (14.312 to 14.325 mm.)
Inside	.34425 to .34475 in. (8.744 to 8.757 mm.)
Fitted height above head	$.625 \pm .016$ in. ($15.87 \pm .40$ mm.)

VALVE SPRINGS

Free length—inlet and exhaust	$2\frac{1}{64}$ in. (51.2 mm.)
Number of working coils	$4\frac{1}{2}$
Pressure:	
Valve open—inlet and exhaust	130 lb. (59 kg.)
Valve closed—inlet and exhaust	77.5 ± 2 lb. ($35.1 \pm .9$ kg.)

TAPPETS

Type	Flat base. Barrel type
Diameter	.81125 to .81175 in. (20.605 to 20.618 mm.)
Length	2.293 to 2.303 in. (58.25 to 58.5 mm.)

ROCKERS

Bore of rocker arms	.7485 to .7495 in. (19.01 to 19.03 mm.)
Rocker ratio	1.4:1

CAMSHAFT

Journal diameters:	
Front	1.78875 to 1.78925 in. (45.43 to 45.44 mm.)
Centre	1.72875 to 1.72925 in. (43.91 to 43.92 mm.)
Rear	1.62275 to 1.62325 in. (41.22 to 41.23 mm.)
End-float	.003 to .007 in. (.076 to .178 mm.)
Bearings: number and type	3 thinwall steel-backed white metal
Outside diameter (before fitting)	Front 1.920 in. (48.76 mm.), centre 1.860 in. (47.24 mm.), rear 1.754 in. (44.55 mm.)
Inside diameter (reamed in position	Front 1.790 in. (45.47 mm.), centre 1.730 in. (43.94 mm.), rear 1.624 in. (41.25 mm.)
Clearance	.001 to .002 in. (.0254 to .0508 mm.)

ENGINE LUBRICATION SYSTEM
Oil pump

Type	Eccentric rotor
Relief pressure valve operates	50 lb./sq. in. (3.52 kg./cm.^{2})
Relief valve spring:	
Free length	2.859 in. (72.638 mm.)
Fitted length	2.156 in. (54.769 mm.) at $13\frac{1}{2}$ lb. (6.12 kg.) load.

Oil filter

Type	Tecalemit or Purolator
Capacity	1 pint (.57 litre)

Oil pressure

Normal running	50 lb./sq. in. (3.52 kg./cm.^{2})
Idling (minimum)	15 lb./sq. in. (1.05 kg./cm.^{2})

TORQUE WRENCH SETTINGS

Cylinder head nuts	40 lb. ft. (5.53 kg. m.)
Main bearing nuts	70 lb. ft. (9.7 kg. m.)
Connecting rod set screws	35 lb. ft. (4.83 kg. m.)
Clutch assembly to flywheel	25 lb. ft. (3.46 kg. m.)
Bevel pinion nut	140 lb. ft. (19.35 kg. m.)
Flywheel securing bolts	35 to 40 lb. ft. (4.84 to 5.53 kg. m.)
Steering-wheel nut	41 lb. ft. (5.76 kg. m.)
Road wheel nuts	60 to 62.5 lb. ft. (8.3 to 8.64 kg. m.)

FUEL SYSTEM

Carburettor

Make and type	S.U. HS2 semi-downdraught
Diameter	$1\frac{1}{4}$ in. (31.75 mm.)
Needle	Standard M
Jet	.090 in. (2.29 mm.)
Piston spring	Red

AIR CLEANER

Type	Cleaner and silencer

FUEL PUMP

Make and type	S.U. electric—PD
Delivery rate	45 pints/hr. (25.5 litres/hr.)
Delivery pressure	2 to 3 lb./sq. in. (.14 to .21 kg./cm.^{2})

COOLING SYSTEM

Type	Pressurized radiator. Thermo-siphon, pump- and fan-assisted
Thermostat setting	70° C. (158° F.)

IGNITION SYSTEM

Sparking plugs	Champion N5
Size	14 mm.
Plug gap	.024 to .026 in. (.625 to .660 mm.)
Coil	Lucas LA12
Distributor	Lucas DM2
Distributor contact points gap	.014 to .016 in. (.35 to .40 mm.)
Timing:	
High Compression	5° B.T.D.C.
Low Compression	T.D.C

CLUTCH

Make and type	Borg & Beck A6–G. Single dry plate
Diameter	8 in. (20.3 cm.)
Facing material	Wound yarn
Pressure springs	6
Colour	Black and yellow
Damper springs	6
Colour	Black and light green
Release lever ratio	4.6:1

GEARBOX

Number of forward speeds	4
Synchromesh	Second, third, and fourth gears
Ratios:	
Top	1.0:1
Third	1.373:1
Second	2.215:1
First	3.637:1
Reverse	4.755:1
Overall ratios:	
Top	4.55:1
Third	6.25:1
Second	10.08:1
First	16.55:1
Reverse	21.64:1
Speedometer gear ratio	9/28

ELECTRICAL EQUIPMENT

System	12-volt. Positive earth
Charging system	Compensated voltage control
Battery	Lucas BT7A, BTZ7A, BT9A, BTZ9A
Battery capacity:	
BT7A, BTZ7A	43 amp.-hr. at 20-hr. rate
BT9A, BTZ9A	58 amp.-hr. at 20-hr. rate
Starter motor	Lucas 4-brush. M35G/1
Dynamo	Lucas C39PV/2
Control box	Lucas RB106/2
Cut-out:	
Cut-in voltage	12.7–13.3
Drop-off voltage	8.5–11.0
Reverse current	5.0 amps. (max.)
Regulator:	
At 1,500 r.p.m. dynamo speed: Open-circuit setting at 20° C. (68° F.)	15.4–16.4 volts

For ambient temperatures other than 20° C. the following allowances should be made to the above setting:

For every 10° C. (18° F.) above 20° C. subtract .1 volt.

For every 10° C. (18° F.) below 20° C. add .1 volt

CAPACITIES

	Imp.	U.S.	Litres
Engine sump (including filter)	8 pts.	9.6 pts.	4.5
Gearbox	$4\frac{1}{2}$ pts.	5.4 pts.	2.56
Rear axle	2 pts.	2.4 pts.	1.14
Cooling system	$11\frac{1}{2}$ pts.	13.8 pts.	6.5
Fuel tank	10 gal.	12 gal.	45.4

MG Magnette Mk III and IV, Riley 4/Sixty-Eight and 4/Seventy-Two engines 1959–69
(data not shown is unchanged from earlier engines)

ENGINE

Type	15GE and 15RB (Magnette Mk III and Riley 4/Sixty-Eight)
Number of cylinders	4
Bore	2.875 in. (73.025 mm.)
Stroke	3.5 in. (88.9 mm.)
Capacity	90.88 cu. in. (1489 c.c.)
Firing order	1, 3, 4, 2
Compression ratio	8.3:1
Capacity of combustion chamber (valves fitted)	2.37 cu. in. (38.9 c.c.)
Valve operation	Overhead by push-rod
B.M.E.P.	140 lb./sq. in. (9.84 kg./cm.^{2}) at 3,300 r.p.m.
Torque	85 lb. ft. (11.75 kg. m.) at 3,300 r.p.m.
Oversize bore:	
1st	.010 in. (.254 mm.)
Max.	.040 in. (1.016 mm.)

VALVES AND VALVE GEAR
Valves

Seat angle	45°
Head diameter:	
Inlet	1.500 to 1.505 in. (38.10 to 38.23 mm.)
Exhaust	1.281 to 1.286 in. (32.54 to 32.67 mm.)
Inlet valve:	
Opens	5° B.T.D.C.
Closes	45° A.B.D.C.
Exhaust valve:	
Opens	40° B.B.D.C.
Closes	10° A.T.D.C.
	From Engine Nos. 15GE–8067 and 15RB–4134
Inlet valve:	
Opens	T.D.C.
Closes	50° A.B.D.C.
Exhaust valve:	
Opens	35° B.B.D.C.
Closes	15° A.T.D.C.

[Check with .021 in. (.5 mm.) rocker clearance.]

VALVE SPRINGS

Free length:	
Inner	$1\frac{31}{32}$ in. (50 mm.)
Outer	$2\frac{3}{64}$ in. (52 mm.)
Fitted length:	
Inner	$1\frac{7}{16}$ in. (36.5 mm.)
Outer	$1\frac{9}{16}$ in. (39.7 mm.)
Number of working coils:	
Inner	$6\frac{1}{2}$
Outer	$4\frac{1}{2}$
Pressure:	
Valve open	Inner 50 lb. (22.7 kg.). Outer 105 lb. (47.6 kg.)
Valve closed	Inner 30 lb. (13.6 kg.). Outer $60\frac{1}{2}$ lb. (275 kg.)

TAPPETS

Type	Spherical base. Barrel type
Diameter	.81125 to .81175 in. (20.605 to 20.618 mm.)
Length	2.293 to 2.303 in. (58.25 to 58.5 mm.)
Clearance	.0005 to .00175 in. (.0127 to .0444 mm.)

ENGINE LUBRICATION SYSTEM
Oil pump

Type	Eccentric rotor
Relief pressure valve operates	75 lb./sq. in. (5.27 kg./cm.^{2})
Relief valve spring:	
Free length	3 in. (76.2 mm.)
Fitted length	2.156 in. (54.77 mm.) at 16 lb. (7.26 kg.) load
Capacity	$3\frac{1}{4}$ gal./min. (31 U.S. pints/min., 14.8 litres/min.) at 1,000 pump r.p.m.

Oil filter

Make and type	Tecalemit or Purolator. Full-flow
Capacity	$1\frac{1}{4}$ pints (1.5 U.S. pints, .71 litre)

Oil pressure

Normal running	75 lb./sq. in. (5.27 kg./cm.^{2})
Idling (minimum)	15 lb./sq. in. (1.05 kg./cm.^{2})

FUEL SYSTEM
Carburettors

Make and type	S.U. twin HD4 semi-downdraught
Diameter	$1\frac{1}{2}$ in. (38.10 mm.)
Jet	.090 in. (2.29 mm.)
Needle	Standard FU. Rich FT. Weak M9
Piston spring	Red

Air cleaner

Type	Cleaner and silencer. Oil bath

Fuel pump

Make and type	S.U. electric—PD
Delivery rate (minimum)	45 pints/hr. (54 U.S. pints/hr., 25.5 litres/hr.)
Delivery pressure	2 to 3 lb./sq. in. (.14 to .21 kg./cm.^{2}).

[To Car Nos. GHS1 15634 and RHS1 10120.]

Make and type	S.U. electric—S.P.
Delivery rate (minimum)	56 pints/hr. (62.7 U.S. pints/hr., 31.8 litres/hr.)
Delivery pressure	2 to 3.8 lb./sq. in. (.14 to .27 kg./cm.^{2})

COOLING SYSTEM

Type	Pressurized radiator. Thermo-siphon, pump- and fan-assisted
Thermostat setting	70° C. (158° F.)
Cars exported to cold	82° C. (180° F.) from Car

countries	Nos. GHS1 15491 and RHS1 9962.

IGNITION SYSTEM

Coil

Resistance at 20° C. (68° F.) primary winding	Lucas 3.2 to 3.4 ohms.
Consumption:	
Ignition switch on at 15° C. (60° F.)	3.6 amps.
At 2,000 r.p.m.	1.25 amps.

Distributor

Cam form	Lucas 25D4 4-cylinder high-lift
Cam closed period	60° ± 3°
Cam open period	30° ± 3°
Automatic advance	Centrifugal and vacuum
Rotation of rotor	Anti-clockwise
Serial number	40644A/B
Automatic advance starts*	700 r.p.m.
Vacuum advance:	
Starts	6 in. (15 cm.) Hg
Ends*	16° at 14 in. (136 cm.) Hg
Maximum advance*	28° at 2,800 r.p.m.
Decelerating check*	20° at 2,000 r.p.m.
	15° at 1,600 r.p.m.
	8° at 1,000 r.p.m.
Contact point gap setting	.014 to .016 in. (.35 to .40 mm.)
Breaker spring tension	18 to 24 oz. (510 to 680 gm.)
Condenser capacity	.18 to .24m F.
Timing marks	Pointers on timing chain case and notch on crankshaft pulley
Static ignition timing	8° B.T.D.C.

Sparking plugs

Size	Champion N5 14 mm. $\frac{3}{4}$ in. (19.0 mm.) reach
Gap	.024 to .026 in. (.625 to .660 mm.)

*Crankshaft degrees and r.p.m.

GEARBOX

Number of forward speeds	4
Synchromesh	Second, third, and fourth gears
Ratios:	
Top	1.0:1
Third	1.373:1
Second	2.215:1
First	3.637:1
Reverse	4.755:1
Overall ratios:	
Top	4.3:1
Third	5.91:1
Second	9.52:1
First	15.64:1
Reverse	20.45:1
Speedometer gear ratio	9/28

ENGINE

Type	16GE, 16RA and 16GF (Magnette Mk IV and Riley 4/Seventy Two)
Number of cylinders	4
Bore	3.0 in. (76.2 mm.)
Stroke	3.5 in. (88.9 mm.)
Capacity	99.08 cu. in. (1622 c.c.)
Firing order	1, 3, 4, 2
Compression ratio	8.3:1
Capacity of combustion chamber (valves fitted)	2.64 cu. in. (43.0 c.c.)
Valve operation	Overhead by push-rod
B.M.E.P.	136 lb./sq. in. (9.63 kg./cm.^{2}) at 2,600 r.p.m.
Torque	89 lb. ft. (12.3 kg. m.) at 2,500 r.p.m.
Oversize bore:	
1st	.010 in. (.254 mm.)
Max.	.040 in. (1.016 mm.)

CONNECTING RODS

Big-end bearings

Material	Steel-backed copper-lead
Bearing side-clearance	.008 to .012 in. (.203 to .305 mm.)
Bearing diametrical clearance	.001 to .0027 in. (.0254 to .068 mm.)

PISTONS

Type	Aluminium alloy. Solid skirt. Anodized.
Clearances:	
Bottom of skirt	.0015 to 0021 in. (.038 to .053 mm.)
Top of skirt	.0035 to .0042 in. (.0889 to .1067 mm.)
Oversizes	+.010 in., +.020 in., +.030 in., +.040 in. (+.254 mm., +.508 mm., +.762 mm., +1.02 mm.)

PISTON RINGS

Compression:	
Plain	Top ring
Tapered	Second and third rings
Width (plain)	.0615 to .0625 in. (1.562 to 1.587 mm.)
Thickness	.119 to .126 in. (3.02 to 3.20 mm.)
Fitted gap	.009 to .014 in. (.229 to .356 mm.)
Clearance in groove	.0015 to .0035 in. (.038 to .089 mm.)
Oil control type	Slotted scraper
Width	.1552 to .1562 in. (3.94 to 3.97 mm.)
Thickness	.119 to .126 in. (3.02 to 3.20 mm.)
Fitted gap	.008 to .013 in. (.20 to .33 mm.)
Clearance in groove	.0018 to .0038 in. (.046 to .096 mm.)

VALVE SPRINGS

Free length:	
Inner	$1\frac{31}{32}$ in. (50 mm.)
Outer	$1\frac{59}{64}$ in. (48.8 mm.)
Fitted length:	
Inner	$1\frac{7}{16}$ in. (36.5 mm.)

Outer	$1\frac{17}{32}$ in. (38.9 mm.)
Number of working coils:	
Inner	$6\frac{1}{2}$
Outer	$4\frac{1}{2}$
Pressure:	
Valve open	Inner 50 lb. (22.7 kg.). Outer 115 lb. (52.15 kg.)
Valve closed	Inner 30 lb. (13.6 kg.). Outer 62 lb. (28.12 kg.)

FUEL SYSTEM
Carburettors

Make and type	S.U. twin HD4 semi-downdraught
Diameter	$1\frac{1}{2}$ in. (38.10 mm.)
Jet	.090 in. (2.29 mm.)
Needle	Standard HB. Rich FU. Weak FK
Piston spring	Red

Fuel pump

Make and type	S.U. electric—SP or AUF204
Delivery rate (minimum)	56 pints/hr. (67.2 U.S. pints/hr., 31.8 litres/hr.)
Delivery pressure	2 to 3.8 lb./sq. in. (.14 to .27 kg./cm.^{2})

COOLING SYSTEM

Thermostat setting:	
Standard	82° C. (180° F.)
Hot countries	74° C. (165° F.)
Cold countries	88° C. (190° F.)

IGNITION SYSTEM
Distributor

Serial number	40823A
Automatic advance starts*	700 r.p.m.
Vacuum advance:	
Starts	6 in. (15 cm.) Hg.
Ends*	24° at 16 in. (41 cm.) Hg.
Maximum advance*	26° at 3,700 r.p.m.
Decelerating check	19° at 2,700 r.p.m.
	10° at 1,400 r.p.m.
	6° at 1,000 r.p.m.
Contact point gap setting	.014 to .016 in. (.35 to .40 mm.)
Ignition timing:	
Static	4° B.T.D.C.
Stroboscopic*	7° B.T.D.C. at 600 r.p.m.

*Crankshaft degrees and r.p.m.

Wolseley Sixteen-Sixty engine 1961–71
(data not shown is unchanged from the Wolseley Fifteen-Sixty)

ENGINE

Type	16AMW
Number of cylinders	4
Bore	3 in. (76.2 mm.)
Stroke	3.5 in. (88.9 mm.)
Capacity	98.9 cu. in. (1622 c.c.)
Firing order	1, 3, 4, 2

Compression ratio	8.3:1 or 7.2:1
Capacity of combustion chamber (valves fitted)	2.64 cu. in. (43.0 c.c.)
Valve operation	Overhead by push-rod
B.M.E.P.:	
High compression	138 lb./sq. in. (9.7 kg./cm.^{2}) at 2,100 r.p.m.
Low compression	128 lb./sq. in. (8.94 kg./cm.^{2}) at 2,000 r.p.m.
Torque:	
High compression	90 lb. ft. (12.4 kg. m.) at 2,100 r.p.m.
Low compression	83 lb. ft. (11.6 kg. m.) at 2,000 r.p.m.
Oversize bore:	
1st	.010 in. (.254 mm.)
Max.	.040 in. (1.016 mm.)
B.H.P. (standard):	
High compression	61 at 4,500 r.p.m.
Low compression	56 at 4,500 r.p.m.

CRANKSHAFT

Main journal diameter	2.0005 to 2.001 in. (50.813 to 50.825 mm.)
Minimum regrind diameter	1.96 in. (49.78 mm.)
Crankpin journal diameter	1.8759 to 1.8764 in. (47.648 to 47.661 mm.)
Crankpin minimum regrind diameter	1.835 in. (46.61 mm.)

Main bearings

Number and type	3 shell-type
Material	Steel-backed copper-lead
Length	1.25 in. (31.75 mm.)
End-clearance	.002 to .003 in. (.051 to .076 mm.)
End-thrust	Taken by thrust washers at centre main bearing
Diametrical clearance	.001 to .0027 in. (.0254 to .068 mm.)

CONNECTING RODS

Length between centres	6.5 in. (165.1 mm.)

Big-end bearings

Material	Steel-backed copper-lead
Bearing side-clearance	.008 to .012 in. (.203 to .305 mm.)
Bearing diametrical clearance	.001 to .0027 in. (.0254 to .068 mm.)

PISTONS

Type	Aluminium alloy. Solid skirt. Anodized
Clearances:	
Bottom of skirt	.0015 to .0021 in. (.038 to .053 mm.)
Top of skirt	.0022 to .0034 in. (.0558 to .0863 mm.)
Oversizes	+.010 in., +.020 in., +.030 in., +.040 in. (+.254 mm., +.508 mm., +.762 mm., +1.02 mm.)

PISTON RINGS

Compression:

Plain	Top ring
Tapered	Second and third rings
Width (plain)	.0771 to .0781 in. (1.95 to 1.98 mm.)
Thickness	.119 to .126 in. (3.02 to 3.20 mm.)
Fitted gap	.012 to .017 in. (.305 to .432 mm.)
Clearance in groove	.0015 to .0035 in. (.038 to .089 mm.)
Oil control type	Slotted scraper
Width	.1552 to .1562 in. (3.94 to 3.99 mm.)
Thickness	.119 to .126 in. (3.02 to 3.20 mm.)
Fitted gap	.008 to .013 in. (.20 to .33 mm.)
Clearance in groove	.0016 to .0036 in. (.040 to .091 mm.)

GUDGEON PIN

Type	Clamped
Fit in piston	.0001 to .00035 in. (.0025 to .009 mm.)
Fit in connecting rod	.0001 to .0006 in. (.0025 to .0150 mm.)
Diameter (outer)	.75 in. (19.05 mm.)

VALVES AND VALVE GEAR

Valves

Seat angle	45°
Head diameter:	
Inlet	1.500 to 1.505 in. (38.1 to 38.3 mm.)
Exhaust	1.281 to 1.286 in. (32.5 to 32.6 mm.)
Stem diameter:	
Inlet	.3422 to .3427 in. (8.691 to 8.704 mm.)
Exhaust	.34175 to .34225 in. (8.680 to 8.693 mm.)
Valve lift	.325 in. (8.25 mm.)
Valve stem to guide clearance:	
Inlet	.0015 to .0025 in. (.038 to .063 mm.)
Exhaust	.002 to .003 in. (.051 to .076 mm.)
Valve rocker clearance:	
Running	.015 in. (.38 mm.) (hot)
Timing	.021 in. (.53 mm.)
Timing markings	Dimples on timing wheels
Chain pitch and number of pitches	$\frac{3}{8}$ in. (9.52 mm.), 52 pitches
Inlet valve:	
Opens	T.D.C.
Closes	50° A.B.D.C.
Exhaust valve:	
Opens	35° B.B.D.C.
Closes	15° A.T.D.C.

[With .021 in. (.53 mm.) rocker clearance (for checking purposes only).]

VALVE SPRINGS

Free length	$2\frac{1}{32}$ in. (51.6 mm.)
Number of working coils	$4\frac{1}{2}$
Pressure:	
Valve open	130 lb. (59 kg.)
Valve closed	79 ± 2 lb. (35.8 ± .9 kg.)

FUEL SYSTEM

Carburettor

Make and type	S.U. HS2 semi-downdraught
Diameter	$1\frac{1}{4}$ in. (31.75 mm.)
Needle	Standard GX. Rich M. Weak GG
Jet	.090 in. (2.29 mm.)
Piston spring	Yellow

IGNITION SYSTEM

Sparking plugs	Champion N5
Size	14 mm.
Plug gap	.024 to .026 in. (.625 to .660 mm.)
Coil	Lucas LA12
Distributor	Lucas 25D4

Riley One-Point-Five and Wolseley 1500 engines 1957–65

ENGINE

Type:	
Wolseley	B.P.15L.WA (revised code 15WA), 15WC, and 15WD
Riley	15R. Later engines: 15RB
Number of cylinders	4
Bore	2.875 in. (73.025 mm.)
Stroke	3.5 in. (88.9 mm.)
Capacity	90.88 cu. in. (1489 c.c.)
Firing order	1, 3, 4, 2
Compression ratio:	
Low: *Wolseley only*	7.2:1
High: *Wolseley and Riley*	8.3:1
Capacity of combustion chamber (valves fitted)	2.4 cu. in. (39.2 c.c.)
Valve operation	Overhead, by push-rod
B.M.E.P.:	
Low compression:	127 lb./sq. in. (8.921 kg./cm.²) at 2,000 r.p.m.
High compression:	
Wolseley	137 lb./sq. in. (9.632 kg./cm.²) at 2,100 r.p.m.
Riley	136 lb./sq. in. (9.56 kg./cm.²) at 2,500 r.p.m.
Torque:	
Low compression:	
Wolseley only	77 lb. ft. (10.65 kg. m.) at 2,000 r.p.m.
High compression:	
Wolseley	82.5 lb. ft. (11.406 kg. m.) at 2,100 r.p.m.
Riley	82 lb. ft. (11.34 kg. m.) at 2,500 r.p.m.
Oversize bore	(First) .010 in. (.254 mm.). (Max.) .040 in. (1.016 mm.)

CRANKSHAFT

Main journal diameter	2.0005 to 2.001 in. (50.813 to 50.825 mm.)
Minimum regrind diameter	1.96 in. (49.78 mm.)
Crankpin journal diameter	1.8759 to 1.8764 in. (47.648 to 47.661 mm.)
Crankpin minimum regrind diameter	1.835 in. (46.61 mm.)

Main bearings

Number and type	3 shell type
Material:	
Bottom half	Steel-backed white metal
Top half	Steel-backed white metal
Length	1.375 in. (34.925 mm.)
End-clearance	.002 to .003 in. (.051 to .076 mm.)
End-thrust	Taken by thrust washers at centre main bearing
Running clearance	.0005 to .002 in. (.0127 to .0508 mm.)

CONNECTING RODS

Length between centres	6.5 in. (165.1 mm.)
Big-end bearings:	
Material:	
Bottom half	Steel-backed, lead-bronze-, lead-indium-, or lead-tin-plated
Top half	Steel-backed, lead-bronze-, lead-indium-, or lead-tin-plated
Bearing side-clearance	.008 to .012 in. (.203 to .305 mm.)
Bearing diametrical clearance	.001 to .0025 in. (.0254 to .063 mm.)

PISTONS

Type	Aluminium alloy. Anodized
Clearances:	
Wolseley:	
Bottom of Skirt	*Part No. 1H 583* .0008/.0014 in. (.0203/.0355 mm.), *Part No. 1H 581* .0007/.0013 in. (.0177/.0330 mm.), *Part No. 1H 700* .0006/.0012 in. (.0152/.0304 mm.)
Top of skirt	*Part No. 1H 583* .0028/.0034 in. (.0711/.0863 mm.), *Part No. 1H 581* .0027/.0033 in. (.0685/.0838 mm.), *Part No. 1H 700* .0022/.0029 in. (.0558/.0736 mm.)
Riley:	
Bottom of skirt	.0017/.0023 in. (.0432/.0584 mm.)
Top of skirt	.0035/.0042 in. (.0899/.1067 mm.)
Oversizes: *Wolseley and Riley*	+.010 in., +.020 in., +.030 in., +.040 in. (+.254 mm., +.508 mm., +.762 mm., +1.02 mm.)

PISTON RINGS

Wolseley

Compression:	
Plain	Top ring
Tapered	Second and third rings
Width	.0771 to .0781 in. (1.95 to 1.98 mm.)
Thickness	.111 to .118 in. (2.81 to 3.0 mm.)
From Engine No. 26816	.119 to .126 in. (3.02 to 3.2 mm.)
Fitted gap	.008 to .013 in. (.20 to .33 mm.)
Clearance in groove	.0015 to .0035 in. (.038 to .089 mm.)
Oil control type	Slotted scraper
Width	.1552 to .1562 in. (3.94 to 3.99 mm.)
Thickness	.111 to .118 in. (2.81 to 3.0 mm.)
From Engine No. 26816	.119 to .126 in. (3.02 to 3.2 mm.)
Fitted gap	.008 to .013 in. (.20 to .33 mm.)
Clearance in groove	.0016 to .0036 in. (.040 to .091 mm.)

Riley

Compression:	
Plain	Top ring
Tapered	Second and third rings
Width	.0615 to .0625 in. (1.56 to 1.58 mm.)
Thickness	.111 to .118 in. (2.81 to 3.0 mm.)
From Engine No. 15R-U-H791	.119 to .126 in. (3.02 to 3.2 mm.)
Fitted gap	.008 to .013 in. (.20 to .33 mm.)
Clearance in groove	.0015 to .0035 in. (.038 to .089 mm.)
Oil control type	Slotted scraper
Width	.1552 to .1562 in. (3.94 to 3.99 mm.)
Thickness	.111 to .118 in. (2.81 to 3.0 mm.)
From Engine No. 15R-U-H791	.119 to .126 in. (3.02 to 3.2 mm.)
Fitted gap	.008 to .013 in. (.20 to .33 mm.)
Clearance in groove	.0018 to .0038 in. (.046 to .096 mm.)

GUDGEON PIN

Type	Clamped
Fit in piston	.0001 to .00035 in. (.0025 to .009 mm.). Hand push fit at 20° C. (68° F.)
Fit in connecting rod	.0001 to .0006 in. (.0025 to .0150 mm.)
Diameter (outer)	.6869 to .6871 in. (17.447 to 17.452 mm.)

VALVES AND VALVE GEAR

Valves:

Seat angle:

Inlet ... 45°

Exhaust ... 45°

Head diameter:

Wolseley: Inlet ... 1.370 to 1.375 in. (34.89 to 34.92 mm.)

Exhaust ... 1.182 to 1.187 in. (30.02 to 30.16 mm.)

Riley: Inlet ... 1.500 to 1.505 in. (38.10 to 38.23 mm.)

Exhaust ... 1.281 to 1.286 in. (32.54 to 32.66 mm.)

Stem diameter:

Inlet ... .3422 to .3427 in. (8.691 to 8.70 mm.)

Exhaust ... .34175 to .34225 in. (8.680 to 8.693 mm.)

Valve lift ... .322 in. (7.937 mm.)

Valve stem to guide clearance:

Inlet ... .0015 to .0025 in. (.038 to .063 mm.)

Exhaust ... .002 to .003 in. (.051 to .076 mm.)

Valve rocker clearance:

Running ... .015 in. (.38 mm.) (cold)

Timing ... .021 in. (.53 mm.)

Timing markings ... Dimples on timing wheels

Chain pitch and number of pitches ... $\frac{3}{8}$ in. (9.52 mm.), 52 pitches

Inlet valve:

Opens ... 5° B.T.D.C.

Closes ... 45° A.B.D.C.

Exhaust valve:

Opens ... 40° B.B.D.C.

Closes ... 10° A.T.D.C.

From Engine Nos. 15WC-U-L12316 and 15RB-U-H5623

Inlet valve:

Opens ... T.D.C.

Closes ... 50° A.B.D.C.

Exhaust valve:

Opens ... 35° B.B.D.C.

Closes ... 15° A.T.D.C.

[With .021 in. (.53 mm.) valve rocker clearance, for checking purposes only]

VALVE GUIDES

Length:

Wolseley:

Inlet ... $1\frac{7}{8}$ in. (47.63 mm.)

Exhaust ... $2\frac{13}{64}$ in. (55.95 mm.)

Riley:

Inlet and exhaust (RB-type engine) ... $1\frac{7}{8}$ in. (47.63 mm.)

Exhaust (R-type engine) ... $2\frac{13}{64}$ in. (55.95 mm.)

Diameter:

Outside ... .5635 to .5640 in. (14.31 to 14.325 mm.)

Inside ... .3442 to .3447 in. (8.74 to 8.75 mm.)

Fitted height above head ... .625 in. (15.87 mm.)

VALVE SPRINGS

Wolseley

Free length ... $2\frac{1}{64}$ in. (51.2 mm.)

Fitted length ... $1\frac{17}{32}$ in. (38.89 mm.)

Number of working coils ... $4\frac{1}{2}$

Pressure:

Valve open ... 130 lb. (59 kg.)

Valve closed ... 77.5 lb. (35.12 kg.)

Riley

Free length: Inlet and exhaust:

Inner ... $1\frac{31}{32}$ in. (50.0 mm.)

Outer ... $2\frac{3}{64}$ in. (51.99 mm.)

Number of working coils:

Inner ... $6\frac{1}{2}$

Outer ... $4\frac{1}{2}$

Pressure:

Valve open: Inlet and exhaust:

Inner ... 50 lb. (22.7 kg.)

Outer ... 105 lb. (47.6 kg.)

Valve closed: Inlet and exhaust:

Inner ... 30 ± 2 lb. ($13.6 \pm .9$ kg.)

Outer ... 60.5 ± 2 lb. ($27.4 \pm .9$ kg.)

TAPPETS

Type ... Flat base. Barrel type

Diameter ... .81125 to .81175 in. (20.605 to 20.618 mm.)

Length ... 2.293 to 2.303 in. (58.25 to 58.5 mm.)

ROCKERS

Bore of rocker arms ... .7485 to .7495 in. (19.01 to 19.03 mm.)

Rocker ratio ... 1.4:1

CAMSHAFT

Journal diameters:

Front ... 1.78875 to 1.78925 in. (45.43 to 45.44 mm.)

Centre ... 1.72875 to 1.72925 in. (43.91 to 43.92 mm.)

Rear ... 1.62275 to 1.62325 in. (41.22 to 41.23 mm.)

End-float ... .003 to .007 in. (.076 to .178 mm.)

Bearing: Number and type ... 3 thinwall steel-backed white metal

Outside diameter (before fitting) ... Front 1.920 in. (48.76 mm.), centre 1.860 in. (47.24 mm.), rear 1.754 in. (44.55 mm.)

Inside diameter (reamed in position) ... Front 1.790 in. (45.47 mm.), centre 1.730 in. (43.94 mm.), rear 1.624 in. (41.25 mm.)

Clearance ... .001 to .002 in. (.0254 to .0508 mm.)

ENGINE LUBRICATION SYSTEM
Wolseley

Oil pump:

Type	Eccentric rotor
Relief pressure valve operates	50 lb./sq. in. (3.5 kg./cm.²)

Relief valve spring:

Free length	2.859 in. (72.638 mm.)
Fitted length	2.156 in. (54.769 mm.) at 13½ lb. (6.12 kg.) load

Oil filter:

Type	Tecalemit or Purolator (element Part No. 8G 683)
Capacity	1¼ pints (1½ U.S. pints, .71 litre)

Oil pressure:

Normal running	50 lb./sq. in. (3.5 kg./cm.²)
Idling (minimum)	15 lb./sq. in. (1.05 kg./cm.²)

RILEY

Oil pump:

Type	Eccentric rotor

Relief valve opens:

Early type	50 lb./sq. in. (3.52 kg./cm.²)
RB type	75 lb./sq. in. (5.27 kg./cm.²)

Relief valve spring:
Free length:

Early type	2.859 in. (72.638 mm.)
RB type	3.0 in. (76.2 mm.)

Fitted length:

Early type	2.156 in. (54.769 mm.) at load of 13½ lb. (6.12 kg.)
RB type	2.156 in. (54.769 mm.) at load of 16 lb. (7.26 kg.)

Oil filter:

Type	Tecalemit or Purolator (element Part No. 8G683)
Capacity	1¼ pints (1½ U.S. pints, .71 litre)

Oil pressure:
Normal running:

Early type	50 lb./sq. in. (3.52 kg./cm.²)
RB type	75 lb./sq. in. (5.27 kg./cm.²)
Idling (minimum)	15 lb./sq. in. (1.05 kg./cm.²)

MG Magnette ZA engine 1953–56

Engine type	BP15GA, prior to Car No. ZA.18101
	BP15HGC, commencing Car No. ZA.18101
Number of cylinders	4
Firing order	1, 3, 4, 2
Bore	2.875 in. (73.025 mm.)
Stroke	3.5 in. (89 mm.)
Cubic capacity	1489 c.c. (90.88 cu. in.)
Compression ratio	7.15:1, prior to Car No. ZA.18101
	8.3:1, commencing Car No. ZA.18101
Capacity of combustion chamber	39.4 c.c. (2.4 cu. in.)

First oversize bore	.010 in. (.254 mm.)
Maximum oversize bore	.040 in. (1.016 mm.)
Number of main bearings	3
Type of main bearings	Steel-backed, white-metal-lined (Thinwall)
Main journal diameter	2 in. (50.8 mm.)
Main journal, minimum regrind diameter	1.960 in. (49.78 mm.)
Main bearing length	1.375 in. (34.925 mm.)
Main bearing end clearance	.002 to .003 in. (.0508 to .0762 mm.)
Main bearing diametrical clearance	.0005 to .002 in. (.0127 to .0508 mm.)
Crankshaft end thrust	Taken at centre main bearing by thrust washers
Crankpin diameter	1.875 in. (47.625 mm.)
Crankpin minimum regrind diameter	1.835 in. (46.61 mm.)
Connecting rod bearings	Steel-backed, white-metal-lined, prior to Car No. ZA.18101
	Lead indium, commencing Car No. ZA.18101
Connecting rod length between centres	6½ in. (165.1 mm.)
Connecting rod bearing side clearance	.008 to .012 in. (.2032 to .305 mm.)
Connecting rod bearing diametrical clearance	.0016 in. (.04 mm.)
Piston type	Aluminium alloy; concave crown, split skirt
Piston clearance, top of skirt	.0016 to .0024 in. (.0406 to .061 mm.), prior to Car No. ZA.18101
	.0035 to .0042 in. (.090 to .106 mm.), commencing Car No. ZA.18101
Piston clearance, bottom of skirt	.0008 to .0014 in. (.0203 to .0356 mm.), prior to Car No. ZA.18101
	.0017 to .0023 in. (.043 to .058 mm.), commencing Car No. ZA.18101
Piston rings, compression	1 plain, 2 taper
Piston rings, oil control	1 slotted
Piston ring gap	.008 to .013 in. (.203 to .330 mm.)
Gudgeon pin type	Clamped in connecting rod
Gudgeon pin fit in piston	Double thumb press, .0001 in. (.00254 mm.) tight to .00035 in. (.00889 mm.) slack
Gudgeon pin diameter	.6869 to .6871 in. (17.4472 to 17.4523 mm.)
Camshaft bearings	Three steel-backed white metal
Camshaft drive	Duplex chain: ⅜ in. pitch, 52 pitches
Camshaft bearing clearance	.001 to .002 in. (.0254 to .0508 mm.)
Camshaft thrust taken on	Front end thrust plate

Valve timing marking	Timing wheels marked		(39.69 mm.) commencing Car No. ZA.18101
Valve timing in degrees:		Valve spring pressure	Shut: 77½ lb. (35.15 kg.). Open: 130 lb. (58.897 kg.)
Inlet:			
Opens	5° B.T.D.C.	Oil pressure relief valve operates	50 lb./sq. in. (3.5 kg./cm.²)
Closes	45° A.B.D.C.		
Exhaust:			
Opens	40° B.B.D.C.	Oil pressure	50 lb./sq. in. (3.5 kg./cm.²) (normal). 15 lb./sq. in. (1.05 kg./cm.²) (idling)
Closes	10° A.T.D.C.		
Valve seat angle	45°		
Inlet valve head diameter	1½ in. (38.1 mm.)	Oil filter (external)	By-pass, prior to Car No. ZA.18101
Inlet valve stem diameter	11/32 in. (8.731 mm.)		Full flow, commencing Car No. ZA.18101
Exhaust valve head diameter	1 9/32 in. (32.54 mm.)	FUEL SYSTEM	
Exhaust valve stem diameter	11/32 in. (8.731 mm.)	Carburettor type	Twin, S.U. H.2 semi-downdraught, 1¼ in. Prior to Car No. ZA.18101
Inlet valve throat diameter	1 5/16 in. (33.337 mm.)		Twin, S.U. H.4 semi-downdraught, 1½ in. Commencing Car No. ZA.18101
Exhaust valve throat diameter	1 5/32 in. (29.368 mm.)		
Valve lift	.322 in. (8.1778 mm.)	Needle	Standard: G.M. Prior to Car. No. ZA.18101
Valve rocker clearance	Running: .015 in. (.381 mm.) hot. For timing: .021 in. (.533 mm.)		Standard: E.Q. Commencing Car No. ZA.18101
Valve spring free length	2 1/64 in. (51.197 mm.), prior to Car No. ZA.18101	Fuel pump	S.U. H.P. Test 10 gals. per hr. Suction lift 33 in.
	Inner: 1 31/32 in. (50 mm.), commencing Car No. ZA.18101	CLUTCH AND GEARBOX	
		Clutch	Borg & Beck, 8 in. (20.32 cm.)
Valve spring free length (fitted)	1 17/32 in. (38.894 mm.), prior to Car No. ZA.18101	Synchromesh	Second, third and top
	Inner: 1 7/16 in. (36.51 mm.) commencing Car No. ZA.18101. Outer: 2 3/64 in. (51.99 mm.) commencing Car No. ZA.18101 (fitted) 1 9/16 in.	Ratios:	
		Top	1.0:1
		Third	1.374:1
		Second	2.214:1
		First	3.64:1
		Reverse	4.76:1

MG MGA: All models

	MGA 1500	MGA 1600
ENGINE		
Type	15GB	
(From Car No. 61504)	15GD	16GA
Number of cylinders	4	
Bore	2.875 in. (73.025 mm.)	2.968 in. (75.39 mm.)
Stroke	3.5 in. (89 mm.)	
Capacity	90.88 cu. in. (1489 c.c.)	96.9 cu. in. (1588 c.c.)
Firing order	1, 3, 4, 2	
Compression ratio	8.3:1	
Capacity of combustion chamber (valves fitted)	2.3 to 2.4 cu. in. (38.2 to 39.2 c.c.)	2.36 cu. in. (38.7 c.c.)
Valve operation	Overhead by push-rod	
B.M.E.P.	130 lb./sq. in. at 3,500 r.p.m.	135 lb./sq. in. (9.5 kg./cm.²) at 4,000 r.p.m.
Torque	77.4 lb. ft. at 3,500 r.p.m.	87 lb. ft. (12.03 kg. m.) at 3,800 r.p.m.
Cooling system	Thermo-siphon, pump- and fan-assisted	
Oversize bore:		
1st	.010 in. (.254 mm.)	
Max.	.040 in. (1.016 mm.)	

	MGA 1500	**MGA 1600**
CRANKSHAFT		
Main journal diameter	2 in. (50.8 mm.)	
Minimum regrind diameter	1.96 in. (49.78 mm.)	
Crankpin journal diameter	1.8759 to 1.8764 in. (47.65 to 47.66 mm.)	
Crankpin minimum regrind diameter	1,8359 in. (46.64 mm.)	
Main bearings		
Number and type	3. Shell-type	
Material:		
Bottom half	Steel-backed. White metal	
Top half	Steel-backed. White metal	
Length	1.375 in. (34.925 mm.)	
End-clearance	.002 to .003 in. (.051 to .076 mm.)	
End-thrust	Taken by thrust washers at centre main bearing	
Running clearance	.0005 to .002 in. (.0127 to .0508 mm.)	
CONNECTING RODS		
Length between centres	6.5 in. (165.1 mm.)	6.5 in. (165.1 mm.)
Big-end bearings		
Material:		
Bottom half	Steel and lead-indium	
Top half	Steel and lead-indium	
Bearing side-clearance	.008 to .012 in. (.203 to .305 mm.)	
Bearing diametrical clearance	.0010 to .0025 in. (.025 to .063 mm.).	−.010 in., −.020 in., −.030 in., −.040 in. (−.254 mm., −.508 mm., −.762 mm., −1.016 mm.)
PISTONS		
Type	Aluminium alloy	
Clearances:		
Bottom of skirt	.0017 to .0023 in. (.043 to .051 mm.)	
Top of skirt	.0035 to .0042 in. (.090 to .106 mm.)	
Oversizes	+.010 in., +.020 in., +.030 in. +.040 in. (+.254 mm., +.508 mm., +.762 mm., +1.016 mm.)	

	MGA 1600 Mk II	**MGA Twin-Cam**
ENGINE		
Type (from Car No. 61504)	16GC	BC16GB
Bore	3.0 in. (76.2 mm.)	2.969 in. (75.41 mm.)
Capacity	99.5 cu. in. (1622 c.c.)	96.906 cu. in. (1588 c.c.)
Compression ratio	8.9:1 or 8.3:1	9.9:1 with pistons AEH681 or 8.3:1 with pistons AEH690
Capacity of combustion chamber (valves fitted)	2.624 cu. in. (43.0 c.c.)	86.6 c.c. (5.28 cu. in.)
Valve operation		Twin overhead camshafts
B.M.E.P.	90 at 5,500 r.p.m. HC	163 lb./sq. in. (11.46 kg./cm.^{2}) at 4,500 r.p.m.
	85 at 5,500 r.p.m. LC	105 lb. ft. (14.5 kg. m.) at 4,500 r.p.m.
	148 lb./sq. in. (10.4 kg./cm.^{2}) at 4,000 r.p.m. HC	
	140 lb./sq. in. (9.84 kg./cm.^{2}) at 3,000 r.p.m. LC	
	97 lb. ft. (13.1 kg. m.) at 4,000 r.p.m. HC	
	92 lb. ft. (12.72 kg. m.) at 3,000 r.p.m. LC	

CRANKSHAFT
Journal length:

Front	1.528 to 1.544 in. (38.817 to 39.224 mm.)	
Intermediate	1.471 to 1.473 in. (37.363 to 37.414 mm.)	
Rear	1.494 to 1.498 in. (37.940 to 38.049 mm.)	
Bearing length	1.25 in. (31.75 mm.)	
Diametrical clearance	.001 to .0027 in. (.0254 to .0685 mm.)	
Small-end bore	.750 to .7512 in. (19.05 to 19.08 mm.)	

CONNECTING RODS

Length between centres	6.5 in. (165.1 mm.)	

Big-end bearings

Bearing side-clearance	.002 to .0037 in. (.051 to .094 mm.)

PISTONS

Type	Flat top (9.9:1 compression ratio)
Material	Aluminium alloy
Clearances:	
Bottom of skirt	.0035 to .0066 in. (.090 to .168 mm.)
Top of skirt	.0058 to .0083 in. (.147 to .211 mm.)
Type	Domed top (8.3:1 compression ratio)
Material	Aluminium alloy
Clearances:	
Bottom of skirt	.0035 to .0041 in. (.090 to .101 mm.)
Top of skirt	.0070 to .0076 in. (.177 to .192 mm.)

PISTON RINGS
Compression:

Plain	Top ring	Top ring
Tapered	2nd and 3rd rings	2nd and 3rd rings
Width	.0615 to .0625 in. (1.56 to 1.58 mm.)	.0615 to .0625 in. (1.56 to 1.58 mm.)
Thickness	.111 to .118 in. (2.81 to 3.0 mm.) to Engine No. 40824 .119 to .126 in. (3.02 to 3.2 mm.) from Engine No. 40825	.141 to .148 in. (3.57 to 3.76 mm.)
Fitted gap	.0008 to .013 in. (.20 to .33 mm.)	.009 to .014 in. (.229 to .356 mm.)
Clearance in groove	.0015 to .0035 in. (.038 to .089 mm.)	
Oil control type	Slotted scraper	
Width	.1552 to .1562 in. (3.94 to 3.99 mm.)	
Thickness	.111 to .118 in. (2.81 to 3.0 mm.) to Engine No. 40824 .119 to .126 in. (3.02 to 3.2 mm.) from Engine No. 40825	.135 to .142 in. (3.43 to 3.61 mm.)
Fitted gap	.008 to .013 in. (.20 to .33 mm.)	.009 to .014 in. (.23 to .36 mm.)
Clearance in groove	.0016 to .0036 in. (.040 to .091 mm.)	.0016 to .0036 in. (.040 to .091 mm.)

GUDGEON PIN

Type	Clamped
Fit	.0001 to .00035 in. (.0025 to .009 mm.). Hand push fit at 68° F. (20° C.)
Diameter	.6869 to .6871 in. (17.447 to 17.4523 mm.)

VALVES AND VALVE GEAR
Valves
Seat angle:

Inlet	45°
Exhaust	45°
Head diameter:	
Inlet	1½ in. (38.1 mm.)

Exhaust	$1\frac{9}{32}$ in. (32.54 mm.)
Stem diameter:	
Inlet	.342 in. (8.68 mm.)
Exhaust	.342 in. (8.68 mm.)
Valve lift	.357 in. (9.06 mm.)
Valve stem to guide clearance:	
Inlet	.00155 to .00255 in. (.0394 to .0635 mm.)
Exhaust	.00105 to .00205 in. (.027 to .052 mm.) to Engine No. 4044 .002 to .003 in. (.051 to .076 mm.) after Engine No. 4045
Valve rocker clearance:	
Running	.017 in. (.432 mm.) (hot)
Timing	.060 in. (1.52 mm.)
Timing markings	Dimples on timing wheels
Chain pitch and number of pitches	$\frac{3}{8}$ in. (9.52 mm.), 52 pitches
Inlet valve:	
Opens	16° B.T.D.C.
Closes	56° A.B.D.C.
Exhaust valve:	
Opens	51° B.B.D.C.
Closes	21° A.T.D.C.

VALVE GUIDES

Length	
Inlet	$1\frac{7}{8}$ in. (47.63 mm.)
Exhaust	$2\frac{9}{32}$ in. (57.94 mm.)
Diameter:	
Inlet: Outside	.5635 in. (14.31 mm.)
Inside	.3438 in. (8.73 mm.)
Exhaust: Outside	.5635 in. (14.31 mm.)
Inside	.3438 in. (8.73 mm.)
Fitted height above head	.625 in. (15.87 mm.)

VALVE SPRINGS

Free length:	
Inner	$1\frac{31}{32}$ in. (50 mm.)
Outer	$2\frac{3}{64}$ in. (51.99 mm.)
Fitted length:	
Inner	$1\frac{7}{16}$ in. (36.51 mm.)
Outer	$1\frac{9}{16}$ in. (39.69 mm.)
Number of working coils:	
Inner	$6\frac{1}{2}$
Outer	$4\frac{1}{2}$
Pressure:	
Valve open	Inner 50 lb. (22.7 kg.). Outer 105 lb. (47.6 kg.)
Valve closed	Inner 30 lb. (13.6 kg.). Outer $60\frac{1}{2}$ lb. (27 kg.)

PISTON RINGS

Compression	
Width	.054 to .055 in. (1.37 to 1.39 mm.)
Thickness	.124 to .131 in. (3.15 to 3.33 mm.)
Fitted gap	.008 to .013 in. (.20 to .33 mm.)
Oil control type	Microland scraper Twin-segment scraper (from engine No. 446)
Thickness	.124 to .131 in. (3.15 to 3.33 mm.)
Fitted gap	.008 to .013 in. (.20 to .33 mm.)
Clearance in groove	.0015 to .0035 in. (.038 to .089 mm.)

GUDGEON PIN

Fit	.0001 to .0006 in. (.0025 to .0152 mm.). Hand push fit at 68° F. (20° C.)	Fully floating. Hand-push fit at room temperature.
Diameter:		
Outer	.7499 to .7501 in. (19.047 to 19.050 mm.)	
Inner	.3215 in. (7.94 mm.)	
Length	2.693 to 2.703 in. (68.402 to 68.656 mm.)	.875 in. (22.22 mm.)

VALVES AND VALVE GEAR
Valves

Head diameter:		
Inlet	1.562 to 1.567 in. (39.6 to 39.8 mm.)	1.59 in. (40.38 mm.)
Exhaust	1.343 to 1.348 in. (34.11 to 34.23 mm.)	1.44 in. (36.58 mm.)
Stem diameter:		
Inlet	.342 in. (8.68 mm.)	
Exhaust	.342 in. (8.68 mm.)	
Valve lift	.350 in. (8.89 mm.)	.375 in. (9.52 mm.)
Valve stem to guide clearance:		
Inlet		.00155 to .00255 in. (.0394 to .0635 mm.)
Exhaust	.002 to .003 in. (.051 to .076 mm.)	.00155 to .00255 in. (.0394 to .0635 mm.)
Valve rocker clearance	.015 in. (.38 mm.) (cold)	.014 to .015 in. (.356 to .381 mm.) (cold)
Chain pitch and number of pitches		.375 in. (9.52 mm.), 132 pitches
Inlet valve:		
Opens		20° B.T.D.C.
Closes		50° A.B.D.C.
Exhaust valve:		
Opens		50° B.B.D.C.
Closes		20° A.T.D.C.

VALVE GUIDES

Length:		
Inlet	$1\frac{5}{8}$ in. (41.275 mm.)	$2\frac{1}{16}$ in. (52.39 mm.)
Exhaust		$2\frac{7}{16}$ in. (61.91 mm.)
Diameter:		
Inlet: Outside	.5635 to .5640 in. (14.31 to 14.32 mm.)	.5645 to 5655 in. (14.33 to 14.36 mm.)
Inside	.34425 to .34475 in. (8.744 to 8.757 mm.)	.3438 to .3443 in. (8.73 to 8.74 mm.)
Exhaust: Outside		.5645 to .5655 in. (14.33 to 14.36 mm.)
Inside		.3438 to .3443 in. (8.73 to 8.74 mm.)
Fitted height above head		.750 in. (19.05 mm.) inlet .844 in. (21.43 mm.) exhaust

VALVE SPRINGS

Free length:		
Inner	$1\frac{59}{64}$ in. (48.8 mm.)	2.3 in. (58.42 mm.)
Outer	1.449 in. (36.8 mm.)	2.54 in. (64.51 mm.)
Fitted length:		
Inner	1.575 in. (40 mm.)	1.62 in. (41.15 mm.)
Outer		1.78 in. (45.21 mm.)
Number of working coils:		
Inner		7.8
Outer		6
Load:		
Full lift: Inlet and exhaust	Inner 50 lb. (22.7 kg.). Outer 113 lb. (51.2 kg.)	Inner 65 lb. (29.5 kg.). Outer 125 lb. (56.7 kg.)

	MGA 1500	MGA 1600
No lift: Inlet	Inner 28 to 32 lb. (12.7 to 14.51 kg.). Outer 53 to 57 lb. (24 to 25.8 kg.)	Inner 42 lb. (19.1 kg.). Outer 84 lb. (38.1 kg.)
Exhaust	Inner and outer 53 to 57 lb. (24 to 25.8 kg.)	

TAPPETS

Type	Barrel with flat base	
Diameter: Body	$\frac{13}{16}$ in. (20.64 mm.)	
Length	2.293 to 2.303 in. (58.25 to 58.5 mm.)	

ROCKERS

Outside diameter before fitting	.751 in. (19.07 mm.)	
Inside diameter (reamed in position)	.616 to .620 in. (15.65 to 15.74 mm.)	
Bore of rocker arms	.7485 to .7489 in. (19.01 to 19.02 mm.)	
Rocker ratio	1.426:1	

CAMSHAFT

Journal diameters:		
Front	1.78875 to 1.78925 in. (45.43 to 45.44 mm.)	
Centre	1.72875 to 1.72925 in. (43.91 to 43.92 mm.)	
Rear	1.62275 to 1.62325 in. (41.22 to 41.23 mm.)	
End-float	.003 to .007 in. (.076 to .178 mm.)	
Bearing: number and type	3. Thinwall steel-backed white metal	
Outside diameter (before fitting)	Front 1.920 in. (48.76 mm.), centre 1.860 in. (47.24 mm.), rear 1.754 in. (44.55 mm.)	
Inside diameter (reamed in position)	Front 1.790 in. (45.47 mm.), centre 1.730 in. (43.94 mm.), rear 1.624 in. (41.25 mm.)	
Clearance	.001 to .002 in. (.0254 to .0508 mm.)	

ENGINE LUBRICATION SYSTEM

Oil pump

Type	Eccentric rotor	
Relief pressure valve operates	75 to 80 lb./sq. in. (5.3 to 5.6 kg./cm.^{2})	50 lb./sq. in. (3.5 kg./cm.^{2})
Relief valve spring:		
Free length	3 in. (76.2 mm.)	
Fitted length	$2\frac{5}{32}$ in. (54.77 mm.) at 16 lb. (7.26 kg.) load	
Identification colour	Red spot	

Oil filter

Type	Tecalemit (element Part No. 1H779) or Purolator (element Part No. 1H1054) up to Engine No. 26932 Tecalemit or Purolator (element Part No. 8G683) from Engine No. 26933	Tecalemit or Purolator
Capacity	$\frac{1}{2}$ pint (.28 litre)	1 pint (.57 litre)

Oil pressure

Normal running:		
Minimum	30 lb./sq. in. (2.1 kg./cm.^{2})	15 lb./sq. in. (1.05 kg./cm.^{2})
Maximum	80 lb./sq. in. (5.6 kg./cm.^{2})	50 lb./sq. in. (3.5 kg./cm.^{2})

TORQUE WRENCH SETTINGS

Cylinder head nuts	50 lb. ft. (6.91 kg. m.)	
Main bearing nuts	70 lb. ft. (9.7 kg. m.)	
Connecting rod set screws	35 lb. ft. (4.83 kg. m.)	
Clutch assembly to flywheel	25 lb. ft. (3.46 kg. m.)	
Road wheel nuts	60 to 62.5 lb. ft. (8.3 to 8.65 kg. m.)	

FUEL SYSTEM
Carburettor
Make and type   S.U. twin H4 semi-downdraught
Diameter   1½ in. (38.1 mm.)
Needle   GS
Jet   .090 in. (2.29 mm.)
Piston spring   Red

	MGA 1600 Mk II	MGA Twin-Cam
TAPPETS		
Type		Inverted bucket
Diameter:		
Body		1.5 in. (38.1 mm.)
Working face		1.5 in. (38.1 mm.)
Length		1.25 in. (31.75 mm.)
(from Engine No. 1087)		1.5 in. (38.1 mm.)
CAMSHAFT		
Journal diameters		1.250 to 1.2505 in. (31.75 to 31.76 mm.)
End-float		.001 to .005 in. (.025 to .127 mm.)
Bearing: number and type		3. D2 bi-metal bearings
Inside diameter		1.2515 to 1.2525 in. (31.788 to 31.813 mm.)
Clearance		.001 to .0025 in. (.0254 to .0635 mm.)
HALF-SPEED SHAFT		
Journal diameters		
Front		1.78875 to 1.78925 in. (45.43 to 45.44 mm.)
Centre		1.72875 to 1.72925 in. (43.91 to 43.92 mm.)
Rear		1.62275 to 1.62325 in. (41.22 to 41.23 mm.)
End-float		.003 to .006 in. (.076 to .152 mm.)
Bearing: number and type		3. Thinwall steel-backed white metal
Inside diameter (reamed in position):		
Front		1.790 in. (45.47 mm.)
Centre		1.730 in. (43.94 mm.)
Rear		1.624 in. (41.25 mm.)
Clearance		.001 to .002 in. (.025 to .051 mm.)
ENGINE LUBRICATION SYSTEM		
Oil filter		
Capacity		½ pint (.6 U.S. pint, .28 litre)
Oil pressure		
Normal running:		
Minimum	15 lb./sq. in. (1.05 kg./cm.^{2}) at 500 r.p.m.	10 to 15 lb./sq. in. (.7 to 1.05 kg./cm.^{2})
Maximum	70 lb./sq. in. (4.9 kg./cm.^{2}) at 30 m.p.h.	50 to 60 lb./sq. in. (3.52 to 4.22 kg./cm.^{2})
TORQUE WRENCH SETTINGS		
Cylinder head nuts		70 lb. ft. (9.68 kg. m.)
Clutch assembly to flywheel		35 to 40 lb. ft. (4.84 to 5.53 kg. m.)
Camshaft bearing nut		33 lb. ft. (4.56 kg. m.)
Steering-wheel nut		42 lb. ft. (5.75 kg.m.)
FUEL SYSTEM		
Carburettor		
Make and type		S.U. twin H6 semi-downdraught
Diameter		1¾ in. (44.45 mm.)
Needle		OA6
Jet		.10 in. (2.54 mm.)
Piston spring		Red, 4½ oz. (128 gm.)

AIR CLEANER
Make and type   Vokes—oil-wetted

FUEL PUMP
Make and type   S.U. electric—high pressure
Delivery test   10 gal. per hr. (45.4 litres per hr.)
Suction lift   33 in. (83.8 cm.)
Output lift   48 in. (121.9 cm.)

COOLING SYSTEM
Type   Pressurized radiator. Thermo-siphon,
                                   pump- and fan-assisted
Thermostat setting   70 to 75° C. (158 to 167° F.)   Crack open 68° C. (154° F.). Fully
                                                                          open 83° C. (181° F.) from Engine
                                                                          No. 16GA4788

Quantity of anti-freeze:
  15° frost   1 pint (.57 litre)
  25° frost   1½ pints (.85 litre)
  35° frost   2 pints (1.1 litres)
Filler cap spring pressure   7 lb. (3.18 kg.) from Car No. 71832

IGNITION SYSTEM
Sparking plugs   Champion N5, was NA8
Size   14 mm
Plug gap   .024 to .026 in. (.625 to .660 mm.)
Coil   Lucas HA12
Distributor   Lucas. Type DM2. Later models
                                   DM2P4
Distributor contact points gap   .014 to .016 in. (.35 to .40 mm.)
Suppressors   Lucas No. 78106A fitted on each
                                   H.T. cable
Timing   7° B.T.D.C.

CLUTCH
Make and type   Borg & Beck A6–G. Single dry-plate
Diameter   8 in. (20.3 cm.)
Facing material   Wound yarn—Borglite
Pressure springs   6
  Colour   Black and yellow
                                 Cream and light green: commencing
                                   Engine No. 16225
Damper springs   6
  Colour   White with light-green stripes
Release lever ratio   9:1

GEARBOX
No. of forward speeds   4
Synchromesh   Second, third, and fourth gears
Ratios:
  Top   1.0:1
  Third   1.374:1
  Second   2.214:1
  First   3.64:1
  Reverse   4.76:1
Overall ratios:
  Top   4.3:1
  Third   5.908:1
  Second   9.520:1
  First   15.652:1
  Reverse   20.468:1
Speedometer gears ratio   5:12

FUEL PUMP
Delivery test   12.5 gal./hr. (54.28 litres/hr.)

COOLING SYSTEM

Thermostat setting | 150:8° F. (66° C.) | 50 to 55° C. (122 to 131° F.)

Quantity of anti-freeze:
15° frost   1½ pints (1.8 U.S. pints, .85 litre)
25° frost   2 pints (2.4 U.S. pints, 1.14 litres)
35° frost   3½ pints (4.2 U.S. pints, 2 litres)

IGNITION SYSTEM

Sparking plugs — Champion N3 Champion N58R (for competition work and other arduous conditions)

Timing — 10° B.T.D.C. (up to Engine No. 4003). HC   T.D.C. (maximum advance)
5° B.T.D.C. (from Engine No. 4004)
10° B.T.D.C. LC

CLUTCH

Make and type — Borg & Beck 8A6–G single dry plate — Borg & Beck 8ARG. Single dry plate
Facing material — Wound yarn
Friction plate damper springs — 6. Maroon and light green
Pressure springs — 6. Light grey
  Minimum free length — 2.27 in. (57.658 mm.)
  Rate — 282 lb. in. (3.24 kg. mm.)
  Total spring load (mean) — 1,200 lb. (544.3 kg.)
  Test length — 1.56 in. (39.624 mm.)
  Load — 195 to 205 lb. (88.45 to 92.98 kg.)
Release lever ratio — 11.7:1

GEARBOX

		Standard gear box	Close ratio gearbox
Ratios:			
Top		1.0:1	1.0:1
Third		1.374:1	1.267:1
Second		2.214:1	1.62:1
First		3.64:1	2.445:1
Reverse		4.67:1	3.199:1
Overall ratios:			
Top	4.1:1	4.3:1	4.3:1
Third	5.633:1	5.908:1	5.449:1
Second	9.077:1	9.520:1	6.966:1
First	14.924:1	15.652:1	10.52:1
Reverse	19.516:1	20.468:1	13.75:1

MGB models with B-series 18G/18GA 3-main bearing engines

ENGINE

Type — 18G,18GA
Number of cylinders — 4
Bore — 3.16 in. (80.26 mm.)
Stroke — 3.5 in. (89 mm.)
Capacity — 1798 c.c. (109.8 cu. in.)
Combustion chamber volume (valves fitted) — 42.5 to 43.5 c.c. (2.59 to 2.65 cu. in.)
Firing order — 1, 3, 4, 2
Valve operation — Overhead by push-rod
Compression ratio:
  H.C. — 8.8:1
  L.C. — 8.0:1
Compression pressure:
  H.C. — 160 lb./sq. in. (11.25 kg./cm.^{2})
  L.C. — 130 lb./sq. in. (9.15 kg./cm.^{2})

Torque:
  H.C. — 110 lb. ft. (15.2 kg. m.) at 3,000 r.p.m.
  L.C. — 105 lb. ft. (14.5 kg. m.) at 3,000 r.p.m.
Engine idle speed (approx.) — 500 r.p.m.
Oversize bore:
  First — .010 in. (.254 mm.)
  Max. — .040 in. (1.016 mm.)

CRANKSHAFT

Main journal diameter — 2.1262 to 2.127 in. (54.01 to 54.02 mm.)
Crankpin journal diameter — 1,8759 to 1.8764 in. (47.648 to 47.661 mm.)
Crankshaft end-thrust — Taken on thrust washers at centre main bearing
Crankshaft end-float — .004 to .005 in. (.10 to .13 mm.)

MAIN BEARINGS
Number and type — Three thinwall
Material — Steel-backed copper-lead
Length — 1⅛ in. (28.5 mm.)
Diametrical clearance — .001 to .0027 in. (.0254 to .068 mm.)
Undersizes — −.010, −.020, −.030 and −.040 in. (−.254, −.508, −.762 and −1.016 mm.)

CONNECTING RODS
Type — Angular-split big-end, split clamp small-end
Length between centres — 6.5 in. (165.1 mm.)

BIG-END BEARINGS
Type — Shell
Material — Steel-backed copper-lead
Length — .995 to 1.005 in. (25.2 to 25.52 mm.)
Diametrical clearance — .001 to .0027 in. (.0254 to .068 mm.)
Undersizes — −.010, −.020, −.030 and −.040 in. (−.254, −.508, −.762 and −1.016 mm.)
End-float on crankpin (nominal) — .008 to .012 in. (.20 to .30 mm.)

PISTONS
Type — Aluminium solid skirt
Clearance in cylinder:
 Top — .0036 to .0045 in. (.091 to .121 mm.)
 Bottom — .0018 to .0024 in. (.045 to .060 mm.)
Number of rings — 4 (3 compression, 1 oil control)
Width of ring grooves:
 Top, Second and Third — .064 to .065 in. (1.625 to 1.651 mm.)
 Oil control — .1578 to .1588 in. (4.008 to 4.033 mm.)
Gudgeon pin bore — .7501 to .7503 in. (19.052 to 19.057 mm.)

PISTON RINGS
Compression:
Type:
 Top — Parallel ⎫ cast-iron
 Second and third — Tapered ⎭ molybdenum filled
Width:
 Top, second and third — .0615 to .0625 in. (1.562 to 1.587 mm.)
Fitted gap
 Top, second and third — .012 to .017 in. (.304 to .431 mm.)
Ring to groove clearance:
 Top, second and third — .0015 to .0035 in. (.038 to .088 mm.)
Oil Control:
Type — Slotted scraper
Width — .1552 to .1562 in. (3.94 to 3.96 mm.)

Fitted gap — .012 to .017 in. (.304 to .431 mm.)
Ring to groove clearance — .0016 to .0036 in. (.04 to .09 mm.)

GUDGEON PIN
Type — Semi-floating
Fit in piston — Free-fit at 20° C. (68° F.)
Diameter (outer) — .7499 to .7501 in. (19.04 to 19.05 mm.)

CAMSHAFT
Journal diameters:
 Front — 1.78875 to 1.78925 in. (45.424 to 45.437 mm.)
 Centre — 1.72875 to 1.72925 in. (43.910 to 43.923 mm.)
 Rear — 1.62275 to 1.62325 in. (41.218 to 41.230 mm.)
Bearing liner inside diameter (reamed after fitting):
 Front — 1.79025 to 1.79075 in. (45.472 to 45.485 mm.)
 Centre — 1.73025 to 1.73075 in. (43.948 to 43.961 mm.)
 Rear — 1.62425 to 1.62475 in. (41.256 to 41.269 mm.)
Diametrical clearance — .001 to .002 in. (0254 to .0508 mm.)
End-thrust — Taken on locating plate
End-float — .003 to .007 in. (.076 to .178 mm.)
Cam lift — .250 in. (6.35 mm.)
Drive — Chain and sprocket from crankshaft
Timing chain — ⅜ in. (9.52 mm.), pitch × 52 pitches

TAPPETS
Type — Barrel with flat base
Outside diameter — 13⁄16 in. (20.64 mm.)
Length — 2.293 to 2.303 in. (58.25 to 58.5 mm.)

ROCKER GEAR
Rocker shaft:
 Length — 14 1⁄32 in. (.356 mm.)
 Diameter — .624 to .625 in. (15.85 to 15.87 mm.)
Rocker arm:
 Bore — .7485 to .7495 in. (19.01 to 19.26 mm.)
Rocker arm bush inside diameter — .6255 to .626 in. (15.8 to 15.9 mm.)
Ratio — 1.4:1

VALVES
Seat angle: Inlet and exhaust — 45½°
Head diameter:
 Inlet — 1.562 to 1.567 in. (38.67 to 38.80 mm.)
 Exhaust — 1.343 to 1.348 in. (34.11 to 34.23 mm.)

Stem diameter:
Inlet .3422 to .3427 in. (8.68 to 8.69 mm.)
Exhaust .3417 to .3422 in. (8.660 to 8.661 mm.)

Stem to guide clearance:
Inlet .0015 to .0025 in. (.0381 to .0778 mm.)
Exhaust .002 to .003 in. (.0508 to .0762 mm.)

Valve lift: Inlet and exhaust .3645 in. (9.25 mm.)

VALVE GUIDES
Length:
Inlet $1\frac{5}{8}$ in. (41.275 mm.)
Exhaust $2\frac{13}{64}$ in. (55.95 mm.)
Outside diameter: Inlet and exhaust .5635 to .5640 in. (14.30 to 14.32 mm.)
Inside diameter: Inlet and exhaust .3442 to .3447 in. (8.73 to 8.74 mm.)
Fitted height above head: Inlet and exhaust $\frac{5}{8}$ in. (15.875 mm.)
Interference fit in head: Inlet and exhaust .0005 to .00175 in. (.012 to .044 mm.)

(Later cars)
Length: Inlet $1\frac{7}{8}$ in. (47.63 mm.)
Fitting height above head: Inlet $\frac{3}{4}$ in. (19 mm.)

VALVE SPRINGS
Free length:
Inner $1\frac{31}{32}$ in. (50.0 mm.)
Outer $2\frac{9}{64}$ in. (54.4 mm.)
Fitted length:
Inner $1\frac{7}{16}$ in. (36.5 mm.)
Outer $1\frac{9}{16}$ in. (39.7 mm.)
Load at fitted length:
Inner 28 to 32 lb. (12.7 to 14.5 kg.)
Outer 72 lb. (32.7 kg.)
Load at top of lift:
Inner 48 to 52 lb. (21.7 to 23.6 kg.)
Outer 117 lb. (53 kg.)
Valve crash speed 6,200 r.p.m.

VALVE TIMING
Timing marks Dimples on camshaft and crankshaft wheels

Rocker clearance:
Running .015 in. (.38 mm.) cold
Timing .055 in. (1.4 mm.)
Inlet valve:
Opens 16° B.T.D.C.
Closes 56° A.B.D.C.
Exhaust valve:
Opens 51° B.B.D.C.
Closes 21° A.T.D.C.

ENGINE LUBRICATION
System Wet sump, pressure fed
System pressure:
Running Between 50 and 80 lb./sq. in. (3.51 and 5.6 kg./cm.^{2})
Idling Between 10 and 25 lb./sq. in. (.7 and 1.7 kg./cm.^{2})

Oil pump Hobourn-Eaton or eccentric rotor
Capacity $3\frac{1}{4}$ gal./min. at 2,000 r.p.m.
Oil filter Tecalemit full-flow felt element
By-pass valve opens 13 to 17 lb./sq. in. (.9 to 1.1 kg./cm.^{2})
Oil pressure relief valve 70 lb./sq. in. (4.9 kg./cm.^{2})
Relief valve spring:
Free length 3 in. (76.2 mm.)
Fitted length $2\frac{5}{32}$ in. (54.7 mm.)
Load at fitted length 15.5 to 16.5 lb. (7.0 to 7.4 kg.)

FUEL SYSTEM
Carburettors Twin S.U. type HS4
Choke diameter $1\frac{1}{2}$ in. (38.1 mm.)
Jet size .090 in. (2.2 mm.)
Needles No. 5 (Standard), No. 6 (Rich), No. 21 (Weak)
Piston spring Red
Air cleaners Copper paper element
Fuel pump
Type (early cars) S.U. electric HP
Minimum flow 7 gal./hr. (31.8 litres/hr., 8.4 U.S. gal./hr.)

DISTRIBUTOR
Make/Type Lucas/25D4
Contact breaker gap .014 to .016 in. (.35 to .40 mm.)
Contact spring tension 18 to 24 oz. (510 to 680 gm.)
Rotation of rotor Anti-clockwise
Dwell angle 60° ± 3°
Centrifugal advance
Crankshaft degrees/speed (vacuum pipe disconnected)

Serial number 40897 (H.C.)	Serial number 40916 (L.C.)
6° at 600 r.p.m.	6° at 600 r.p.m.
6° at 700 r.p.m.	8° at 800 r.p.m.
9° at 900 r.p.m.	9° at 1,000 r.p.m.
15° at 1,600 r.p.m.	18° at 3,000 r.p.m.
20° at 2,200 r.p.m.	24° at 4,400 r.p.m.

Vacuum advance
Starts 5 in. Hg (127 mm. Hg), 40897 (H.C.). 4 in. Hg (101.6 mm. Hg), 40916 (L.C.)
Finishes 13 in. Hg (330.2 mm. Hg), 40897 (H.C.). 12 in. Hg (304.8 mm. Hg), 40916 (L.C.)
Total crankshaft degrees 20° ± 2°, 40897 (H.C.). 16° ± 2°, 40916 (L.C.)

IGNITION COIL
Make/Type Lucas/HA12
Resistance: Primary 3.1 to 3.5 ohms at 20° C. (68° F.)

ELECTRICAL
Dynamo Lucas C40/1
Battery Lucas BT9E or BTZ9E
Volts/Polarity 12-volt/Positive earth
Starter Lucas M4 18G Inertia-type
Control unit Lucas RB.340

All MGB 18GB 5-main bearing engines
(to be used in conjunction with 18G/18GA data)

ENGINE

Type	18GB

MAIN BEARINGS

Number and type	5 thin-wall
Length:	
Front, centre and rear	$1\frac{1}{8}$ in. (28.5 mm.)
Intermediate	$\frac{7}{8}$ in. (22.23 mm.)

CONNECTING RODS

Type	Angular-split big-end, bushed small-end

BIG-END BEARINGS

Length	.775 to .785 in. (19.68 to 19.94 mm.)

PISTONS

Gudgeon pin bore	.8126 to .8129 (20.610 to 20.167 mm.)
Clearance in cylinder skirt:	
Top	.0012 to .0006 in. (.030 to .015 mm.)
Bottom	.0033 to .0021 in. (.080 to .050 mm.)

GUDGEON PIN

Type	Fully floating
Fit in piston	.0001 to .00035 in. (.0025 to .007 mm.)
Diameter (outer)	.8124 to .8127 (20.608 to 20.615 mm.)

FUEL SYSTEM

Carburettor needles	FX (Standard); No. 6 (Rich); No. 21 (Weak)

REAR AXLE (GT)

Type	Hypoid, semi-floating
Ratio	3.909:1 (11.43)

All MGB models with 18GD (GHN4 and GH and 18GG (GHN5 and GHD5) engines
(to be used in conjunction with 18G/18GA/18GB data)

ENGINE

Type	18GD–18GG

PISTONS

Type	Aluminium solid skirt, three rings
Clearance of skirt in cylinder:	
Top	.0021 to .0033 in. (.053 to .084 mm.)
Bottom	.006 to .0012 in. (.015 to .030 mm.)
Number of rings	Three; 2 compression, 1 oil control
Width of ring grooves:	
Compression	.064 to .065 in. (1.625 to 1.651 mm.)
Oil control	.1578 to .1588 in. (4.01 to 4.033 mm.)

PISTON RINGS

Type: Compression:	
Top	Plain, sintered alloy
Second	Tapered, sintered alloy–marked 'TOP'
Oil control	Two chrome-faced rings with expander, Apex
Fitted gap:	
Compression	.012 to .022 in. (.305 to .600 mm.)
Oil control	.015 to .045 in. (.38 to 1.14 mm.)
Width:	
Compression	.0615 to .0625 in. (1.56 to 1.59 mm.)
Oil control	.152 to .158 in. (3.86 to 4.01 mm.)
Thickness: Compression:	
Top	.124 to .127 in. (3.14 to 3.22 mm.)
Second	.104 to .111 in. (2.64 to 2.81 mm.)

GUDGEON PIN

Type	Press fit in connecting rod
Diameter	.8125 to .8127 in. (20.63 to 20.64 mm.)
Fit in:	
Piston	Hand push fit at 16° C. (60° F.)
Small end	12 lb. ft. (1.7 kg. m.) minimum using 18G 1150 and adaptor type C

CONNECTING RODS

Type	Horizontal split big-end, solid small-end
Length between centres	6.5 in. (165.1 mm.)
Locking method big-end	Multi-sided nut

COOLING SYSTEM

Fan belt:	
Width	$\frac{15}{32}$ in. (11.9 mm.)
Length	$35\frac{1}{2}$ in. (90.2 cm.) at $\frac{3}{8}$ in. width equivalent
Thickness	$\frac{27}{64}$ in. (10.7 mm.)
Tension	$\frac{1}{2}$ in. (12.8 mm.) movement at midway of longest run
Thermostat:	
Normal	82° C. (180° F.)
Hot climates	74° C. (165° F.)
Cold climates	88° C. (190° F.)

CLUTCH

Fluid	Lockheed Disc Brake Fluid (Series 329)

GEARBOX AND OVERDRIVE

Number of forward gears	4
Synchromesh	All forward gears
Gearbox ratios:	
Reverse	3.095:1

First	3.44:1
Second	2.167:1
Third	1.382:1
Fourth	1.000:1

Overdrive
Type	Laycock L.H.
Ratio	.82:1

Overall gear ratios:
Reverse	12.098:1
First	13.45:1
Second	8.47:1
Third	5.4:1
Fourth	3.909:1

Overdrive:
Third	4.43:1
Fourth	3.2:1

Top gear speed per
1,000 r.p.m.:
Standard	18 m.p.h. (29 km.p.h.)
Overdrive	22 m.p.h. (35 km.p.h.)

Speedometer gear ratio:
Standard	10:26
Overdrive	8:21

AUTOMATIC GEARBOX
Torque converter ratio	2.2:1 to 1:1

Gearbox ratios:
Reverse	2.09:1
First	2.39:1
Second	1.45:1
Top	1.00:1

Overall gear ratio
(converter at 1:1):
Reverse	8.17:1
First	9.34:1
Second	5.668:1
Top303.909:1	
Speedometer gear ratio	10:26

ELECTRICAL
System	12-volt, negative earth

BATTERIES
Type (two 6-volt)	Lucas BT9E or BTZ9E. Later cars: Lucas CA9E

Capacity:
10-hour rate	51 amp.-hour. Later cars: 53 amp.-hour
20-hour rate	58 amp.-hour. Later cars: 60 amp.-hour
Plates per cell	9
Electrolyte to fill one cell	1 pint (570 c.c., 1.2 U.S. pints)

CONTROL BOX
Type	4TR Electronic
Voltage setting	14.3 to 14.7 volts at 5,000 r.p.m.

ALTERNATOR
Type	Lucas 16AC, 18GD engine. Lucas 16ACR, 18GG engine
Output at 14 volts and 6,000 r.p.m.	34 amps
Maximum permissible rotor speed	12,500 r.p.m.

Pulley ratio–alternator/ crankshaft	1.795:1
Stator phases	3
Rotor poles	12
Rotor winding resistance	4.33 ohms ± 5% at 20° C. (68° F.)
Brush length (new)	½ in. (12.6 mm.)
Brush spring tension	7 to 10 oz. (198–283 gm.) with brush face flush with brush box

STARTER
Type	Lucas M418G Pre-engaged
Light running current	70 amp. at 5,800 to 6,500 r.p.m.
Lock torque	17 lb. ft. (2.35 kg. m.) at 465 amps
Torque at 1,000 r.p.m.	7 lb. ft. (.97 kg. m.) at 260 amps

Solenoid:
Closing coil resistance	.13 to .15 ohm
Hold-on coil resistance	.63 to .73 ohm
Brush spring tension	36 oz. (1.02 kg.)

STARTER MOTOR RELAY
Type	Lucas Model 6RA-33243
Winding resistance	76 ohms

Bobbin core to
underside of armature
air gap:
Contacts open	0.030 ± 0.005 in. (0.76 ± 0.13 mm.)
Con4acts closed	0.010 ± 0.003 in. (0.25 ± 0.08 mm.)
Cut-in voltage	4.0 to 7.5 volts
Drop-off voltage	5 volts (maximum)

Static ignition timing:
H.C.	10° B.T.D.C.
L.C.	8° B.T.D.C.

Stroboscopic ignition
timing:
H.C.	14° B.T.D.C. at 600 r.p.m.
L.C.	12° B.T.D.C. at 600 r.p.m.
Timing mark location	Pointer on timing case, notch on crankshaft pulley

DISTRIBUTOR
Make/Type	Lucas/25D4
Contact breaker gap	.014 to .016 in. (.35 to .40 mm.)
Contact spring tension	18 to 24 oz. (510 to 680 gm.)
Rotation of rotor	Anti-clockwise
Dwell angle	60° ± 3°

CENTRIFUGAL ADVANCE
Crankshaft degrees/Speed (vacuum pipe disconnected)

Serial Number 40897 (H.C.)	Serial Number 40916 (L.C.)
4° at 600 r.p.m.	6° at 600 r.p.m.
6° at 700 r.p.m.	8° at 800 r.p.m.
9° at 900 r.p.m.	9° at 1,000 r.p.m.
15° at 1,600 r.p.m.	18° at 3,000 r.p.m.
20° at 2,200 r.p.m.	24° at 4,400 r.p.m.

VACUUM ADVANCE

Starts	5 in. Hg (127 mm. Hg) (H.C.). 4 in. Hg (101.6 mm. Hg) (L.C.)
Finishes	13 in. Hg (330.2 mm. Hg) (H.C.). 12 in Hg (304.8 mm. Hg) (L.C.)
Total crankshaft degrees	20° ± 2° (H.C.). 16° ± 2° (L.C.)

IGNITION COIL

Make/Type	Lucas/HA12
Resistance: Primary	3.1 to 3.5 ohms at 20° C. (68° F.)

SPARKING PLUGS

Make/Type	Champion/N9Y
Gap	.024 to .026 (.625 to .66 mm.)

CARBURETTORS

Make/Type	SU/HS4
Jet	.090 in. (2.2 mm.)
Needle	Standard, FX; Rich, No. 5; Weak, GZ
Piston spring	Red

'Emission Control' engines fitted to the MGB

ENGINE

Type (1967–69)	18GF (EEC)
Type (1969–70)	18GH (EEC, Carburettor crankcase ventilation)
Type (1969–70)	18GJ (EEC, ELC, Carburettor crankcase ventilation)
Type (1970–1)	18GK (EEC, ELC)
Type (1971–2)	18V 584Z (EEC, ELC—Non overdrive)
Type (1971–2)	18V 585Z (EEC, ELC—Overdrive)
Type (1972–4)	18V 672Z (EEC, ELC—Non overdrive)
Type (1972–4)	18V 673Z (EEC, ELC—Overdrive)

Abbreviations: EEC, Exhaust Emission Control; ELC, Evaporative Loss Control.

FUEL SYSTEM

Fuel tank capacity (Engine types 18GJ and 18GK)	12 U.S. gallons (45.4 litres)

Carburettor needle:

18GF	FX
18GH–18GJ	AAE
18GK	AAL
18V 584Z and 18V 585Z	AAU
18V 672Z and 18V 673Z	ABD

DISTRIBUTOR

Make/type	Lucas 25D4
Serial number:	
18GF	40897
18GH–18GJ	41155
18GK	41339
18V 584Z and 18V 585Z	41370
18V 672Z and 18V 673Z	41491

ENGINE

Type:	
Synchromesh gearbox	18V 581F–18V 581Y
Synchromesh gearbox with overdrive	18V 582F–18V 582Y
Automatic transmission	18V 583F–18V 583Y

VALVES

Inlet valve:	
Seat angle	45½°
Head diameter	1.625 to 1.630 in. (41.27 to 41.40 mm.)
Stem diameter	0.3429 to 0.3434 in. (8.70 to 8.72 mm.)
Stem to guide clearance	0.0008 to 0.0018 in. (0.020 to 0.046 mm.)

VALVE SPRING

Free length	1.92 in. (48.77 mm.)
Fitted length	1.44 in. (36.58 mm.)
Load at fitted length	82 lb. (37.2 kg.)
Load at top of lift	142 lb. (64.4 kg.)

ELECTRICAL

Starter motor

Type	Lucas 2M100 Pre-engaged
Brush spring tension	36 oz. (1.02 kg.)
Minimum brush length	⅜ in. (9.5 mm.)
Minimum commutator thickness	0.140 in. (3.5 mm.)
Lock torque	14.4 lb. ft. (2.02 kg. m.) with 463 amps.
Torque at 1,000 r.p.m.	7.3 lb. ft. (1.02 kg. m.) with 300 amps
Light running current	40 amp. at 6,000 r.p.m. (approx.)
Maximum armature end-float	0.010 in. (0.25 mm.)
Solenoid:	
Closing (series) winding resistance	0.25 to 0.27 ohm
Hold-on (shunt) winding resistance	0.76 to 0.80 ohm

18V engines with the following suffixes: 581F, 582F, 583F, 581Y, 582Y and 583Y

ENGINE

Type	18V (1798 c.c.)
Displacement	109.8 cu. in. (1798 c.c.)
Firing order	1, 3, 4, 2
Compression ratio:	
H.C.	9.0:1
L.C.	8.0:1
Cranking pressure	Nominal 170 lbf./sq. in. (11.95 kgf./cm.²) at 275 r.p.m.
Idle speed	750 to 800 r.p.m.

Valve rocker clearance:

Set cold	.015 in. (.38 mm.)
Set hot	.013 in. (.33 mm.)

Static ignition timing:

H.C.	10° B.T.D.C.
L.C.	10° B.T.D.C.

Stroboscopic ignition timing:

H.C.	13° B.T.D.C. at 600 r.p.m.
L.C.	13° B.T.D.C. at 600 r.p.m.
Timing mark location	Pointer on timing case, notch on crankshaft pulley

DISTRIBUTOR

Make/Type	Lucas/25D4
Contact breaker gap	.014 to .016 in. (.35 to .40 mm.)
Contact spring tension	18 to 24 oz. (510 to 680 gm.)
Rotation of rotor	Anti-clockwise
Dwell angle	60° ± 3°

CENTRIFUGAL ADVANCE

Crankshaft degrees/Speed (vacuum pipe disconnected)

Serial Number 41288 (H.C.)	Serial Number 41290 (L.C.)
0 to 6° at 600 r.p.m.	0 to 6° at 600 r.p.m.
4 to 9° at 700 r.p.m.	6 to 10° at 800 r.p.m.
7 to 11° at 900 r.p.m.	7 to 11° at 1,000 r.p.m.
13 to 17° at 1,600 r.p.m.	16 to 20° at 3,000 r.p.m.
18 to 22° at 2,200 r.p.m.	22 to 26° at 4,400 r.p.m.

VACUUM ADVANCE

Starts	5 in. Hg (127 mm. Hg), (H.C.). 4 in. Hg (101.6 mm. Hg), (L.C.)
Finishes	13 in. Hg (330.2 mm. Hg), (H.C.). 12 in. Hg (304.8 mm. Hg), (L.C.)
Total crankshaft degrees	20° ± 2°, (H.C.). 16° ± 2°, (L.C.)

IGNITION COIL

Make/Type	Lucas/HA12
Resistance: Primary	3.1 to 3.5 ohms at 20°C. (68°F.)

SPARKING PLUGS

Make/Type	Champion/N9Y
Gap	.024 to .026 in. (.625 to .66 mm.)

CARBURETTORS

Make/type	SU/HS4
Jet	.090 in. (2.2 mm.)
Needle	AAU
Piston spring	Red

ELECTRICAL

Alternator	Lucas 16ACR
Battery	Lucas BT9E, BTZ9E, CA9E, SG9E or Exide 3XCK9L
Volts/Polarity	12 volt/negative earth
Starter	Lucas 2M100 Pre-engaged

18V engines to ECE 15 European emission control requirements

ENGINE

Type	18V
Displacement	109.8 cu. in. (1798 c.c.)
Firing order	1, 3, 4, 2
Compression ratio	9.0:1
Cranking pressure	Nominal 170 to 190 lbf./sq. in. (12 to 13.4 kgf./cm.^{2})

Valve rocker clearance:

set cold	.015 in. (.38 mm.)
Idle speed	750 r.p.m.
Fast idle speed	1,100 to 1,200 r.p.m.
Stroboscopic ignition timing	15° B.T.D.C. at 1,000 r.p.m.
Static ignition timing	5° B.T.D.C.
Timing mark location	Pointer on timing case, notch on crankshaft pulley

DISTRIBUTOR

Make/Type	Lucas/25D4
Contact breaker gap	.014 to .016 in. (.35 to .40 mm.)
Contact spring tension	18 to 24 o. (510 to 680 gm.)
Rotation of rotor	Anti-clockwise
Dwell angle	60° ± 3°
Serial number	41032

CENTRIFUGAL ADVANCE

Crankshaft degrees/ Speed (vacuum disconnected)	0 to 3° at 600 r.p.m.
	0 to 4° at 700 r.p.m.
	2 to x° at 900 r.p.m.
	10 to 14° at 1,600 r.p.m.
	17 to 21° at 2,200 r.p.m.

VACUUM ADVANCE

Starts	3 in. Hg. (76 mm. Hg.)
Finishes	8 in. Hg. (203 mm. Hg.)
Total crankshaft degrees	14° ± 2°

IGNITION COIL

Make/Type	Lucas/HA12
Resistance: Primary	3.1 to 3.5 ohms at 20°C. (68°F.)

SPARKING PLUGS

Make/Type	Champion/N9Y
Gap	.024 to .026 (.625 to .66 mm.)

CARBURETTORS

Make/Type	SU/HIF4
Specification	AUD 434
Jet	.090 in. (2.2 mm.)
Needle	AAU
Piston spring	Red

EXHAUST EMISSION

Exhaust gas analyser reading at engine idle speed	3 to 4.5% CO

Austin and Morris 1800 and Wolseley 18/85 (Mk I) engines 1967–68

ENGINE

Types	18AMW, 18C, 18WB, 18H197
Number of cylinders	4
Bore	3.160 in. (80.26 mm.)
Stroke	3.5 in. (88.9 mm.)
Capacity	109.75 in.^{3} (1798 cm.^{3})
Combustion chamber volume (valve fitted)	2.59 to 2.65 in.^{3} (42.5 to 43.5 cm.^{3})
Valve operation	Overhead by push-rod
B.M.E.P.: 8.4:1	136 lbf./in.^{2} (9.56 kgf./cm.^{2}) at 2500 rev./min. 18WB and from 18AMW/U/H101631
8.2:1	134.5 lbf./in.^{2} (9.46 kgf./cm.^{2}) at 2500 rev./min. Between 18AMW/U/H 27523 to H97273, and L20548 to L97810. 136 lbf./in.^{2} (9.56 kgf./cm.^{2}) at 2100 rev./min. All other 18AMW engines
6.8:1	—
Torque:	
8.4:1	99 lbf. ft. (13.7 kgf. m.) at 2500 rev./min. 18WB and from 18AMW/U/H101631
8.2:1	100 lbf. ft. (13.8 kgf. m.) at 2100 rev./min. Between 18AMW/U/H 27523 to H97273, and L20548 to L97810. 99 lbf. ft. (13.7 kgf. m.) at 1200 rev./min. All other 18AMW engines
6.8:1	—
Oversize bores	+0.010 in., +0.020 in., +0.030 in., +0.040 in., (+0.254 mm., +0.508 mm., +0.762 mm., +1.016 mm.)

CRANKSHAFT

Main journal diameter	2.1262 to 2.127 in. (54.01 to 54.02 mm.)
Min. regrind diameter	2.0865 in. (52.997 mm.)
Crankpin journal diameter	1.8759 to 1.8764 in. (47.648 to 47.661 mm.)
Min. regrind diameter	1.836 in. (45.632 mm.)
Crankshaft end-thrust	Taken on thrust washers at centre main bearing
Crankshaft end-float	0.001 to 0.005 in. (0.03 to 0.13 mm.)

MAIN BEARINGS

Number and type	5 thin-wall type
Material	Steel-backed copper-lead or reticular tin
Length:	
Front, centre and rear	1$\frac{1}{8}$ in. (28.5 mm.)
Intermediate	$\frac{7}{8}$ in. (22.23 mm.)
Diametrical clearance	0.001 to 0.0027 in. (0.025 to 0.068 mm.)
Undersizes	0.010 in., 0.020 in., 0.030 in., 0.040 in., (0.254 mm., 0.508 mm., 0.762 mm., 1.016 mm.)

CONNECTING RODS

Type	Angular-split big-end, bushed small-end
Length between centres	6.5 in. (165.1 mm.)

BIG-END BEARINGS

Type and material	Steel-backed copper-lead or VP3
Length	0.775 to 0.785 in. (19.68 to 19.94 mm.)
Diametrical clearance	0.0015 to 0.0032 in. (0.038 to 0.081 mm.)
End-float on crankpin (nominal)	0.008 to 0.012 in. (0.20 to 0.30 mm.)
Undersizes	0.010 in., 0.020 in., 0.030 in., 0.040 in., (0.254 mm., 0.508 mm., 0.762 mm., 1.016 mm.)

PISTONS

Type	Aluminium solid skirt
Clearance of skirt in cylinder:	
Top	0.0036 to 0.0045 in. (0.091 to 0.121 mm.)
Bottom	0.0018 to 0.0024 in. (0.045 to 0.061 mm.)
Number of rings	4 (3 compression, 1 oil control)
Width of ring grooves:	
Top, Second and Third	0.064 to 0.065 in. (1.625 to 1.651 mm.)
Oil control	0.1578 to 0.1588 in. (4.01 to 4.033 mm.)
Gudgeon pin bore	0.8128 to 0.813 in. (20.610 to 20.617 mm.)

PISTON RINGS

Compression:

Type:	
Top	Plain (cast iron molybdenum filled)
Second and third	Tapered (cast iron molybdenum filled)
Width:	
Top, second and third	0.0615 to 0.0625 in. (1.562 to 1.587 mm.)
Fitted gap:	
Top, second and third	0.012 to 0.017 in. (0.304 to 0.431 mm.)
Ring to groove clearance:	
Top, second and third	0.0015 to 0.0035 in. (0.038 to 0.088 mm.)

Oil control:

Type	Slotted scraper
Width	0.1552 to 0.1562 in. (3.94 to 3.96 mm.)
Fitted gap	0.012 to 0.017 in. (0.304 to 0.431 mm.)
Ring to groove clearance	0.0016 to 0.0036 in. (0.04 to 0.09 mm.)

GUDGEON PIN

Type	Fully floating
Fit in piston	Hand push fit at 16° C. (60° F.)

Outside diameter	0.8125 to 0.8127 in. (20.637 to 20.64 mm.)

CAMSHAFT

Journal diameters:	
Front	1.78875 to 1.78925 in. (45.424 to 45.437 mm.)
Centre	1.72875 to 1.72925 in. (43.910 to 43.923 mm.)
Rear	1.62275 to 1.62325 in. (41.218 to 41.230 mm.)
Bearing liner inside diameter (reamed after fitting):	
Front	1.79025 to 1.79075 in. (45.472 to 45.485 mm.)
Centre	1.73025 to 1.73075 in. (43.948 to 43.961 mm.)
Rear	1.62425 to 1.62475 in. (41.256 to 41.269 mm.)
Bearings	White-metal-lined, steel-backed
Diametrical clearance	0.001 to 0.002 in. (0.025 to 0.051 mm.)
End-thrust	Taken on locating plate
End-float	0.003 to 0.007 in. (0.076 to 0.178 mm.)
Drive	Chain and sprocket from crankshaft
Timing chain	$\frac{3}{8}$ in. (9.52 mm.) pitch × 52 pitches

TAPPETS

Type	Barrel with flat base
Outside diameter	$\frac{13}{16}$ in. (20.64 mm.)
Length	2.293 to 2.303 in. (5825 to 58.5 mm.)
Push-rod length	8.78 to 8.81 in. (223 to 224 mm.)

ROCKER GEAR

Rocker shaft

Length	$14\frac{1}{32}$ in. (356 mm.)
Diameter	0.624 to 0.625 in. (15.85 to 15.87 mm.)

Rocker arm

Bore	0.7485 to 0.7495 in. (19.01 to 19.26 mm.)
Rocker arm bush inside diameter (reamed)	0.6255 to 0.626 in. (15.8 to 15.9 mm.)
Ratio	1.4:1

VALVES

Seat angle: Inlet and exhaust	$45\frac{1}{2}°$
Head diameter:	
Inlet	1.562 to 1.567 in. (39.67 to 39.80 mm.)
Exhaust	1.343 to 1.348 in. (34.11 to 34.23 mm.)
Stem diameter:	
Inlet	0.3429 to 0.3434 in. (8.709 to 8.722 mm.)
Exhaust	0.3423 to 0.3428 in. (9.694 to 8.707 mm.)

Stem guide to clearance:	
Inlet	0.0008 to 0.0018 in. (0.020 to 0.046 mm.)
Exhaust	0.0014 to 0.0024 in. (0.035 to 0.061 mm.)
Valve lift: Inlet and exhaust	0.347 in. (8.81 mm.)[3], 0.342 in. (8.67 mm.)[2], 0.314 in. (7.98 mm.)[1]

VALVE GUIDES

Length:	
Inlet	1.88 in. (47.75 mm.)
Exhaust	2.22 in. (56.39 mm.)
Outside diameter: Inlet and exhaust	0.5635 to 0.5640 in. (14.30 to 14.32 mm.)
Inside diameter: Inlet and exhaust	0.3441 to 0.3448 in. (8.743 to 8.755 mm.)
Fitted height above head:	
Inlet	$\frac{3}{4}$ in. (19 mm.)
Exhaust	$\frac{5}{8}$ in. (15.89 mm.)
Interference fit in head: Inlet and exhaust	0.0005 to 0.00175 in. (0.012 to 0.044 mm.)

VALVE SPRINGS *Double spring*

Free length	$2\frac{9}{64}$ in. (54 mm.), *outer.* $1\frac{31}{32}$ in. (50.0 mm.), *inner*
Fitted length	$1\frac{9}{16}$ in. (39.7 mm.), *outer.* $1\frac{7}{16}$ in. (36.5 mm.), *inner*
Load at fitted length	60.5 lbf. (24.7 kgf.), *outer.* 30 lbf. (13.6 kgf.), *inner*
Load at top of lift	105 lbf. (47.6 kgf.), *outer.* 50 lbf. (22.7 kgf.), *inner*
Valve crash speed	5700 rev./min.

VALVE TIMING

Timing marks	Marks on camshaft and crankshaft wheels
Rocker clearance:	
Running (cold)	0.013 in. (0.33 mm.)[1], 0.018 in. (0.46 mm.)[2], 0.013 in. (0.33 mm.)[3]
Timing	0.020 in. (0.51 mm.)[1], 0.020 in. (0.51 mm.)[2], 0.020 in. (0.51 mm.)[3]
Inlet valve:	
Opens	T.D.C.[1], 5° B.T.D.C.[2], 5° B.T.D.C.[3]
Closes	50° A.B.D.C.[1], 45° A.B.D.C.[2], 45° A.B.D.C.[3]
Exhaust valve:	
Opens	35° B.B.D.C.[1], 51° B.B.D.C.[2], 40° B.B.D.C.[3]
Closes	15° A.T.D.C.[1], 21° A.T.D.C.[2], 10° A.T.D.C.[3]

LUBRICATION

System	Wet sump, pressure-fed
System pressure:	
Running	50 to 70 lbf./in² (3.5 to 4.9 kgf./cm²)
Idling	15 to 25 lbf./in² (1.0 to 1.8 kgf./cm²)
Oil pump	Hobourn-Eaton rotor type

Capacity	3¼ gal. (14.8 litres, 4 U.S. gal.)/min. at 1000 rev./min.
Oil filter	Full flow with renewable element
By-pass valve opens	8 to 12 lbf./in² (0.6 to 0.8 kgf./cm²)
Oil pressure relief valve	70 lbf./in² (4.9 kgf./cm²)
Relief valve spring:	
Free length	3 in. (76 mm.)
Fitted length	2$\frac{5}{32}$ in. (54.77 mm.)
Load at fitted length	15.5 to 16.5 lbf. (7.0 to 7.4 kgf.)
Oil pressure warning light switch	6 to 10 lbf./in² (0.4 to 0.7 kgf./cm²)

[1]Between 18AMW/U/H27523 to H97273, and L20547 to L97811.
[2]Up to 18AMW/U/H27272, L20546; and between 18AMW/U/H9724 to H101630, and L97811 to 97850. Up to 18WB/SB/U/H3063, A/H3936.
[3]From 18AMW/U/H101631, L97851 and 18WB/U/H3064, A/H3937. Camshaft identified by three grooves on end of shaft.

IGNITION SYSTEM

Coil, Distributor, Spark plugs	Refer to 'Additional data'

COOLING SYSTEM

Type	Pressurized spill return system with thermostat control, pump- and fan-assisted
Thermostat settings:	
Standard	82° C. (180° F.)
Hot countries	74° or 77° C. (165° or 170° F.)
Cold countries	88° C. (190° F.)
Pressure cap	13 lbf./in² (0.91 kgf./cm²)
Fan belt:	
Outside length	36.75 in. (93 cm.), *standard*. 41.12 in. (104 cm.), *power steering*. 38.5 in. (98 cm.), *11AC alternator*
Hot climates	35.5 in. (90 cm.), *standard*. 40 in. (101 cm.), *power steering*. 40 in. (101 cm.), *11AC alternator*
Tension	0.5 in. (13 mm.) deflection on longest run

FUEL SYSTEM

Carburettor	Refer to 'Additional data'

AIR CLEANER

Type	Paper element with warm/cold air intake and silencer

FUEL PUMP

Make and type	S.U. electric; AUF 200 type (AUF 209 or 215 model)
Delivery rate (minimum)	7 gal./hr. (8½ U.S. gal./hr., 32 litres/hr.)
Delivery pressure	2 to 3.8 lbf./in² (0.14 to 0.27 kgf./cm²)

CLUTCH

Make and type	Borg & Beck 8 in. diaphragm type (narrow)
Clutch plate diameter	8 in. (20.32 cm.)
Facing material	Wound yarn (RY2, WR7, M54 or 2124F)
Number of damper springs	6
Damper spring colours:	
Diaphragm spring blue	2: orange/light grey
	1: white/light grey, black/buff, violet/yellow, dark green/light blue
Diaphragm spring blue	2: orange/light grey, violet/yellow
	1: white/light grey, black/buff
Diaphragm spring light green—early units only	White/light green
Clutch release bearing	Carbon
Early units	Graphite (MY3D)
Master cylinder:	
Make/type	Girling, centre valve with integral reservoir
Bore diameter	$\frac{5}{8}$ in. (15.87 mm.)
Slave cylinder bore diameter	1 in. (25.4 mm.)

ADDITIONAL DATA

ENGINE

Type	18AMW, 18C, 18WB
Capacity	109.8 in³ (1798 cm³)
Compression ratio:	
H.C.	8.4:1 [1]
L.C.	6.8:1
Firing order	1, 3, 4, 2
Compression pressure:	
H.C.	150 to 160 lbf./in² (10.5 to 11.2 kgf./cm²)
L.C.	120 to 140 lbf./in² (8.4 to 9.8 kgf./cm²)
Idling speed	600 rev./min.
Fast idle speed	1000 rev./min.
Ignition timing:	
Stroboscopic at 600 rev./min.*†	16° B.T.D.C.
Advance check at 2,000 rev./min.*†	23° to 27° B.T.D.C.
Timing marks	Pointers on front cover and groove in crankshaft pulley
Valve rocker clearance (cold)	0.013 in. (0.33 mm.)

DISTRIBUTOR

Make/type	Lucas 25D4
Rotation of rotor	Anti-clockwise
Dwell angle	60° ± 3°
Contact breaker gap	0.014 to 0.016 in. (0.35 to 0.40 mm.)
Condenser capacity	0.18 to 0.24 microfarad
Serial No.	41034 (H.C.), 40970 (L.C.)

CENTRIFUGAL ADVANCE

Decelerating check*†	20° at 3800 rev./min. H.C. 32° at 4600 rev./min. L.C.
	16° at 2600 rev./min. H.C. 18° at 2400 rev./min. L.C.
	11° at 2000 rev./min. H.C. 15° at 2000 rev./min. L.C.
	4° at 1200 rev./min. H.C. 3° at 1000 rev./min. L.C.

No advance below	500 rev./min. H.C. 700 rev./min. L.C.	Oil control	0.1578 to 0.1588 in. (4.01 to 4.033 mm.)

VACUUM ADVANCE
Maximum*   (2–15–10) H.C. (4–12–8) L.C.
20° at 15 in. (380 mm.) Hg H.C. 16° at 12 in. (305 mm.) Hg L.C.

Starts   2 in. (50 mm.) Hg H.C. 4 in. (102 mm.) Hg L.C.

*Crankshaft degrees and r.p.m.
†Vacuum pipe disconnected

SPARK PLUGS
Make/type   Champion N–9Y or N5
Gap   0.025 in. (0.65 mm.)

IGNITION COIL
Make/type   Lucas HA12
Primary resistance at 20° C. (68° F.)   3.1 to 3.5 ohms
Consumption   3.9 A

CARBURETTOR
Make/type   S.U. HS6 at 30° AUD 147, AUD 223

Piston spring   Yellow
Jet size   0.100 in.
Needle:
   Standard   TW
   Rich   SW
   Weak   C1W
[1]From 18AMW/U/H101631 and 18WB

1800 and 18/85 Mk II engines 1968–72

ENGINE
Type   18H
Combustion chamber volume (valves fitted)   2.32 to 2.38 in^3 (38 to 39 cm^3)
B.M.E.P.: H.C.   138 lbf./in^2 (9.5 kgf./cm^2) at 3000 rev./min.
Torque: H.C.   101 lbf. ft. (14 kgf. m.) at 3000 rev./min.

CONNECTING RODS
Type   Horizontal split big-end, solid small-end
Length between centres   6.5 in. (165.1 mm.)
Locking method, big-end   Multi-sided nut

PISTONS
Type   Aluminium solid skirt
Clearance of skirt in cylinder:
   Top   0.0021 to 0.0037 in. (0.053 to 0.094 mm.)
   Bottom   0.0006 to 0.0016 in. (0.015 to 0.041 mm.)
Number of rings   Three; 2 compression, 1 oil control
Width of ring grooves:
   Compression   0.064 to 0.065 in. (1.625 to 1.651 mm.)

PISTON RINGS
Compression:
   Type: Top   Plain, sintered alloy
      Second   Tapered, sintered alloy—top face marked 'TOP'
   Fitted gap   0.012 to 0.017 in. (0.30 to 0.43 mm.)
   Width   0.0615 to 0.0625 in. (1.56 to 1.59 mm.)
   Thickness: Top   0.124 to 0.127 in. (3.14 to 3.22 mm.)
       Second   0.104 to 0.111 in. (2.64 to 2.81 mm.)
Oil control:
   Type   Two chrome-faced rings with expander
   Fitted gap (rings)   0.015 to 0.045 in. (0.38 to 1.14 mm.)
   Width (rings)   0.152 to 0.156 in. (3.86 to 3.96 mm.)

GUDGEON PIN
Type   Press fit in connecting rod
Diameter   0.8124 to 0.8127 in. (20.63 to 20.64 mm.)
Fit in:
   Piston   Hand push fit at 16° C. (60° F.)
   Small end   12 lbf. ft. (1.7 kgf. m.) minimum using 18G 1150/D

VALVES
Head diameter: Inlet   1.625 to 1.630 in. (41.27 to 41.40 mm.)

FUEL SYSTEM
Carburettor   Refer to 'Additional data'
Fuel pump
Make/type   S.U. mechanical; AUF 700 (AUF 704 model)
Suction (min.)   6 in. (152 mm.) Hg
Pressure (min.)   3 lbf./in^2 (0.21 kgf./cm^2)

ADDITIONAL DATA
ENGINE
Type   18H
Capacity   109.8 in.^{3} (1798 cm.^{3})
Compression ratio:
   H.C.   9.0:1
   L.C.[1]   8.0:1
Firing order   1, 3, 4, 2
Compression pressure:
   H.C.   170 to 195 lbf./in^2 (11.9 to 13.7 kgf./cm.^{2})
   L.C.[1]   150 to 160 lbf./in^2 (10.5 to 11.2 kgf./cm.^{2})
Idling speed   700 rev./min.
Fast idle speed   1,100 rev./min.
Ignition timing:
   Stroboscopic at 600 rev./min.*†   12° B.T.D.C. *H.C.* 17° B.T.D.C. *L.C.*[1]

Advance check at 2000 rev./min.*†	22° to 26° B.T.D.C. *H.C.* 27° to 31° B.T.D.C. *L.C.* [1]
Timing marks	Pointers on front cover and groove in. crankshaft pulley
Valve rocker clearance (cold)	0.013 in. (0.33 mm.)

DISTRIBUTOR

Make/type	Lucas 25D4
Rotation of rotor	Anti-clockwise
Dwell angle	60° ± 3°
Contact breaker gap	0.014 to 0.016 in. (0.35 to 0.40 mm.)
Condenser capacity	0.18 to 0.24 microfarad
Serial No.	41234 *H.C.* 41035 *L.C.* 41260 *L.C.*

CENTRIFUGAL ADVANCE

Decelerating check*†	26° at 4400 rev./min., 41234 *H.C.* 32° at 4600 rev./min., 41035 *L.C.* 30° at 5000 rev./min., 41260 *L.C.*
	20° at 3200 rev./min., 41234 *H.C.* 18° at 2400 rev./min., 41035 *L.C.* 22° at 3400 rev./min., 41260 *L.C.*
	12° at 2200 rev./min., 41234 *H.C.* 15° at 2000 rev./min., 41035 *L.C.* 16° at 2400 rev./min., 41260 *L.C.*
	4° at 1200 rev./min., 41234 *H.C.* 3° at 1000 rev./min., 41035 *L.C.* 14° at 1200 rev./min., 41260 *L.C.*
No advance below	500 rev./min., 41234 *H.C.* 500 rev./min., 41035 *L.C.* 600 rev./min., 41260 *L.C.*

VACUUM ADVANCE

	(1–7–6), 41234 *H.C.* (4–15–8), 41035 *L.C.* (6–13–7), 41260 *L.C.*
Maximum*	12° at 7 in. (180 mm.) Hg, 41234 *H.C.* 16° at 15 in. (380 mm.) Hg, 41035 *L.C.* 14° at 13 in. (330 mm.) Hg, 41260 *L.C.*
Starts	1 in. (25 mm.) Hg, 41234 *H.C.* 4 in. (102 mm.) Hg, 41035 *L.C.* 6 in. (152 mm.) Hg, 41260 *L.C.*

*Crankshaft degrees and rev./min.
†Vacuum pipe disconnected

SPARK PLUGS

Make/type	Champion N–9Y
Gap	0.025 in. (0.65 mm.)

IGNITION COIL

Make/type	Lucas HA12 or Lucas BA7 with ballast resistor
Primary resistance at 20° C. (68° F.)	3.1 to 3.5 ohms or 1.4 to 1.6 ohms with ballast resistor
Consumption	3.9 A or 4.15 A with ballast resistor

CARBURETTOR

Make/type	S.U. HS6 at 20°
Specification:	
Manual gearbox	AUD 280, AUD 524, AUD 565 (AUD 561 *Canada*)
Automatic gearbox	AUD 291, AUD 525, AUD 568
Piston spring	Yellow
Jet size	0.100 in.
Needle:	
Standard	ZH (BAJ *Canada*)
Rich	SA
Weak	C1W

[1]L.C. (export, territories with fuel below 91 R.O.N.) 6.9:1
Compression pressure 120 to 140 lbf./in² (8.4 to 9.8 kgf./cm.²)
Ignition timing, stroboscopic at 600 rev./min. 15 B.T.D.C.

1800 and 18/85 'S' Mk II engines 1968–72

ENGINE

Type	18H
Combustion chamber volume (valves fitted)	2.22 to 2.28 in.³ (36.44 to 37.44 cm.³)
Compression ratio	9.5:1
Compression·pressure	175 to 200 lbf./in² (12.3 to 14.1 kgf./cm.²)
B.M.E.P.	145 lbf./in² (10.2 kgf./cm.²) at 3000 rev./min.
Torque	106 lbf. ft. (14.66 kgf. m.) at 3000 rev./min.

VALVES

Head diameter: Inlet (marked '20')	1.625 to 1.630 in. (41.27 to 41.40 mm.)

VALVE TIMING

Timing marks	Dimples on camshaft and crankshaft wheels
Rocker clearance:	
Running (cold)	0.013 in. (0.33 mm.)
Timing	0.020 in. (0.51 mm.)
Inlet valve:	
Opens	16° B.T.D.C.
Closes	56° A.B.D.C.
Exhaust valve:	
Opens	51° B.B.D.C.
Closes	21° B.T.D.C.
Depth of cylinder head	3.437 +0.040 in., −0.000 in. (87.31 +1.02 mm., −0.00 mm.)

FUEL SYSTEM

Carburettor	Refer to 'Additional data'
Air cleaner	
Type	Twin paper element with warm/cold air in.take and silencer tube

MANUAL GEARBOX

Gearbox ratios: Second	2.06:1
Overall ratios: Second	7.99:1
Road speed at 1000 rev./min. in. top gear	18.2 m.p.h. (29.3 km./h.)

BRAKES
Front
Disc diameter	9.7 in. (246 mm.)
Pad area (total)	27.6 in.² (178 cm.²)
Swept area (total)	195 in.² (1258 cm.²)
Lining material	Ferodo 2430 F

GENERAL DIMENSIONS
Overall length	166.67 in. (4233 mm.)
Overall width	66.68 in. (1694 mm.)
Overall height*	56.5 in. (1435 mm.)
Wheelbase*:	
Power steering	106.4 in. (2703 mm.)
Manual steering	106.16 in. (2696 mm.)
Ground clearance*	6.5 in. (165 mm.)

*Unladen condition

ADDITIONAL DATA

ENGINE
Type	18H
Capacity	109.8 in³ (1798 cm³)
Compression ratio: H.C.	9.5:1
Firing order	1, 3, 4, 2
Compression pressure: H.C.	180 to 200 lbf./in² (12.6 to 14 kgf./cm²)
Idling speed	700 to 800 rev./min.
Fast idle speed	1000 rev./min.
Ignition timing:	
Stroboscopic at 600 rev./min.*†	12° B.T.D.C.
Advance check at 2000 rev./min.*†	23° to 27° B.T.D.C.
Timing marks	Pointers on front cover and groove in crankshaft pulley
Valve rocker clearance (cold)	0.013 in. (0.33 mm.)

DISTRIBUTOR
Make/type	Lucas 25D4
Rotation of rotor	Anti-clockwise
Dwell angle	60° ± 3°
Contact breaker gap	0.014 to 0.016 in. (0.35 to 0.40 mm.)
Condenser capacity	0.18 to 0.24 microfarad
Serial No.	41238

CENTRIFUGAL ADVANCE
Decelerating check*†	20° to 24° at 5000 rev./min.
	11° to 15° at 2800 rev./min.
	8° to 12° at 2000 rev./min.
	4° to 7° at 1200 rev./min.
No advance below	600 rev./min.

VACUUM ADVANCE
	(4–11–7)
Maximum*	14° at 11 in. (280 mm.) Hg
Starts	4 in. (100 mm.) Hg

*Crankshaft degrees and r.p.m.
†Vacuum pipe disconnected

SPARK PLUGS
Make/type	Champion N–9Y
Gap	0.025 in. (0.65 mm.)

IGNITION COIL
Make/type	Lucas HA12
Primary resistance at 20° C. (68° F.)	3.1 to 3.5 ohms
Consumption	3.9 A

CARBURETTOR
Make/type	S.U. Twin HS6 at 30° AUD 171
Piston spring	Red
Jet size	0.100 in.
Needle:	
Standard	TZ
Rich	C1
Weak	C1W

1800 and 18/85 (Mk III) engines 1973–75

ENGINE
Type	18H
Combustion chamber volume (valves fitted)	2.32 to 2.38 in³ (38 to 39 cm³)
B.M.E.P.: H.C.	138 lbf./in² (9.5 kgf./cm²) at 3000 rev./min.
Torque: H.C.	101 lbf. ft. (14 kgf. m.) at 3000 rev./min.

CONNECTING RODS
Type	Horizontal split big-end, solid small-end
Length between centres	6.5 in. (165.1 mm.)
Locking method, big-end	Multi-sided nut

PISTONS
Type	Aluminium solid skirt
Clearance of skirt in cylinder:	
Top	0.0021 to 0.0037 in. (0.053 to 0.094 mm.)
Bottom	0.0006 to 0.0016 in. (0.015 to 0.041 mm.)
Number of rings	Three; 2 compression, 1 oil control
Width of ring grooves:	
Compression	0.064 to 0.065 in. (1.625 to 1.651 mm.)
Oil control	0.1578 to 0.1588 in. (4.01 to 4.033 mm.)

PISTON RINGS
Compression:	
Type: Top	Plain, sintered alloy
Second	Tapered, sintered alloy—top face marked 'TOP'
Fitted gap	0.012 to 0.017 in. (0.30 to 0.43 mm.)
Width	0.0615 to 0.0625 in. (1.56 to 1.59 mm.)
Thickness: Top	0.124 to 0.127 in. (3.14 to 3.22 mm.)
Second	0.104 to 0.111 in. (2.64 to 2.81 mm.)

Oil control

Type	Two chrome-faced rings with expander
Fitted gap (rings)	0.015 to 0.045 in. (0.38 to 1.14 mm.)
Width (rings)	0.152 to 0.156 in. (3.86 to 3.96 mm.)

GUDGEON PIN

Type	Press fit in connecting rod
Diameter	0.8124 to 0.8127 in. (20.63 to 20.64 mm.)

Fit in:

Piston	Hand push fit at 16° C. (60° F.)
Small end	12 lbf. ft. (1.7 kgf. m.) minimum using 18G 1150/D

TAPPETS

Type	Bucket with radiused base
Outside diameter	0.812 in. (20.624 mm.)
Length	1.500 to 1.505 in. (38.10 to 38.22 mm.)
Push-rod length	10.38 to 10.41 in. (263.7 to 264.4 mm.)

Valves

Seat angle: Inlet and Exhaust	$45\frac{1}{2}°$

Head diameter:

Inlet	1.625 to 1.630 in. (41.27 to 41.40 mm.)
Exhaust	1.343 to 1.348 in. (34.11 to 34.23 mm.)

Stem diameter:

Inlet	0.3429 to 0.3434 in. (8.709 to 8.722 mm.)
Exhaust	0.3423 to 0.3428 in. (8.694 to 8.707 mm.)

Stem to guide clearance:

Inlet	0.0008 to 0.0018 in. (0.0203 to 0.0457 mm.)
Exhaust	0.0014 to 0.0024 in. (0.0355 to 0.0609 mm.)
Valve lift: Inlet and exhaust	0.347 in. (8.81 mm.)

VALVE SPRING*

Free length	1.92 in. 48.77 mm.) approx.
Fitted length	1.44 in. (36.58 mm.)
Load at fitted length	82 lbf. (37 kgf.)
Load at top of lift	142 lbf. (64 kgf.)
Number of working coils	$4\frac{1}{2}$
Valve crash speed	5500 rev./min.

VALVE TIMING

Timing marks	Marks on camshaft and crankshaft wheels

Rocker clearance:

Running (cold)	0.013 in. (0.33 mm.)
Timing	0.020 in. (0.51 mm.)

Inlet valve:

Opens	5° B.T.D.C.
Closes	45° A.B.D.C.

Exhaust valve:

Opens	40° B.B.D.C.
Closes	10° A.T.D.C.

IGNITION SYSTEM

Coil, Distributor and Spark plugs	Refer to 'Additional data'

FUEL SYSTEM

Carburettor	Refer to 'Additional data'

AIR CLEANER

Type:

Standard	Paper element with warm/cold air intake tube
Emission control (ECE 15)	Paper element with an air temperature control valve on the air intake tube

FUEL PUMP

Make/type	S.U. mechanical; AUF 700 or AUF 800
Suction (min.)	6 in. (152 mm.) Hg
Pressure (min.)	3 lbf./in^2 (0.21 kgf./cm^2)

ADDITIONAL DATA

ENGINE

Type	18H
Capacity	109.8 in.^{3} (1798 cm^3)

Compression ratio:

H.C.	9.0:1
L.C.	8.0:1 (6.9:1 available)
Firing order	1, 3, 4, 2

Compression pressure:

H.C.	170 to 195 lbf./in^2 (11.9 to 13.7 kgf./cm^2)
L.C.	150 to 160 lbf./in^2 (10.5 to 11.2 kgf./cm^2)
Idling speed	750 rev./min.
Fast idle speed	1000 rev./min.

Ignition timing

Stroboscopic at 1000 rev./min.	14° B.T.D.C., H.C. 19° B.T.D.C., L.C.
Advance check at 2000 rev./min.	22° to 26° B.T.D.C., H.C. 27° to 31° B.T.D.C., L.C.
Timing marks	Pointers on front cover and groove in crankshaft pulley
Valve rocker clearance (cold)	0.013 in. (0.33 mm.)

DISTRIBUTOR

Make/type	Lucas 25D4 or 45D4
Rotation of rotor	Anti-clockwise
Dwell angle: 25D4	60° ± 3°
45D4	51° ± 5°
Contact breaker gap	0.014 to 0.016 in. (0.35 to 0.40 mm.)
Condenser capacity	0.18 to 0.24 microfarad
Serial No.: 25D4	41234, H.C. 41260 L.C.
45D4	41415 H.C. 41421 L.C.

CENTRIFUGAL ADVANCE

Decelerating check*†	24° to 28° at 4400 rev./min. H.C. 28° to 32° at 5000 rev./min. L.C.

	18° to 22° at 3200 rev./min. *H.C.* 20° to 24° at 3400 rev./min. *L.C.* 10° to 14° at 2200 rev./min. *H.C.* 14° to 18° at 2400 rev./min. *L.C.* 2° to 6° at 1200 rev./min. *H.C.* 12° to 16° at 1200 rev./min. *L.C.*
No advance below	500 rev./min. *H.C.* 600 rev./min. *L.C.*
VACUUM ADVANCE	(1–7–6) *H.C.* (6–13–7) *L.C.*
Maximum	12° at 7 in. (180 mm.) Hg *H.C.* 14° at 13 in. (330 mm.) Hg *L.C.*
Starts	1 in. (25 mm.) Hg *H.C.* 6 in. (152 mm.) Hg *L.C.*

*Crankshaft degrees and rev./min.
†Vacuum pipe disconnected
*Early units as 1800 Mk II

SPARK PLUGS

Make/type	Champion N–9Y
Gap	0.025 in. (0.65 mm.)

IGNITION COIL

Make/type	Lucas HA12 or Lucas BA7 with ballast resistor
Primary resistance at 20° C. (68° F.)	3.1 to 3.5 ohms or 1.4 to 1.6 ohms with ballast resistor
Consumption	3.9 A or 4.15 A with ballast resistor

CARBURETTOR

Make/type	S.U. HS6 at 20°
Specification:	
Manual gearbox	AUD 564, AUD 355
Automatic gearbox	AUD 356, AUD 570
Piston spring	Yellow
Jet size	0.100 in.
Needle	BBF
Exhaust gas analyser reading at engine idle speed	3.0 to 4.5% CO

Morris Marina 1.8 engine

ENGINE

Type	18V
Number of cylinders	4
Bore	3.160 in. (80.26 mm.)
Stroke	3.5 in. (88.9 mm.)
Capacity	109.7 in³ (1798 cm³)
Combustion chamber volume (valves fitted)	2.32 to 2.38 in³ (38 to 39 cm³)
Firing order	1, 3, 4, 2
Valve operation	Overhead by push-rod
Compression ratio:	
H.C.	9.0:1
L.C.	8.0:1
Cranking pressure:	
H.C.	190 lbf./in² (13.4 kgf./cm²)
L.C.	170 lbf./in² (12 kgf./cm²)

Oversize bores	+0.010 in., +0.020 in., +0.030 in., +0.040 in., (0.254 mm., +0.508 mm., +0.762 mm., +1.016 mm.)

CRANKSHAFT

Main journal diameter	2.1262 to 2.127 in. (54.005 to 54.025 mm.)
Minimum regrind diameter	2.0865 in. (52.997 mm.)
Crankpin journal diameter	1.8759 to 1.8764 in. (47.647 to 47.660 mm.)
Minimum regrind diameter	1.836 in. (46.534 mm.)
Crankshaft end-thrust	Taken on thrust washers at centre main bearing
Crankshaft end-float	0.002 to 0.003 in. (0.050 to 0.0076 mm.)

MAIN BEARINGS

Number and type	5 thin wall type
Material	Steel-backed copper-lead or reticular tin
Length:	
Front, centre and rear	1.125 in. (28.57 mm.)
Intermediate	0.875 in. (22.22 mm.)
Diametrical clearance	0.001 to 0.0027 in. (0.025 to 0.068 mm.)
Undersizes	0.010 in., 0.020 in., 0.030 in., 0.040 in. (0.254 mm., 0.508 mm., 0.762 mm., 1.016 mm.)

CONNECTING RODS

Type	Horizontal, split big-end
Length between centres	6.5 in. (165.1 mm.)

BIG-END BEARINGS

Type and material	Steel-backed copper-lead or VP3
Length	0.775 to 0.785 in. (19.68 to 19.94 mm.)
Diametrical clearance	0.0015 to 0.0032 in. (0.038 to 0.081 mm.)
End-float on crankpin (nominal)	0.008 to 0.012 in. (0.20 to 0.30 mm.)
Undersizes	0.010 in., 0.020 in., 0.030 in., 0.040 in. (0.254 mm., 0.508 mm., 0.762 mm., 1.016 mm.)

GUDGEON PIN

Type	Pressed in connecting rod
Fit in piston	Hand push-fit at 16° C. (60° F.)
Diameter (outer)	0.8125 to 0.8127 in. (20.637 to 20.642 mm.)

PISTONS

Type	Aluminium, solid skirt
Clearance of skirt in cylinder:	
Top	0.0021 to 0.0037 in. (0.0533 to 0.0939 mm.)
Bottom	0.0018 to 0.0024 in. (0.045 to 0.060 mm.)
Number of rings	3 (2 compression, 1 oil control)

Width of ring grooves:

Top and second	0.064 to 0.065 in. (1.625 to 1.651 mm.)
Oil control	0.1578 to 0.1588 in. (40.01 to 40.03 mm.)
Gudgeon pin bore	0.8130 to 0.8132 in. (21.650 to 21.925 mm.)

PISTON RINGS

Compression:

Type:	
Top	Plain, sintered alloy
Second	Tapered, sintered alloy
Width: Top, second	0.0615 to 0.0625 in. (1.562 to 1.587 mm.)
Fitted gap: Top, second	0.012 to 0.017 in. (0.304 to 0.431 mm.)
Ring to groove clearance: Top, second	0.0015 to 0.0035 in. (0.038 to 0.088 mm.)

Oil control:

Type	Slotted scraper
Width	0.1552 to 0.1562 in. (3.942 to 3.967 mm.)
Fitted gap	0.015 to 0.045 in. (0.381 to 1.143 mm.)
Ring to groove clearance	0.0016 to 0.0036 in. (0.040 to 0.091 mm.)

CAMSHAFT

Journal diameters:

Front	1.78875 to 1.78925 in. (45.434 to 45.446 mm.)
Centre	1.72875 to 1.72925 in. (43.910 to 43.923 mm.)
Rear	1.62275 to 1.62325 in. (41.218 to 41.230 mm.)

Bearing liner inside diameter (reamed after fitting):

Front	1.79025 to 1.79075 in. (45.472 to 45.485 mm.)
Centre	1.73025 to 1.73075 in. (43.948 to 43.961 mm.)
Rear	1.62425 to 1.62475 in. (41.256 to 41.269 mm.)
Bearings: Type	White metal lined, steel-backed
Diametrical clearance	0.001 to 0.002 in. (0.0254 to 0.0508 mm.)
End-thrust	Taken on locating plate
End-float	0.003 to 0.007 in. (0.076 to 0.178 mm.)
Drive	Chain and sprocket from crankshaft
Timing chain	0.375 in. (9.52 mm.) pitch × 52 pitches

TAPPETS

Type	Bucket with radiused base
Outside diameter	0.8125 in. (20.624 mm.)
Length	1.5 to 1.505 in. (38.1 to 38.22 mm.)
Push-rod length	10.38 to 10.41 in. (263.6 to 264.4 mm.)

ROCKER GEAR

Rocker shaft:

Length	14.032 in. (356.4 mm.)
Diameter	0.624 to 0.625 in. (15.85 to 15.87 mm.)

Rocker arm:

Bore	0.7485 to 0.7495 in. (19.004 to 19.037 mm.)
Bush inside diameter (reamed in position)	0.6255 to 0.626 in. (15.887 to 15.9 mm.)

VALVES

Seat angle:

Inlet	$45\frac{1}{2}°$
Exhaust	$45\frac{1}{2}°$

Head diameter:

Inlet	1.562 to 1.567 in. (39.675 to 39.802 mm.)
Exhaust	1.343 to 1.348 in. (34.11 to 34.23 mm.)

Stem diameter:

Inlet	0.3429 to 0.3434 in. (8.709 to 8.722 mm.)
Exhaust	0.3423 to 0.3428 in. (8.694 to 8.707 mm.)

Stem to guide clearance:

Inlet	0.0008 to 0.0018 in. (0.0203 to 0.0457 mm.)
Exhaust	0.0014 to 0.0024 in. (0.0355 to 0.0609 mm.)
Valve lift: Inlet and exhaust	0.360 in. (9.14 mm.)

VALVE GUIDES

Length:

Inlet	1.875 in. (47.62 mm.)
Exhaust	2.203 in. (55.95 mm.)
Outside diameter: Inlet and exhaust	0.5635 to 0.5640 in. (14.312 to 14.325 mm.)
Inside diameter: Inlet and exhaust	0.3442 to 0.3447 in. (8.743 to 8.755 mm.)

Fitted height above head:

Inlet	0.75 in. (19.05 mm.)
Exhaust	0.625 in. (15.87 mm.)
Interference fit in head: Inlet and exhaust	0.0005 to 0.00175 in. (0.012 to 0.0443 mm.)

VALVE SPRINGS

Free length	1.92 in. (48.77 mm.) approx.
Fitted length	1.44 in. (36.58 mm.)
Load at fitted length	82 lbf. (37 kgf.)
Load at top of lift	142 lbf. (64 kgf.)
Number of working coils	$4\frac{1}{2}$

VALVE TIMING

Timing marks	Dimples in camshaft and crankshaft wheels

Rocker clearance:

Running (cold)	0.013 in. (0.33 mm.)
Timing	0.020 in. (0.51 mm.)

Inlet valve:

Opens	5° B.T.D.C.*†, 16° B.T.D.C.*†

Closes	45° A.B.D.C.*†, 56° A.B.D.C.*×
Exhaust valve:	
Opens	40° B.B.D.C.*×, 51° B.B.D.C.*†
Closes	10° A.T.D.C.*×, 21° A.T.D.C.*†

LUBRICATION

System	Wet sump, pressure fed
System pressure:	
Running	50 to 70 lbf./in² (3.5 to 4.9 kgf./cm²)
Idling	15 to 25 lbf./in² (1.0 to 1.8 kgf./cm²)
Oil pump	Hobourn-Eaton rotor type
Capacity	3.25 gal. (4 U.S. gal., 14.8 litres) per minute at 1,000 rev./min.

× Cars with model series letter 'K' in the prefix from number 101.
*Single carburettor automatic and manual
†GT and HL automatic and manual

Oil filter	Full flow; disposable cartridge type
By-pass valve opens	8 to 12 lbf./in² (0.56 to 0.84 kgf./cm²)
Oil pressure relief valve	60 lbf./in.² (4.2 kgf./cm.²)
Relief valve spring:	
Free length	3 in. (76 mm.)
Fitted length	2.156 in. (54.76 mm.)
Load at fitted length	15.5 to 16.5 lbf. (7.0 to 7.4 kgf.)

TRANSMISSION

Gearbox

Synchromesh	All forward gears
Ratios:	
Top	1.000:1
Third	1.307:1
Second	1.916:1
First	3.111:1
Reverse	3.422:1
Overall ratios:	
Top	3.636:1
Third	4.751:1
Second	7.003:1
First	11.313:1
Reverse	12.444:1
Road speed per 1,000 rev./min. in top gear	18.1 m.p.h. (29.1 km./h.)

AUTOMATIC

Torque converter

Diameter	9.5 in. (240 mm.)
Identification (stamped on converter)	118
Ratio range	1:1 to 2:1

Gearbox

Ratios:	
First	2.39:1
Second	1.45:1

Top	1.00:1
Reverse	2.09:1
Final drive ratios	3.636:1
Speed at 1,000 rev./min. in top	18.1 m.p.h. (29.1 km./h.)

Austin Marina engine (export only)

Type	Without catalyst
Manual	18V 795 AE
Automatic	18V 850 AE
Compression ratio	8.0:1
Cranking pressure	130 lbf./in²
Oversize bores	+0.010 in., +0.020 in., +0.030 in., +0.040 in.
Torque (S.A.E. J.245 net)	87.8 lbf. ft. at 2,500 rev./min.

VALVES

Seat angle:	
Inlet	45°
Exhaust	45°

Austin Morris ½-ton van and pick-up (1500) engines to 1971

ENGINE

Type	15AC
Number of cylinders	4
Bore	2.875 in. (73.025 mm.)
Stroke	3.5 in. (88.9 mm.)
Capacity	1489 c.c. (90.88 cu. in.)
Combustion chamber volume (valves fitted)	2.4 cu. in. (39.2 c.c.)
Firing order	1, 3, 4, 2
Valve operation	Overhead by push-rod
Compression ratio:	
H.C.	8.3:1
L.C.	7.2:1
B.M.E.P.:	
H.C.	135 lb./sq. in. (9.49 kg./cm.²) at 2,000 r.p.m.
L.C.	123 lb./sq. in. (8.65 kg./cm.²) at 2,100 r.p.m.
Torque:	
H.C.	81 lb. ft. (11.2 kg. m.) at 2,000 r.p.m.
L.C.	74 lb. ft. (10.2 kg. m.) at 2,100 r.p.m.
Cranking pressure (compression):	
H.C.	150 lb./sq. in. (10.5 kg./cm.²)
L.C.	125 lb./sq. in. (8.79 kg./cm.²)

CRANKSHAFT

Main journal diameter	2.0005 to 2.0010 in. (50.81 to 50.82 mm.)
Crankpin journal diameter	1.8759 to 1.8764 in. (47.65 to 47.66 mm.)
Crankshaft end-thrust	Taken on thrust washer at centre main bearing

Crankshaft end-float — .002 to .003 in. (.051 to .076 mm.)

MAIN BEARINGS

Number and type — Three shell type
Material — Copper-lead
Length — 1.25 in. (31.75 mm.)
Diametrical clearance — .001 to .0027 in. (.0254 to .068 mm.)
Undersizes — .010 to .040 in. (.254 to 1.016 mm.)

CONNECTING RODS

Type — Angular split big-end, split clamp small-end
Length between centres — 6.5 in. (165.1 mm.)

BIG-END BEARINGS

Type — Shell type
Material — Copper-lead
Length — 1.0 in. (2.54 mm.)
Diametrical clearance — .001 to .0027 in. (.0254 to .068 mm.)
Undersizes — .010 to .040 in. (.254 to 1.016 mm.)
End-float on crankpin (nominal) — .008 to .012 in. (.203 to .305 mm.)

PISTONS

Type — Aluminium alloy, split skirt, anodized
Clearance in cylinder:
  Top — .0022 to .0034 in. (.056 to .087 mm.)
  Bottom — .0006 to .0014 in. (.015 to .035 mm.)
Number of rings — 4 (3 compression, 1 oil control)
Width of ring grooves:
  Top, second, and third — .0796 to .0806 in. (2.02 to 2.04 mm.)
  Oil control — .1578 to .1588 in. (4.01 to 4.04 mm.)
Gudgeon pin bore — .6870 to .68725 in. (17.450 to 17.456 mm.)

PISTON RINGS

Compression:
  Type: Top — Parallel chrome
        Second and third — Tapered cast iron
  Width — .0771 to .0781 in. (1.95 to 1.98 mm.)
Oil control:
  Type — Slotted scraper
  Width — .1552 to .1562 in. (3.94 to 3.99 mm.)
  Fitted gap — .008 to .013 in. (.20 to .33 mm.)
  Ring to groove clearance — .0016 to .0036 in. (.040 to .091 mm.)

CAMSHAFT

Journal diameters:
  Front — 1.78875 to 1.78925 in. (45.43 to 45.44 mm.)
  Centre — 1.72875 to 1.72925 in. (43.91 to 43.92 mm.)
  Rear — 1.62275 to 1.62325 in. (41.22 to 41.23 mm.)
Bearing liner inside diameter (reamed after fitting):
  Front — 1.79025 to 1.79075 in. (45.47 to 45.48 mm.)
  Centre — 1.73025 to 1.73075 in. (43.95 to 43.96 mm.)
  Rear — 1.62425 to 1.62475 in. (41.25 to 41.26 mm.)
Diametrical clearance — .001 to .002 in. (.0254 to .0508 mm.)
End-thrust — Taken on locating plate
End-float — .003 to .007 in. (.076 to .178 mm.)
Cam lift — .250 in. (16.35 mm.)
Drive — Chain and sprocket from crankshaft
Timing chain — $\frac{3}{8}$ in. (9.52 mm.) pitch × 52 pitches

TAPPETS

Type — Barrel with spherical base
Outside diameter — .81125 to .81175 in. (20.605 to 20.618 mm.)
Length — 2.293 to 2.303 in. (58.25 to 58.5 mm.)

ROCKER GEAR

Rocker shaft:
  Length — 14$\frac{1}{32}$ in. (356 mm.)
  Diameter — .624 to .625 in. (15.85 to 15.87 mm.)
Rocker arm:
  Bore — .7485 to .7495 in. (19.01 to 19.26 mm.)
Rocker arm bush inside diameter — .625 to .626 in. (15.8 to 15.9 mm.)
Ratio — 1.4:1

VALVES

Seat angle — 45°
Head diameter:
  Inlet — 1.370 to 1.375 in. (34.89 to 34.92 mm.)
  Exhaust — 1. 82 to 1.187 in. (30.02 to 30.16 mm.)
Stem diameter:
  Inlet — .3422 to .3427 in. (8.691 to 8.704 mm.)
  Exhaust — .34175 to .34225 in. (8.680 to 8.693 mm.)
Stem to guide clearance:
  Inlet — .0015 to .0025 in. (.038 to .063 mm.)
  Exhaust — .002 to .003 in. (.051 to .076 mm.)
Valve lift — .312 in. (7.925 mm.)

VALVE GUIDES

Length:
  Inlet — 1$\frac{7}{8}$ in. (47.63 mm.)

Exhaust $2\frac{13}{64}$ in. (55.95 mm.)

Outside diameter .5635 to .5640 in. (14.30 to 14.32 mm.)

Inside diameter:

Inlet .34425 to .34475 in. (8.74 to 8.76 mm.)

Exhaust .3442 to .3447 in. (8.73 to 8.75 mm.)

Fitted height above head $\frac{5}{8}$ in. (15.9 mm.)

Interference fit in head .0005 to .00175 in. (.012 to .044 mm.)

VALVE SPRINGS

Free length $2\frac{1}{64}$ in. (51.2 mm.)

Fitted length $1\frac{17}{32}$ in. (38.9 mm.)

Load at fitted length 75.5 to 79.5 lb. (34.25 to 36.06 kg.)

Load at top of lift 130 lb. (59 kg.)

Valve crash speed 5,500 r.p.m.

VALVE TIMING

Timing marks Dimples on camshaft and crankshaft wheels

Rocker clearance:

Running .015 in. (.38 mm.) cold

Timing .021 in. (.53 mm.)

Inlet valve:

Opens T.D.C.*

Closes 50° A.B.D.C.*

Exhaust valve:

Opens 35° B.B.D.C.*

Closes 15° A.T.D.C.*

*With .021 in. (.53 mm.) rocker clearance (for timing check only)

LUBRICATION

System Wet sump, pressure-fed

System pressure:

Running 30 to 50 lb./sq. in. (2.1 to 3.5 kg./cm.²)

Idling 10 to 15 lb./sq. in. (.7 to 1.05 kg./cm.²)

Oil pump Hobourn-Eaton rotor

Capacity $3\frac{1}{4}$ gal. (14.8 litres, 4 U.S. gal./min.

Oil filter Tecalemit full-flow felt element

Capacity $2\frac{1}{2}$ gal. (11.4 litres, 3 U.S. gal.)/min.

By-pass valve opens 13 to 17 lb./sq. in. (.9 to 1.1 kg./cm.²)

Oil pressure relief valve 50 lb./sq. in. (3.5 kg./cm.²)

Release valve spring:

Free length $2\frac{55}{64}$ in. (72.64 mm.)

Fitted length $2\frac{5}{32}$ in. (54.77 mm.)

Load at fitted length 13 to 14 lb. (5.90 to 6.35 kg.)

Pressure feed to Main bearings, big-end bearings, camshaft bearings, pump spindle, rockers, timing chain tensioner, and rocker ball pins

Leak feed to Cylinders, small-ends, tappets, distributor drive, timing chain and tensioner, and valves

Splash feed to Cylinder walls, distributor drive, tappets, timing chain and tensioner

Mist feed to Valves and rocker tips

FUEL SYSTEM

Carburettor Zenith 30VIG-10

Choke 27 mm.

Main jet 72

Correction jet 95

Pilot jet 50

Air cleaners Oil-wetted (oil bath for export)

Fuel pump A.C.-Delco Type 'U'

Working pressure $1\frac{1}{2}$ to $2\frac{1}{2}$ lb./sq. in. (.105 to .175 kg./cm.²)

COOLING SYSTEM

Type Pressurized. Impeller and fan-assisted with thermostat control

Thermostat setting 83°C. (180° F.)

Pressure cap 7 lb. (3.175 kg.)

Fan blades 4, 13 in. (33.02 cm.) diameter

Fan belt:

Width $\frac{3}{8}$ in. (9.5 mm.)

Outside length $34\frac{7}{8}$ in. (86.5 cm.)

Thickness $\frac{5}{16}$ in. (7.9 mm.)

Tension $\frac{1}{2}$ in. (12.8 mm.) movement

Type of pump Centrifugal

Pump drive Belt from crankshaft pulley

IGNITION SYSTEM

Coil Lucas LA 12

Primary winding resistance at 20° C. (68° F.) 3.2 to 3.4 ohms

Consumption:

Ignition switch on at 15° C. (60° F.) 3.6 amps

At 2,000 r.p.m. 1.25 amps

Distributor Lucas 25D4

Cam form 4-cylinder high-lift

Cam closed period 60° ± 3°

Cam open period 30° ± 3°

Automatic advance Centrifugal and vacuum

Rotation of rotor Anti-clockwise

Serial number 40778A *H.C.* 40776A *L.C.*

Automatic advance starts* 600 r.p.m. *H.C.* 760 r.p.m. *L.C.*

Vacuum advance starts 5 in. (13 cm.) Hg *H.C.* 6 in. (15 cm.) Hg *L.C.*

Ends* 20° at 17 in. (44 cm.) Hg *H.C.* 16° at 14 in. (36 cm.) Hg *L.C.*

Maximum advance* 24° at 4,800 r.p.m. *H.C.* 34° at 5,000 r.p.m. *L.C.*

Decelerating check* 20° at 3,000 r.p.m. *H.C.* 30° at 4,200 r.p.m. *L.C.*

14° at 2,260 r.p.m. *H.C.* 18° at 2,660 r.p.m. *L.C.*

3° at 900 r.p.m. *H.C.* 10° at 1,900 r.p.m. *L.C.*

Contact point gap setting .014 to .016 in. (.35 to .40 mm.)

Breaker spring tension 18 to 24 oz. (510 to 680 gm.)

Condenser capacity .18 to .24 mF

Timing marks	Pointer on timing chain case and notch on crankshaft pulley
Static ignition timing:	
H.C.	5° B.T.D.C. (premium grade fuel)
L.C.	T.D.C. (commercial grade fuel) 10° B.T.D.C. (premium grade fuel)

CLUTCH

Make and type	Borg & Beck single dry plate
Clutch plate:	
Diameter	8 in. (20.32 cm.)
Facing material	Wound yarn
Number of damper springs	6
Damper spring colour	Black/light green
Pressure springs:	
Number	6
Colour	Yellow
Clutch release bearing	Graphite (MY3D)
Release lever ratio	4.26:1
Clutch fluid	Castrol Girling Brake and Clutch Fluid Amber (Spec. 70.R.3)

GEARBOX

Number of forward gears	4
Gearbox ratios:	
Reverse	5.15:1
First	3.95:1
Second	2.41:1
Third	1.49:1
Fourth	1.00:1
Overall ratios:	
Reverse	25.15:1
First	19.23:1
Second	11.73:1
Third	7.26:1
Fourth	4.875:1
Speedometer gear ratio	9/28
Top gear speed at 1,000 r.p.m.	16.5 m.p.h. (26 km.p.h.)

*Crankshaft degrees and r.p.m.

Commercials engines (1622) pre-Sherpa

ENGINE

Type	16AC;16AD;16AE
Number of cylinders	4
Bore	3 in. (76.2 mm.)
Stroke	3.5 in. (88.9 mm.)
Capacity	99.1 cu. in. (1622 c.c.)
Firing order	1, 3, 4, 2
Compression ratio	8.3:1 or 7.2:1
Capacity of c/mbustion chamber (valves fitted)	2.64 cu. in. (43.0 c.c.)
B.M.E.P.:	
High-compression engine	138 lb./sq. in. (9.7 kg./cm.^{2}) at 2,100 r.p.m.
Low-compression engine	128 lb./sq. in. (8.99 kg./cm.^{2}) at 2,000 r.p.m.

Torque:	
High-compression engine	90 lb. ft. (12.4 kg. m.) at 2,100 r.p.m.
Low-compression engine	83 lb. ft. (11.6 kg. m.) at 2,000 r.p.m.

PISTONS

Type	Aluminium alloy. Solid skirt. Anodized
Clearances:	
Bottom of skirt	.0015 to .0021 in. (.038 to .053 mm.)
Top of skirt	.0022 to .0034 in. (.0559 to .0863 mm.)
Oversizes	+.010 in., +.020 in., +.030 in., +.040 in. (+.254 mm., +.508 mm., +.762 mm., +1.02 mm.)

PISTON RINGS

Compression:	
Plain	Top ring
Tapered	Second and third rings
Width (plain)	.0771 to .0781 in. (1.95 to 1.98 mm.)
Thickness	.119 to .126 in. (3.02 to 3.20 mm.)
Fitted gap	.012 to .017 in. (.305 to .432 mm.)
Clearance in groove	.0015 to .0035 in. (.038 to .089 mm.)
Oil control type	Slotted scraper
Width	.1552 to .1562 in. (3.94 to 3.99 mm.)
Thickness	.119 to .126 in. (3.02 to 3.20 mm.)
Fitted gap	.008 to .013 in. (.20 to .33 mm.)
Clearance in groove	.0016 to .0036 in. (.040 to .091 mm.)

VALVES AND VALVE GEAR
Valves

Head diameter:	
Inlet	1.500 to 1.505 in. (38.1 to 38.3 mm.)
Exhaust	1.281 to 1.286 in. (32.5 to 32.6 mm.)
Valve lift	.325 in. (8.25 mm.)

VALVE SPRINGS

Free length	$2\frac{3}{16}$ in. (51.6 mm.)
Number of working coils	$4\frac{1}{2}$
Pressure: Valve open	130 lb. (59 kg.)
Valve closed	79 ± 2 lb. (35.8 ± .9 kg.)
Valve crash speed	5,400 r.p.m.

FUEL SYSTEM
Carburettor

Make and type	S.U. HS2 semi-downdraught
Diameter	$1\frac{1}{4}$ in. (31.75 mm.)
Needle:	
Standard	GX
Rich	M
Weak	GG

Jet   .090 in. (2.29 mm.)
Piston spring   Yellow
Air cleaner   Paper element

IGNITION SYSTEM
Distributor   Lucas 25D4
Serial number   40822 B *H.C.* 40821 *L.C.*
Automatic advance commences*   750 r.p.m. *H.C.* 600 r.p.m. *L.C.*
Vacuum advance:
   Starts   5 in. (13 cm.) Hg *H.C.* 6 in. (15 cm.) Hg *L.C.*
   Ends*   20° at 17 in. (44 cm.) Hg *H.C.* 16° at 14 in. (36 cm.) Hg. *L.C.*
Maximum advance*   26° at 4,600 r.p.m. *H.C.* 30° at 5,000 r.p.m. *L.C.*
Decelerating check*   26° at 3,700 r.p.m. *H.C.* 30° at 4,200 r.p.m. *L.C.*
   18° at 2,700 r.p.m. *H.C.* 20° at 3,000 r.p.m. *L.C.*
   10° at 1,400 r.p.m. *H.C.* 4° at 900 r.p.m. *L.C.*
Ignition timing:
   Static   5° B.T.D.C. *H.C.* 6° B.T.D.C. *L.C.*
   Stroboscopic (at 600 r.p.m.*)   8° B.T.D.C. *H.C.* 9° B.T.D.C. *L.C.*

*Crankshaft degrees and r.p.m.

GEARBOX
Overall ratios:
   Top   4.55:1
   Third   6.25:1
   Second   10.08:1
   First   16.55:1
   Reverse   21.64:1
Top gear speed at 1,000 r.p.m.   17.5 m.p.h. (28 k.p.h.)

Sherpa (commercials) 1622 and 1798 petrol

ENGINE—PETROL 1622 CC
Type   16V
Number of cylinders   4
Bore   3.0 in. (76.2 mm.)
Stroke   3.5 in. (88.9 mm.)
Capacity   99.55 in³ (1622 cm³)
Firing order   1, 3, 4, 2
Valve operation   Overhead by push-rod
Compression ratio   7.5:1
Torque (gross)   82.5 lbf. ft. (11.25 kgf. m.) at 2,000 rev./min.
Static ignition (for assembly purposes)   11° B.T.D.C.

CRANKSHAFT
Main journal diameter   2.0005 to 2.0010 in. (50.80 to 50.82 mm.)
Minimum regrind diameter   1.9605 to 1.9610 in. (49.78 to 49.82 mm.)

Crankpin journal diameter   1.8759 to 1.8764 in. (47.64 to 47.66 mm.)
minimum regrind diameter   1.8359 to 1.8364 in. (46.632 to 46.645 mm.)
Crankshaft end-thrust   Taken on thrust washers at centre main bearing
Crankshaft end-float   0.002 to 0.003 in. (0.051 to 0.076 mm.)

MAIN BEARINGS
Length   1.213 to 1.223 in. (30.81 to 31.06 mm.)
Diametrical clearance   0.001 to 0.0027 in. (0.03 to 0.07 mm.)
Undersizes   0.010 in., 0.020 in., 0.030 in., 0.040 in., (0.25 mm., 0.51 mm., 0.76 mm., 1.02 mm.)

CONNECTING RODS
Type   Diagonally split big-end, clamped small end
Length between centres   6.5 in. (165.1 mm.)

BIG-END BEARINGS
Length   0.995 to 1.005 in. (25.27 to 25.53 mm.)
Diametrical clearance   0.001 to 0.0027 in. (0.03 to 0.07 mm.)
Undersizes   0.010 in., 0.020 in., 0.030 in., 0.040 in. (0.25 mm., 0.51 mm., 0.76 mm., 1.02 mm.)

GUDGEON PIN
Type   Clamped
Fit in piston   0.00035 in. (0.008 mm.) clearance to 0.00005 in. (0.0012 mm.) interference

PISTONS
Type   Solid skirt
Clearances:
   Bottom of skirt   0.0015 to 0.0021 in. (0.04 to 0.05 mm.)
   Top of skirt   0.0028 to 0.0037 in. (0.07 to 0.09 mm.)
Oversizes   0.020 and 0.040 in. (0.51 and 1.02 mm.)

PISTON RINGS
Compression:
Type:
   Top   Chrome-faced
   Second and third   Tapered, cast iron alloy
Width:
   Top   0.0771 to 0.776 in. (1.96 to 1.97 mm.)
   Second and third   0.0771 to 0.0781 in. (1.96 to 1.98 mm.)
   Fitted gap   0.012 to 0.017 in. (0.30 to 0.43 mm.)
Ring to groove clearance:
   Top   0.002 to 0.0035 in. (0.05 to 0.09 mm.)
   Second and third   0.0015 to 0.0035 in. (0.04 to 0.09 mm.)

Oil control:

Type	Slotted scraper
Width	0.1552 to 0.1562 in. (3.94 to 3.97 mm.)
Fitted gap	0.012 to 0.017 in. (0.30 to 0.43 mm.)

CAMSHAFT

Journal diameters:

Front	1.78875 to 1.78725 in. (45.43 to 45.45 mm.)
Centre	1.72875 to 1.72925 in. (43.91 to 43.92 mm.)
Rear	1.62275 to 1.62325 in. (41.22 to 41.23 mm.)

Bearing liner inside diameter (reamed after fitting):

Front	1.79025 to 1.79075 in. (44.47 to 44.48 mm.)
Centre	1.73025 to 1.73075 in. (43.95 to 43.96 mm.)
Rear	1.62425 to 1.62475 in. (41.26 to 41.27 mm.)
Diametrical clearance	0.001 to 0.002 in. (0.02 to 0.05 mm.)
End-thrust	Taken in locatin plate

ROCKER GEAR

Rocker shaft diameter	0.624 to 0.625 in. (15.85 to 15.87 mm.)
Rocker bush inside diameter (reamed in position)	0.6255 to 0.6260 in. (15.89 to 15.90 mm.)

TAPPETS

Type	Bucket
Outside diameter	0.8125 in. (20.65 mm.)
Length	1.495 to 1.505 in. (37.97 to 38.23 mm.)

VALVES

Seat angle:

Inlet	45°
Exhaust	45°

Head diameter:

Inlet	1.500 to 1.505 in. (38.10 to 38.23 mm.)
Exhaust	1.281 to 1.286 in. (32.54 to 32.66 mm.)

Stem diameter:

Inlet	0.3422 to 0.3427 in. (8.69 to 8.70 mm.)
Exhaust	0.34175 to 0.34225 in. (8.68 to 8.69 mm.)

Stem to guide clearance:

Inlet	0.0014 to 0.0026 in. (0.035 to 0.066 mm.)
Exhaust	0.0018 to 0.0030 in. (0.047 to 0.077 mm.)

VALVE GUIDES

Length: Inlet	1.88 in. (47.74 mm.)
Exhaust	2.22 in. (56.39 mm.)
Outside diameter: Inlet and exhaust	0.5635 to 0.5640 in. (14.31 to 14.33 mm.)
Inside diameter (reamed after fitting): Inlet and exhaust	0.3441 to 0.3448 in. (8.74 to 8.76 mm.)
Fitted height above spring seat: Inlet and exhaust	0.625 in. (15.86 mm.)

VALVE SPRINGS

Free length	2.031 to 2.051 in. (51.59 to 52.09 mm.)
Fitted length	1.53 in. (38.89 mm.)
Load at fitted length	79 ± 2 lbf. (35.8 ± 0.91 kgf.)
Load at top of lift	131 lbf. (59.4 kgf.)
Number of working coils	4½ to 5

VALVE TIMING

Timing marks	Dimples on timing wheels, marks on flywheel

Rocker clearance:

Running	0.015 in. (0.38 mm.) cold
Timing	0.021 in. (0.53 mm.)

Up to engine number 16V/760E/7805:

Inlet valve:

Opens	5o° T.D.C
Closes	5o° A.B.D.C.

Exhaust valve:

Opens	35° B.B.D.C.
Closes	15° A.T.D.C.

From engine number 16V/760E/7806:

Inlet valve:

Opens	4° B.T.D.C.
Closes	46° A.B.D.C.

Exhaust valve:

Opens	39° B.B.D.C.
Closes	11° A.T.D.C.

LUBRICATION

System	Wet sump, pressure fed

System pressure:

Running	50 lbf./in² (3.52 kgf./cm²)
Idling	15 lbf./in² (1.05 kgf./cm²)
Oil pump	Rotor type
Oil filter	Full flow; disposable cartridge type
Oil pressure relief valve	50 lbf./in² (3.52 kgf./cm²)

Relief valve spring:

Free length	2.86 in. (72.62 mm.)
Fitted length	2.156 in. (54.77 mm.)
Load at fitted length	13 to 14 lbf. (5.9 to 6.3 kgf.)

ENGINE PETROL 1798 CC

Type	18V
Number of cylinders	4
Bore	3.16 in. (80.26 mm.)
Stroke	3.5 in. (88.9 mm.)
Capacity	109.7 in³ (1798 cm³)
Firing order	1, 3, 4, 2
Valve operation	Overhead by push-rod

Compression ratio:

Low compression	6.9:1
High compression	9.0:1

Torque (gross):

L.C.	91.71 lbf. ft. (12.2 kgf. m.) at 2,000 rev./min.
H.C.	96 lbf. ft. (13.25 kgf. m.) at 2,000 rev./min.

Static ignition timing (for assembly purposes):

L.C. Temperate and cold climates	13° B.T.D.C.
Hot climates	12° B.T.D.C.
H.C.	3° B.T.D.C.

CRANKSHAFT

Main journal diameter	2.1262 to 2.1270 in. (54.00 to 54.02 mm.)
Minimum regrind diameter	2.0862 to 2.087 in. (52.989 to 53.009 mm.)
Crankpin journal diameter	1.8759 to 1.8764 in. (47.64 to 47.66 mm.)
Minimum regrind diameter	1.8359 to 1.8364 in. (46.632 to 46.645 mm.)
Crankshaft end-thrust	Taken on thrust washers at centre main bearing
Crankshaft end-float	0.002 to 0.003 in. (0.050 to 0.071 mm.)

MAIN BEARINGS

Number and type	5 Steel backed lead indium
Length:	
Front, centre and rear	1.120 to 1.130 in. (28.45 to 28.70 mm.)
Intermediate	0.760 to 0.770 in. (19.30 to 19.55 mm.)
Diametrical clearance	0.001 to 0.0027 in. (0.03 to 0.07 mm.)
Undersizes	0.010 in., 0.020 in., 0.030 in., 0.040 in., (0.25 mm., 0.51 mm., 0.76 mm., 1.02 mm.)

CONNECTING RODS

Type	Horizontally split big-end, plain small end
Length between centres	6.498 to 6.502 in. (165.05 to 165.15 mm.)

BIG-END BEARINGS

Type	Steel backed lead indium
Length	0.775 to 0.785 in. (19.68 to 19.93 mm.)
Diametrical clearance	0.001 to 0.0027 in. (0.03 to 0.07 mm.)
Undersizes	0.010 in., 0.020 in., 0.030 in., 0.040 in., (0.25 mm., 0.51 mm., 0.76 mm., 1.02 mm.)

GUDGEON PIN

Type	Press-fit in connecting rod
Fit in piston	Hand push-fit at 16° C. (60° F.)
Fit in connecting rod	0.001 to 0.0017 in. (0.02 to 0.04 mm.) interference
Diameter (outer)	0.8125 to 0.8127 in. (20.63 to 20.64 mm.)

PISTONS

Type	Aluminium alloy, solid skirt, dished crown
Clearances:	
Up to engine number 18V/764E/L2294:	
Top of skirt	0.0021 to 0.0037 in. (0.053 to 0.094 mm.)
Bottom of skirt	0.006 to 0.0016 in. (0.015 to 0.040 mm.)
From engine number 18V/764E/L2295:	
Top of skirt	0.0012 to 0.0028 in. (0.030 to 0.071 mm.)
Bottom of skirt	0.0008 to 0.0018 in. (0.020 to 0.046 mm.)
Oversizes	0.020 and 0.040 in. (0.51 and 1.02 mm.)

PISTON RINGS

Compression:	
Type: Top	Chrome-faced
Second	Tapered or stepped, cast iron alloy
Width	0.0615 to 0.0625 in. (1.56 to 1.59 mm.)
Fitted gap: Top	0.012 to 0.022 in. (0.304 to 0.559 mm.)
Second: Tapered	0.012 to 0.022 in. (0.304 to 0.559 mm.)
Stepped	0.012 to 0.017 in. (0.304 to 0.432 mm.)
Ring to groove clearance	0.0015 to 0.0035 in. (0.028 to 0.088 mm.)
Oil control:	
Type	Two chrome faced nails with expander
Width	0.151 to 0.156 in. (3.83 to 3.96 mm.)
Fitted gap	0.015 to 0.045 in. (0.38 to 1.14 mm.)

CAMSHAFT

Journal diameters:	
Front	1.78875 to 1.78925 in. (45.43 to 45.44 mm.)
Centre	1.72875 to 1.72925 in. (43.91 to 43.93 mm.)
Rear	1.62275 to 1.62325 in. (41.22 to 41.23 mm.)
Bearing liner inside diameter (reamed after fitting):	
Front	1.79025 to 1.79075 in. (45.47 to 45.48 mm.)
Centre	1.73025 to 1.73075 in. (43.95 to 43.96 mm.)
Rear	1.62425 to 1.62475 in. (40.26 to 40.27 mm.)
Diametrical clearance	0.001 to 0.002 in. (0.02 to 0.05 mm.)
End-thrust	Taken on locating plate
End-float	0.003 to 0.007 in. (0.08 to 0.18 mm.)

ROCKER GEAR

Rocker shaft diameter	0.624 to 0.625 in. (15.85 to 15.87 mm.)
Rocker bush inside diameter (reamed in position)	0.6255 to 0.6260 in. (15.89 to 15.90 mm.)

TAPPETS

Type	Bucket
Outside diameter	0.8125 in. (20.65 mm.)
Length	1.495 to 1.505 in. (37.97 to 38.23 mm.)

VALVES

Seat angle:	
Inlet	$45\frac{1}{2}°$
Exhaust	$45\frac{1}{2}°$
Head diameter:	
Inlet	1.562 to 1.567 in. (39.67 to 39.80 mm.)
Exhaust	1.343 to 1.348 in. (34.11 to 34.23 mm.)
Stem diameter	
Inlet	0.3429 to 0.3434 in. (8.70 to 8.72 mm.)
Exhaust	0.3423 to 0.3428 in. (8.69 to 8.70 mm.)
Stem to guide clearance:	
Inlet	0.0007 to 0.0019 in. (0.02 to 0.05 mm.)
Exhaust	0.0013 to 0.0025 in. (0.03 to 0.06 mm.)
Valve lift: Inlet and exhaust	0.36 in. (9.14 mm.)

VALVE GUIDES

Length: Inlet	1.88 in. (47.75 mm.)
Exhaust	2.22 in. (56.39 mm.)
Outside diameter: Inlet and exhaust	0.5635 to 0.5640 in. (14.31 to 14.33 mm.)
Inside diameter: Inlet and exhaust	0.3441 to 0.3448 in. (8.74 to 8.76 mm.)
Fitted height above spring seat:	
Inlet	0.75 in. (19.05 mm.)
Exhaust	0.625 in. (15.37 mm.)
Interference fit in head: Inlet and exhaust	0.0005 to 0.00175 in. (0.01 to 0.04 mm.)

VALVE SPRINGS

Free length	1.92 to 1.94 in. (48.77 to 49.27 mm.)
Fitted length	1.44 in. (36.57 mm.)
Load at fitted length	82 lbf. (37.19 kgf.)
Load at top of lift	142 lbf. (64.4 kgf.)
Number of working coils	$4\frac{1}{2}$

VALVE TIMING

Timing marks	Dimples on timing wheels, marks on flywheel
Rocker clearance:	
Running	0.013 in. (0.33 mm.) cold
Timing	0.020 in. (0.51 mm.)

Up to engine numbers 18V/760E/H4652, 18V/761E/H165, 18V/764E/L18408 and 18V/765E/315:	
Inlet valve:	
Opens	5° B.T.D.C.
Closes	45° A.B.D.C.
Exhaust valve:	
Opens	40° B.T.D.C.
Closes	10° A.T.D.C.
From engine numbers 18V/760E/H4653, 18V/761E/H166, 18V/764E/L18409 and 18V/765E/L316:	
Inlet valve:	
Opens	9° B.T.D.C.
Closes	41° A.B.D.C.
Exhaust valve:	
Opens	44° B.B.D.C.
Closes	6° A.T.D.C.

LUBRICATION

System	Wet sump, pressure fed
System pressure:	
Running	70 lbf./in^2 (4.92 kgf./cm^2)
Idling	15 lbf./in^2 (1.05 kgf./cm^2)
Oil pump	Rotor type
Oil filter	Full flow; disposable cartridge type
Oil pressure relief valve	60 lbf./in^2 (4.21 kgf./cm^2)
Relief valve spring:	
Free length	3 in. (76 mm.)
Fitted length	2.156 in. (54.77 mm.)
Load at fitted length	15.5 to 16.5 lbf. (7.0 to 7.4 kgf.)

Hindustan Ambassador 1500 engine

ENGINE

Bore	2.875 in. (73.02 mm.)
Stroke	3.5 in. (88.9 mm.)
Cubic capacity	90.88 cu. in. (1489 c.c.)
Compression ratio	7.2:1. Gross BHP 50 at 4200 r.p.m. Gross torque 74 lbs. ft. at 3000 r.p.m.
R.A.C. rating	13.225 h.p.
Type of main bearings	Steel-backed, white-metal-lined (Thinwall)
Main journal diameter	2 in. (50.8 mm.)
Main journal, minimum regrind diameter	1.960 in. (49.78 mm.)
Main bearing length	1.375 in. (34.92 mm.)
Main bearing end-clearance	.002 to .003 in. (.05 to .08 mm.)
Main bearing diametrical clearance	.0005 to .002 in. (.01 to .05 mm.)
Crankshaft end-thrust taken by	Renewable thrust plates at centre main bearing
Crankpin diameter	1.875 in. (47.62 mm.)
Crankpin minimum regrind diameter	1.835 in. (46.61 mm.)

Connecting rod bearings	Steel-backed, lead-indium or lead tin lined
Connecting rod length between centres	6.5 in. (16.51 cm.)
Connecting rod bearing side-clearance	.008 to .012 in. (.20 to .30 mm.)
Connecting rod diametrical clearance	.001 to .0025 in. (.025 to .063 mm.)
Piston type	Aluminium alloy, concave crown, split skirt
Piston clearance, top of skirt	.0022 to .0029 in. (.056 to .074 mm.)
Piston clearance, bottom of skirt	.0006 to .0012 in. (.015 to .030 mm.)
Piston rings, compression	1 plain, 2 taper
Piston rings, oil control	1 slotted
Piston ring gap	.008 to .013 in. (.20 to .33 mm.)
Gudgeon pin type	Clamped in connecting rod
Gudgeon pin fit in piston	Double thumb press, .0001 in. (.002 mm.) tight to .0003 in. (.007 mm.) slack
Gudgeon pin diameter	.6869 to .6871 in. (17.44 to 17.45 mm.)
Camshaft bearings	3 steel-backed white-metal
Camshaft drive	Duplex chain: $\frac{3}{8}$ in. pitch, 52 pitches
Camshaft bearing clearance	.001 to .002 in. (.025 to .05 mm.)
Camshaft thrust taken by	Front end thrust plate
Valve timing marking	Timing wheels marked
Valve timing in degrees:	
Inlet	Opens 5° B.T.D.C.* Closes 45° A.B.D.C.*
Exhaust	Opens 40° B.B.D.C.* Closes 10° A.T.D.C.*

*With .022 in. (.56 mm.) valve rocker clearance (for checking purposes only Engine cold also Inlet valve opens as T.D.C. with .027 in. (.69 mm.) Rocker Clearance).

Valve seat angle	45°
Inlet valve head diameter	$1\frac{3}{8}$ in. (34.9 mm.). Stem diameter .3422/.3427 in. (8.692/8.705 mm.)
Exhaust valve head diameter	$1\frac{3}{16}$ in. (30.2 mm.). Stem diameter .3417/.3422 in. (8.679/8.692 mm.)
Inlet valve throat diameter	$1\frac{1}{4}$ in. (31.75 mm.)
Exhaust valve throat diameter	$1\frac{3}{32}$ in. (27.68 mm.)
Valve lift	.325 in. (8.25 mm.)
Valve rocker clearance	Running: .015 in. (.38 mm.) hot
Valve spring free length	$2\frac{1}{32}$ in. (51.6 mm.). Fitted: $1\frac{17}{32}$ in. (38.9 mm.)
Valve spring pressure	Shut: 79 lb. (35.8 kg.). Open: 131 lb. (59.4 kg.)
Carburettor type	S.U. semi-downdraught, $1\frac{1}{4}$ in.
Carburettor needle	Standard
Oil oressure relief valve operates	50 lb./sq. in. (3.5 kg./cm^2)

Oil pressure (normal running)	50 lb./sq. in. (3.5 kg./cm^2)
Oil filter (external)	Full-flow with felt element or paper element
Oil pressure (idling)	15 lb./sq. in. (1.05 kg./cm^2)

CLUTCH AND GEARBOX

Clutch disc diameter	8 in. (20.32 cm.)
Synchromesh operation on	Second, third and top
Ratios:	
Top	1.0:1
Third	1.506:1
Second	2.253:1
First	3.807:1
Reverse	3.807:1
Overall ratios:	
Top	4.875:1
Third	7.342:1
Second	10.983:1
First	18.559:1
Reverse	18.559:1
Speedometer drive gear to pinion ratio	7:17

Austin Freeway and Wolseley 24/80 (Australian) B-series 6-cylinder engines

ENGINE

Type	24Y—Blue Streak Six
Number of cylinders	6
Bore	3.00 in.
Stroke	3.50 in.
Capacity	2,433 c.c.
Firing order	1, 5, 3, 6, 2, 4
Compression ratio	7.7:1
Capacity of combustion chamber (valves fitted)	38.7 to 39.7 c.c.
B.H.P.	80 at 4,350 r.p.m. gross
R.A.C. rating	21.6 h.p.
B.M.E.P.	125 lb./sq. in. gross at 1,650 r.p.m.
Torque	123 lbs./ft. gross at 1,650 r.p.m.
Cooling system	Pump and 8 blade fan assisted (radiator pressurized to 13 P.S.I.)

CRANKSHAFT

Main journal diameter	2.1265/2.1270 in. (10 micro in. finish)
Oil return thread diameter	2.2615/2.2625 in.
Clearance	.0085/.010 in.
Crankpin journal diameter	1.8759/1.8764

MAIN BEARINGS

Tunnel bore	2.271/2.2715 in.
Number	4
Material	Steel backed lead bronze lead tin plated

Length	1.125 in.
End clearance	.002/.006 in.
End thrust	Rear middle main bearing (No. 3)
Running clearance	.001/.0027 in.

CONNECTING RODS

Length between centre	6.498/6.502 in.
Tunnel bore	2.0210/2.0215 in.
Big-end bearing material	Steel backed lead bronze lead tin plated
Bearing side clearance	.008/.012 in.
Bearing diametrical clearance	.001/.0027 in.

PISTONS

Type	4 ring (one oil ring below gudgeon pin) (aluminium alloy tin plated)
Clearances:	
Bottom of skirt	.0001/.0011 in.
Top of skirt	.0003/.0011 in.

PISTON RINGS

Compression:	
Top ring	Torsional chrome
2nd ring	Serrated
Width	.0775/.0780 in.
Thickness	.140/.150 in.
Fitted gap	.008/.016 in.
Clearance in groove	.002/.0035 in.
Oil control, 3rd and 4th (4th below gudgeon pin)	Slotted scraper
Width	.1860/.1865 in.
Thickness	.129/.139 in.
Fitted gap	.008/.016 in.
Clearance in groove	.0015/.003 in.

GUDGEON PIN

Type	Clamp in rod
Fit in piston	.0001/.0003 in. clearance
Fit in connecting rod	−.0002/+.0006 in.
Diameter (outer)	.6869/.6872 in.

VALVES AND VALVE GEAR
Valves

Seat angle:	
Inlet	45°
Exhaust	45°
Head diameter:	
Inlet	1.370/1.375 in.
Exhaust	1.182/1.187 in.
Stem diameter:	
Inlet	.3422/.3427 in.
Exhaust	.3417/.34225 in.
Valve lift	$\frac{5}{16}$ in. nominal
Valve stem to guide clearance:	
Inlet	.0015/.0025 in.
Exhaust	.002/.003 in.
Valve rocker clearance:	
Running	.015 in.
Timing	.021 in.
Timing markings	Dimples on timing wheels

Chain pitch and number of pitches	$\frac{3}{8}$ in., 52 pitches
Inlet valve:	
Opens	T.D.C.*
Closes	50° A.B.D.C.*
Exhaust	
Opens	35° B.B.D.C.
Closes	15° A.T.D.C.

*With .021 in. valve rocker clearance for timing check only.

VALVE GUIDES

Length:	
Inlet	$1\frac{7}{8}$ in.
Exhaust	$2\frac{13}{64}$ in.
Diameter:	
Inlet—Outside	.5635/.5640 in.
Inside	.34425/.34475 in. after assembly
Exhaust—Outside	.5635/.5640 in.
Inside	.34425/.34475 in. after assembly
Fitted height above head	.625 in. above machined surface of valve spring seat, ± $\frac{1}{64}$ in.

VALVE SPRINGS

Free length	$2\frac{1}{32}$ in.
Fitting length	$1\frac{17}{32}$ in.
Number of working coils	$4\frac{1}{2}$
Pressure:	
Valve open	131 lbs.
Valve closed	79 lbs. ± 2

TAPPETS

Type	Spherical base barrel type
Diameter	.81125/.81175 in.
Length	2.293/2.303 in.

ROCKERS

Bore of rocker arm	.7485/.7495 in.
Rocker ratio	1.43:1
Bush diameter	.6255/.626 in.

CAMSHAFT

Journal diameter:	
Front	1.84375/1.84425 in.
Front middle	1.78875/1.78925 in.
Rear middle	1.72875/1.72925 in.
Rear	1.62275/1.62325 in.
End float	.003/.007 in.
Bearings, number and type	4 thin wall steel backed white metal
Tunnel bore diameter:	
Front	1.970/1.971 in.
Front middle	1.915/1.916 in.
Rear middle	1.855/1.856 in.
Rear	1.749/1.750 in.
Bearing diameter (reamed in position):	
Front	1.84525/1.84575 in.
Front middle	1.79025/1.79075 in.
Rear middle	1.73025/1.73075 in.
Rear	1.62425/1.62475 in.
Clearance	.001/.002 in.

FLYWHEEL AND STARTER RING GEAR

Number of teeth on starter ring	120
Flywheel outside diameter	10.823/10.826 in.
Starter ring inside diameter	10.779/10.782 in.
Starter ring to flywheel interference	.041/.047 in.
'Run-out' of flywheel on assembly	Zero to .003 in. on clutch friction face at 4 in. radius from centre
Maximum thickness of metal to be removed during 'skimming'	.0625 in.

ENGINE LUBRICATION SYSTEM

Oil Pump

Type	Hobourn Eaton HE 4920
Flow rate	6.48 gals. at 2000 pump r.p.m.
Spindle diameter	.498/.4985 in.
Spindle bore	.500/.501 in.
Number of teeth on driving shaft	9
Clearance between rotor lobes	.005/.0055 in.
End-float of pump rotors	.001/.0025 in.

Oil Filter

Type	Full flow throw away paper element

Oil Pressure

Normal running	40 lbs./sq. in. hot
Idling (minimum)	10 lbs./sq. in. hot

Oil Pressure Relief Valve

Relief pressure valve operates	50 lbs./sq. in.
Diameter of relief valve	.609/.611 in.
Relief valve seat angle (included)	60°
Spring free length	$2\frac{55}{64}$ in.
Spring fitted length	$2\frac{5}{32}$ in.
Load to compress spring to fitted length	13/14 lbs.

IGNITION SYSTEM

Spark plugs	Champion N5
Size	14 mm. $\frac{3}{4}$ in. reach
Plug gap	.025 in.
Ignition coil:	
Type	Lucas LA 12
Current consumption running	2 amp.
Stall	3.75 amp.
Distributor	Lucas 25D6
Contact breaker gap	.014/.016 in.
Dist. centrifugal advance	2,100 r.p.m., 14–16°, 1,100 r.p.m. 8–10°, 600 r.p.m. 5–7°. 200–300 in. r.p.m. No advance
Dist. vacuum advance	Vacuum commences at 3 in. of mercury, finishes at 9 in. of mercury with 8° distributor advance
Timing	3° B.T.D.C.

COOLING SYSTEM

Type	13 p.s.i. Pressurized radiator, pump and fan assisted
Thermostat setting	80° C., 176° F.
Water pump	Vane type-combined spindle with one piece bearing
Clearance pump body and vane	.020/.030 in.

FUEL SYSTEM

Carburettor

Type	Zenith 34 VN, internally vented
Choke	29 mm.

Jets

Main	120
Compensating	90
Slow running	55
Full throttle bleed	1.5
Part throttle bleed	2.5
Pump	7.0
Plug over slow running	50
Progression	1 × 120 (first)
Slow running feed	.6
Slow running outlet	.9
Emulsion block	5.5
Needle seat	1.75 mm. plus 1.6 mm. washer
Fuel·level	22.5 mm. ($\frac{7}{8}$ in. approx.) from top of float bowl with float in position and bowl removed (18 mm. assembled)

AIR CLEANER	Dual horn container, chemically treated paper

FUEL PUMP

Make and type	S.U. Electric/SP
Delivery rate	10 gallon per hour
Suction head	2 ft. approximately
Delivery head with pipe bore, $\frac{1}{4}$ in.	4 ft. approximately

CLUTCH

Make and type	Borg & Beck—diaphragm spring type, DS/G
Diameter	$8\frac{1}{2}$ in.
Facing material	Wound yarn Raybestos WR 7
Pressure springs	Diaphragm
Damper springs	6
Colour	Red and violet
Release bearing	Carbon graphite

GEARBOX

Type	Constant mesh synchromesh on 2nd and top
Gear control	Lever steering column
Number of gears	3 forward, 1 reverse
Type of gears	Helical synchromesh

Gear Ratios

First	3.09:1
Second	1.62:1

Top	1:1
Reverse	3.67:1
Layshaft bearings:	
Quantity	Two
Material	Split steel backed copper lead tin overlay
Dimensions	Finished bore in lay gear .7519/.7524 in.
Mainshaft spigot needle rollers:	
Quantity	18
Dimensions	28 mm. × 3 mm.
Mainshaft rear ball bearing	
Make	R & M
Type	MJ, $1\frac{1}{8}$ in.
Size	$2\frac{13}{16} \times 1\frac{1}{8} \times \frac{13}{16}$ in.
First motion shaft ball bearing:	
Make	R & M
Type	LJ $1\frac{3}{8}$ in.
Size	$3 \times 1\frac{3}{8} \times \frac{11}{16}$ in. with spring ring

TORQUE WRENCH SETTINGS

Cylinder head set bolts	40 lbs./ft.
Main bearing nuts	70 lbs./ft.
Connecting rod set screws	35 lbs./ft.
Clutch assembly to flywheel	16 lbs./ft.
Flywheel securing bolts	35 lbs./ft.
Rocker shaft	16 lbs./ft.
Rear engine plate	30 lbs./ft.
Gudgeon pin clamp	25 lbs./ft.
Manifold	16 lbs./ft.
Water pump	16 lbs./ft.
Bellhousing	16 lbs./ft.
Crown wheel to diff.	50 lbs./ft.
Diff. carrier bearing cap nuts	60 lbs./ft.
Bevel pinion nut	140 lbs./ft.
Road wheel nuts	60 lbs./ft.

Newage/BMC Navigator engines (marine)

ENGINE

Bore	2.875 in. (73.025 mm.)
Stroke	3.5 in. (88.9 mm.)
Capacity	90.88 cu. in. (1489 c.c.)
Compression ratio:	
Petrol engine	7.2:1
V.O. engine	5.85:1
Maximum b.h.p.:	
Petrol engine	35 at 3,000 r.p.m.
V.O. engine	28.5 at 3,000 r.p.m.

Recommended economical maximum b.h.p. for continuous cruising (12-hour rating):	
Petrol engine	27.5 at 2,200 r.p.m.
V.O. engine	25 at 2,500 r.p.m.
Oil pressure release valve operates	50 lb./sq. in. (3.5 kg./cm^2)
Crankpin diameter (standard)	1.8759 to 1.8764 (47.648 to 47.661 mm.)
Crankpin:	
First regrind size	Std. −.020 in. (.508 mm.)
Second regrind size	Std. −.040 in. (1.016 mm.)
Number of main bearings and type	3. Shimless, steel-backed, white-metal-lined
Main journal diameter (standard)	2.0005 to 2.001 in. (50.813 to 50.825 mm.)
Main journal:	
First regrind size	Std. −.020 in. (.508 mm.)
Second regrind size	Std. −.040 in. (1.016 mm.)
Rocker arm bush inner diameter (reamed in position)	.6255 to .626 in. (15.888 to 15.901 mm.)
Camshaft drive (type)	Chain, double roller
Camshaft chain pitch	$\frac{3}{8}$ in. (9.525 mm.)
Camshaft chain, number of links	88
Valve timing marks	Dimples on camshaft and crankshaft chain wheels. Pointer under cover on flywheel housing and groove in flywheel
Valve seat angle	45°
Inlet valve opens	5° B.T.D.C.
Inlet valve closes	45° A.B.D.C.
Exhaust valve opeNs	40° B.B.D.C.
Exhaust valve closes	10° A.T.D.C.
Valve rocker clearance	.015 in. (.38 mm.) hot
Valve guide clearance (inlet)	.0015 to .0025 in. (.038 to .064 mm.)
Valve guide clearance (exhaust)	.0010 to .0020 in. (.025 to .050 mm.)
Carburettor	Solex updraught, type 26 V.N.
Ignition	Coil 12-volt (standard). (Lucas magneto optional fitting)
Reducing gear ratio (optional)	2:1 and 3:1. Left- or right-hand rotation
Oil capacities:	
Sump and filter	9 Imp. pints (5.11 litres)
Reverse gear	4 Imp. pints (2.27 litres)
Reduction gear:	
(2:1 ratio)	1 Imp. pint (.57 litre)
(3:1 ratio)	$1\frac{1}{2}$ Imp. pints (.85 litre)
Maximum variation of engine from horizontal with craft under way	10°
Running temperature	78° C. (173° F.)
Cooling by flexible neoprene vane-type pump	

5 Thumbnail sketches of B-series powered cars

Austin 10

The Austin Ten 1932–47

Writing in *Veteran and Vintage* magazine in 1974, Bill Boddy referred to 'The universal Ten', the car that was the utterly reliable, rather basic family car: the next step up from the once ubiquitous Austin Seven. The 1928 Sixteen had remained 'antique' in flavour, still with coil ignition, but the Ten was something much more modern, mechanically at least, even though it was utterly conventional. The 10/4 (10 horsepower/4 cylinders) started as a four-door saloon with plated radiator shell surround and side-valve engine following a similar arrangement to the unsuccessful 12/6, an engine layout which forms a common chain linking together the various stages of the B-series story. There was a Zenith 24 UH carburettor, a camshaft-driven fuel pump on the side of the block and a four-speed gearbox with 'silent third' gear. The cable brakes almost worked. In 1933, a proper synchromesh was fitted to third gear, the chassis was strengthened and a sports four-seater introduced, while 12-volt electrics were fitted and the V-type Zenith carburettor was used. (It was later superseded by the more power-inducing down-draught Zenith that had been fitted to the Ripley Sports Ten.)

Various body types were available over the years and, in 1935, the plated radiator shell was dropped, which killed the 'vintage' appeal of the cars, but improved brakes and synchromesh on second made the cars easier to live with for the owner of the time. In 1938 the engine was revised, probably following Harry Weslake's involvement, and given an aluminium cylinder head, larger inlet valves, improved breathing and a higher compression ratio. All the mechanical improvements were carried over to a new Ten (called a 'Cambridge' but not it seems contemporaneously) with rounded styling, rear quarter-lights, a split rear screen and chassis and floorpan combined. The car was built throughout the war for use by the armed forces and slotted straight into the postwar model range but came back with a cast-iron head. A quieter postwar timing set-up was achieved by inserting a rubber ring into the camshaft timing cog arrangement which had the effect of pushing the chain outwards and taking up the slack. The idea was continued with the car's successor.

Austin A40 Somerset

A40 Devon/Dorset and Somerset 1947–54

The A40 Devon (four-door) and Dorset (two-door) were central to Leonard Lord's vision of a brave new world of modern Austin motor cars. Surprisingly, they reverted back to a separate chassis type of construction, but the engine was, in essence, an overhead-valve development, or perhaps evolvement, of the Ten engine, using a similar crank, crank throw, bore centres, camshaft/crankshaft centres and general arrangement, except that the camshaft now drove pushrods of course, instead of acting directly on the valve stems. The A40s were similar in size and weight to their predecessors, but were substantially wider, generally more rotund and so a lot more spacious.

Road tester seemed to genuinely like the car, commenting on the 'cheerful' plastic wipe-clean headlining and the 'quality' fittings such as concealed running boards, hidden behind the skirts on the door bottoms, the concealed hinges and the leather upholstery. Devon and Dorset models were basically similar apart from the number of doors, and the two-door Dorsets were mainly built for export. When the A40 Somerset

replaced both cars in 1952, the car had grown somewhat. Its youthful elegance was replaced by more than a touch of portliness and the car looked very much like the larger A70 Hereford. However, its increase in weight and seating capacity were accompanied by engine improvements giving 6 per cent more engine power and better fuel consumption. In virtually every sense the car was more practicable, with larger screen, wider-opening doors, more leg room and width and a 50 per cent increase in torsional body stiffness due to the contribution of the body panels to overall strength. The A40 Sports cylinder head was fitted to the Somerset and was responsible for the increased power; the Sports itself had been bodied by Jensen Motors from 1950 to 1953 using aluminium panels in a smoother style, but still with 2 + 2 seating. Austin themselves produced the now extremely rare A40 Somerset Coupé, easily recognizable as a drophead Somerset. More than 600,000 A40 chassis were built.

Austin A40 and A50 Cambridge, inc. Countryman (1954–57)
A55 Mk I (1957–58)

Although not the first car to be introduced with the B-series engine, the new Austin was the one in which it found its natural home, the B-series being a Longbridge-evolved engine. Called 'Cambridge', the new car reintroduced an old name, but in spite of that the car was all new. There was no chassis, the integral construction giving great interior space savings. Its wind-tunnel developed body (Longbridge inherited the wartime aircraft producer's wind tunnel at East Works) was $2\frac{3}{4}$ in. longer than the Somerset, $2\frac{1}{2}$ in. lower and $1\frac{1}{2}$ in. narrower. The front seat, however, was $2\frac{3}{4}$ in. wider and the rear seat an extraordinary $12\frac{3}{4}$ in. further across, thanks to the longer wheelbase taking the wheel wells out of the seating space. The engine, as is made clear elsewhere in this book, was a direct development of the A40 unit, with a stouter crank, larger bearings and longer block. The smaller 1200 cc engine fitted to the A40 version was noted for its sewing machine smoothness, although the extra power of the 1500 unit, around which the newly developed engine was based, was welcomed. A newly designed gearbox was also used. A40-type front suspension was again preferred (both cars are prone to wallowing badly when the shock absorbers are over the hill!) but the body construction closely followed A30 chassisless principles, except that 'chassis' legs were retained, front-to-rear, to carry engine, gearbox and rear spring mountings. Wheels at 15 in. were an inch smaller than those used on the Somerset, but when the A55 appeared in 1957, their size shrank again to 14 in. In addition, the A55 became longer at the rear end by $4\frac{5}{8}$ in. and some restyling was carried out there. The more powerful engine had a standard compression ratio of 8.3:1, while a low compression unit with Austin favourite 7.2:1 (previously used on so many engines) could be specified. The 'Countryman' estate model was not made available on the A55. It would seem that Manumatic semi-automatic gearchanging, made by Lockheed, had been around since 1956. There was a gear change but no clutch, that side of things being taken care of automatically. It seems a shame that clutch-free driving with full driver control of the gears did not catch on, but the system was complex, failure-prone and phased out with the A55 Mk I at the end of 1958.

Austin A50/A55

Austin Cambridge A55 Mk II

Cambridge A55 Mk II (1959–61) and Countryman (1960–61)

Body styling changes were almost everything to this model of the Austin Cambridge. Fed up with their staid image, BMC went to the Italian Farina styling house for the design of their newly bodied car. 'Farina' styling needs no description here, but in addition to 'sharper' looks, the extra $11\frac{1}{4}$ in. of length and a 2 in. increase in width (slightly offset by a $\frac{1}{2}$ in. reduction in height) gave much improved accommodation and increase in weight of 80 lb. Acceleration was slightly worse than that of the Mk II's chubby older-sibling and top speed was down from 80 to 76 mph. Improved induction and an SU carburettor gave an extra 4 per cent in power, but that was not quite enough. The standard car was fitted with a floor gear change, but those who hankered for the column change of the Mk I could order it at no extra charge. Road testers seemed to like the rear wing fins—they were in vogue at the time—especially since they helped to make the car's size easy to judge when parking.

The Countryman, reintroduced in Austin guise in September 1960, was fitted with full bench seats, an all-metal body and an upper and lower hinged tailgate.

There was no automatic or semi-automatic option available.

Cambridge A60 Countryman and diesel

The A60 showed the degree of confidence that surrounded BMC at the time: they took a commercially successful car and improved upon it. The A60 was *not* simply a face-lift A55, but essentially a new car. Less frontal overhang reduced overall length by 4 in., while moving the rear axle back and both front and rear wheels outwards and lowering the spring heights gave greatly improved cornering ability and much more room in the rear seats. The car was 50-odd pounds heavier, once again, but the revamped 1622 cc engine endowed it with six extra bhp, leading to better acceleration, top speed and fuel economy, aided by the higher final drive ratio now used. The cars continued to be upholstered in leather and a column change was still available. An automatic option was reintroduced with this model—BMC had clearly been waiting for the new Borg-Warner model 35 auto. box, and the A60 was the first car to receive it. It proved to be an excellent, sturdy gearbox and *The Motor* actually found that it gave an improvement of over 3 mpg in fuel consumption over their manual model—which perhaps goes to show how road testers love to stir the gear stick! Externally, the cars looked identical.

In October 1961, a 1500 cc diesel version of the car was introduced into export markets and sold in the UK from August 1962. From June 1963, the penny dropped and BMC fitted extra sound deadening, but the 1500 diesel engine was always an uncouth, rackety, sluggish engine for the car and relatively few saloon or Countryman models were sold in the UK.

This model was probably the best of those using the early-type three-main bearing B-series engine. Like the engine itself, the cars were solid, very reliable, built with a hint of 'quality' and well regarded if totally unexciting.

Austin A60 Countryman

1800 Mk I, II, III and 1800S

After the Cambridge, came the 1800, which was meant to replace it but was not at first good enough, reflecting the failure of management and the success of the erratic and obstinate Alec Issigonis in having his way on the basis of his enormous past successes, but in the face of all common sense. Hydrolastic suspension coupled with a very long wheelbase (the Citroën influence on Issigonis again) gave a tremendously comfortable ride, and the vast width of the car, coupled with the transverse mounting of the new five-main bearing 1800 B-series engines meant that the 1800 had almost too much passenger space. Its four-square appearance has earned the 1800 the deserved nickname of 'Land-Crab'! Problems with new cars were legion, including valve crash (MGBs had stronger valve springs), poor oil consumption and hosts of other problems both of a fundamental and of a niggling nature. By the time BL had sorted them out, the Land-Crab had become as reliable as its predecessors. Mk Is are identifiable by their grille, which is of mesh with a central horizontal bar bearing the nameplate. Mk IIs have a grille with four twin horizontal bars with intermittent vertical bars and badge. Their rear wings extend to fins, incorporating a vertical light cluster and the boot lid bears the 'Mk II' legend. Larger wheels were also fitted and the engine was of higher bhp output. The Mk III saloon had a black grille with two sets of triple horizontal chrome bars and central badge and the new rod-operated gear lever was a great improvement. From July 1969 to March 1972, the 1800S was produced, giving 97 bhp from its Daniel Richmond-designed cylinder head (which was thus different to the MGB's). The 1800 was sold as an Austin and as a Morris from August 1967 to February 1975 and as a Wolseley 18/85 to March 1972. The Wolseley carried grille and interior trim embellishments and power-assisted steering as standard, while on the Austin and Morris models it became an option from September 1967. Six-cylinder versions using an E-series engine and the same body were also built.

18–22 and Princess (1975–78) (not Princess II)

From March 1975 to September of the same year, the Harris-Mann-designed wedge-shaped car was sold as Austin and Morris 18–22 Series. Then the makers' names were dropped and the car christened just Princess. The car was extraordinarily roomy by virtue of its long wheelbase and transversely mounted engine and the hydragas suspension evened out bumps in a very smooth style, although the handling was unsporting and the steering incredibly heavy, while the gear-change continued the Maxi tradition—it was well below par. The startling styling was not widely admired and neither were the car's woolly qualities, but for a comfortable, reliable family outing, it was another medium-sized car in the Austin tradition in that it did its job unexcitingly but competently. It was generally considered, like the 1800, to be an excellent tow car, the torquey determination of the engine adding to the surefootedness of the wheel-in-each-corner. Right from the start, the E-series six-cylinder engine was available as an option (the 2200 having trapezoidal headlamps while the Austin's and Princess' were round) and from July 1978 until the car's demise in 1980, the Princess became the first recipient of the B-series successor, the O-series engine, in 1700 or 2000 cc form, when it became known as Princess 2. The 2200 continued in production, too.

Austin 1800

Princess

MG ZA and ZB Magnette

When the Magnette appeared at the 1953 London Motor Show, it was the first car to be fitted with the new B-series engine, itself BMC's first new engine. Its body was an extensive development of the Gerald Palmer-designed Wolseley 4/44 body, announced 12 months earlier, mounted lower down and with alterations to every panel save the roof and doors. The ZB Varitone model had a chrome waistline, wrap-around rear window and usually, but not invariably, two-tone bodywork. Inside the car, the leather, walnut and MG octagonalisms gave a sporting, high-class air, while the monocoque construction made for a relatively roomy car. With the introduction of the ZB and the Varitone option came a further option, that of Manumatic semi-automatic transmission (see Austin Cambridge A50 for details). While there were virtually no body modifications when the ZB was introduced, except that the later car had a curved rather than a straight wing flash, the ZB's engine was almost up to MGA levels at 68.5 bhp (60 for ZA), while the higher rear axle ratio gave a genuine 85 mph maximum, making the ZB the fastest 1½-litre production saloon at the time. *The Autocar* called it 'one of the finer cars *The Autocar* has tested' even in ZA form and, bearing in mind the context of the time, the 1956–59 ZB Magnette was arguably the finest saloon car to be fitted with a B-series engine.

MG Magnette Mk III and Mk IV

Unlike the Austin, Morris and Wolseley 'Farina' cars, the Magnette did not receive a facelift between Mk III and IV versions. In September 1961, though the wheelbase was made longer by a mere inch and track became broader, too. The Mk III had become a slightly more sporting version of the 'Farina' range of cars, although its performance was below that of the old ZB Magnette. The Mk IV, however, received the 1622 cc engine, which, although below the MGA state of tune, equalled the bhp output of the ZB, although the car was no faster. In spite of the 1500 ZA/ZB Magnettes', engines being notably smooth, contemporary testers spoke of the roughness of the 1622 cc engine when fitted to the Magnette, which was certainly not typical of it. The car was certainly not what any MG purist wanted to see wearing an MG badge but was instead a quicker version of an honest but mundane motor car. The Borg-Warner automatic box also became available on the Mk IV Magnette.

Magnette Mk III

MG ZA/ZB

MG MGA 1500, 1600 and 1600 Mk II

This range of cars covers all the pushrod MGAs, from the early 1489 cc cars, through 1588 cc to 1622 cc. After the antique-looking TF, the new MGA looked startlingly sleek and modern with a distinct visual connection to the three cars which had run at Le Mans in June 1955, four months before the car's introduction. The streamlined body allowed a higher top speed from a smaller engine than had previously been the case and the 1500 B-series engine, tuned to MG's own standards under the close supervision of Sid Enever, gave excellent performance, especially after the engine was uprated to 72 bhp. A fixed-head coupé version was introduced in October 1956. In the summer of 1959, the MGA 1600 was introduced, its block commonized with the Twin-Cam MGA described in the next 'thumbnail sketch'. The 1588 cc engine was the only pushrod engine of that size made by BMC, but it meant that the MGA became a genuine 100 mph car. In April 1961, after production engineers had been able to stand the hiccoughs in production caused by this odd-sized engine no longer, the 1622 engine was fitted to the MGA, just a few months before its use in the rest of the B-series line-up (apart from Wolseley 1500/Riley 1.5, of course). The MGA 1600 used front disc brakes in place of the earlier car's drums, while amber-coloured front flasher lenses along with completely separate lenses at the rear for flashing indicators and tail lamps were the only visually distinguishing features. The Mk II is easier to recognize because its grille was well recessed at the base of its grille bars and the rear lamps were arranged in a single horizontal strip lens.

MGA Twin-Cam (1958–60)

The Italians produced exciting, production overhead camshaft engines, so why shouldn't the British? Two experimental twin overhead camshaft engines were developed, one by 'Doc' Weaving at Longbridge, the other by Eddie Maher at Coventry. The Morris development was chosen—and was a terrible flop! An enormous amount of engine redevelopment was carried out and it was very expensive to produce. It was also very temperamental in use and gained an instant bad reputation, so that in less than two years only 2111 were built. The Twin-Cam chassis was almost identical to that of the standard cars, except for the following major differences: the steering rack was moved forward one inch and the steering arms lengthened accordingly (which, incidentally, gave less responsive steering), spring rates were revised because of the slightly heavier engine, centre-lock Dunlop disc wheels were fitted (wires were not an option) and Dunlop disc brakes were fitted. The only visual difference apart from the wheels was the oval ventilation hole on each side of the bonnet panel. However, after the Twin-Cam ceased production, a few MGA De-Luxe were sold (although never officially catalogued), with all the Twin-Cam chassis changes but with a pushrod engine, some 1588 cc, others 1622 cc.

Ironically, the only overhead camshaft B-series engine was made more reliable just before production was scrapped. The 5-star petrol compression ratio was too high and led to burned-out pistons: it was lowered (*see* Specifications) and heavy oil burning caused by the juxtaposition of chrome-alloy piston rings and chrome molybdenum treatment of the bores was also cured.

Although the Twin-Cam ceased production in 1960, some De-Luxe hybrids and possibly some Twin-Cams themselves were sold as late as 1962, when the MGA proper ceased production.

MGA Twin-Cam

MGB (1962–81)

If you measure a sports car's success on the level of its sales, or on the degree of affection and respect which its adherents feel for it, then the MGB on either count has to be the most successful sports car ever built. Like all successful MGs, it was sold heavily in the USA and, in very rough terms, a third of production went to California alone, a third went to the rest of North America, while a third stayed in the UK. In all, over half a million MGBs were built. The B-series 1800 engine takes much of the credit for the car's character. Fast in 1962 terms, the engine rapidly became outdated in terms of raw performance, but its ruggedness, lazy torque, the throaty rasp from the exhaust and lack of strain from under the bonnet make the MGB an *enjoyable* sports car. And no matter how many facts and performance figures you throw at it, that's all a sports car needs to be! The sturdiness of the engine was matched by the strength of the body and the predictability of the MGB's safe and fairly rapid handling, all thanks to MG's chief at the time, Sid Enever. He was also the man responsible for the 1800 going to five-main bearings in September 1964, the MGB's competition use pointing out the excessive crank whip experienced on the early three-main 1800 engines. At the same time, the rear oil seal was altered from the relatively inefficient scroll type to the artificial rubber type. Even though the modern and on-paper highly successful TR7 was intended to replace the MGB, the venerable MG always outsold the new Triumph, the latter being killed off only a year after the 'B' ceased production. In October 1965, the MGB GT was introduced with improved rear axle. In October 1967, this axle was commonized with the roadster and both cars received the excellent all-synchromesh gearbox in place of the 3-synchro box which was weak on second gear synchro anyway. In October 1969, a black recessed grille was fitted and vinyl used instead of leather on the seats, which were more comfortably shaped. In the same month of 1971, another grille change and other cosmetic details took place, but December 1974 saw the last of the 'chrome bumper' MGBs as a high-suspension, black crash-resistant-bumper MGB was introduced to take account of US crash regulations for the 1975 model-year. In addition, emission control equipment, which had been becoming gradually more strangulatory from the mid-1960s, affected the performance of US cars drastically, so much so that the latest of the Californian cars had only a 70 mph speedometer, reflecting the top speed of the cars. In May 1975, BL built the MGB GT Jubilee, with British Racing Green bodywork, special decorative transfers and gold MGB GT V8 wheels. The final few MGBs built in 1981 were painted in gold or pewter colour schemes and called Limited Edition MGBs. All of the 'limited edition' MGBs have taken additional collector's status, the last cars especially so.

From October 1967 to August 1969, a development of the C-series engine was fitted to open and closed cars which were called MGC, and from August 1973 to July 1976, the ex-Buick, Rover V8 3.5-litre was fitted to some GTs, which were then known as the MGB GT V8.

Morris Cowley (1954–56), Cowley 1500 (1956–59), Oxford Series (II 1954–56), Oxford Series III (1956–59), including Oxford Traveller and Series IV Traveller (all-metal)

These models were the last distinctly Morris—as opposed to corporate BMC—cars to be built. The 1500 cc Oxford Series II saloon was the first to appear in May 1954, replacing the MO Oxford, which looked like an over-inflated Morris Minor, followed closely by the 1200 cc Cowley in July and the 'Traveller' Estate and less well-appointed Oxford, known as the Cowley 1500, in October. All continued the Oxford's torsion bar front suspension but were styled with a new body and were fitted with the ubiquitous B-series engine and gearbox with column change. Unlike their predecessors, the Traveller's rear-end woodwork did not form a structural part of the car (with the exception of the woodwork between the roof and upper window frame), although it was cleverly recessed into the steel frame to appear structural. The Series III Oxfords were built from October 1956 only with the 1500 cc engine (the 1200 cc B-series was never to be used again) and received minor styling changes such as fluted sides to the bonnet, finned rear wings and hooded headlamps. From June 1957, a strange piece of 'Series' nomenclature took place—the Traveller was built without timbering to the rear but with four side doors, a tailgate and two fuel filler caps, one each side of the body. Known as 'Series IV', it was the only Series IV Oxford built. It ceased production after the Series V had been introduced, the last one being built in April 1960. Manumatic semi-automatic gear changing was available from October 1956 to 1958.

Morris Oxford Series V and Series VI, including Traveller and diesel

These models of the Oxford were absolute clones of the Austin Cambridge models of the corresponding era. The Traveller, first made available from September 1960 to March 1961, also used a wood overlay construction rear end, but then became an all-metal construction. The Morris, like its Austin counterpart, was also available as a diesel from March 1962 to January 1969.

Morris Oxford V/VI

Morris Oxford II/IV

Morris 1800 (1966–75)

Because it was introduced two years after the Austin 1800, the more horrendous of the cars' earlier faults are not to be found on the Morris version. The 1800 (albeit in Austin form) was popular in Australia, where it was voted 'car of the year' and carried the best second-hand values of any car. It was also sold as a 'Ute' utility vehicle. Mk II models had a raised 9:1 compression ratio and the rear wing 'humps' were atrophied. The Morris 1800S was the first 'tuned' 1800, appearing in September 1968, Austin and Wolseley versions following a year later.

Morris 1800

Morris Marina 1.8 (1971–80)

The Morris Marina was produced by BL at a time when an orthodox challenger to the Ford Cortina was needed but when the company had less cash for development than they really needed. The Austin range, it was decided, would be based on transverse-engined roughly 'Issigonis' lines, while Morris cars would be cost reduced and conventional. Thus the Marina used the existing A-series 1275 cc engine or B-series 1800, Morris Minor-type front suspension and steering, Triumph gearbox and brakes but with a new body and new production facilities at Cowley. It was fairly successful, but never reached the absurd planned level of almost a third of a million per annum (in all $1\frac{1}{4}$ million were built in nine years). There were, over the years, permutations between saloon, coupé, estate, van and pick-up body styles with the two main engine sizes, although the light commercial vehicles only used the 1098 or 1275 cc petrol engine. The 1.8 TC in saloon or, for a time, coupé form, then later the GT, were to MGB standards of engine tune. The only major difference was that while all MGBs used the original forged crank, all Marinas were fitted with the new cast iron cranks, built specially for the cars. The 1.3 was introduced with drum brakes and radial ply tyres, but the rest of the range had 'Triumph' disc brakes and radial ply tyres. Early Marinas, especially the heavier-nosed 1.8 models, suffered from very poor handling, but the problem was largely alleviated by modifying the front suspension. At the 1978 Motor Show, the Marina was introduced with 1700 O-series engine, and the 1993 cc O-series with automatic gearbox (the Triumph manual box wasn't up to the job) appeared a year later, just after the car was

Morris Marina 1.8

restyled and renamed the Ital. The Marina was also sold in Australia and the Ital/Marina will probably go into production in Pakistan, fulfilling a similar role to that of the Ambassador/Oxford in India and it could be that the Pakistan car reverts to B-series engine usage, at least in diesel form.

Riley One-Point-Five, Wolseley Fifteen Hundred (1957–65)

These cars were successful, low-volume attempts to sell an up-market Morris Minor fitted with a B-series engine. The rebodying, re-trim and 'new' engine thoroughly disguised the antecedents of the cars' chassis. Both Riley and Wolseley (quickly known as 1.5 and 1500) were relatively quick and luxurious, the Riley the more so in both respects. It also had larger brakes, twin carburettors and a higher rear axle ratio and was a close-ish successor to the MG ZA/ZB Magnette. The cars were sold in Australia under the Wolseley and Austin names and there the body was expanded and remodelled once again and sold as the Morris Major Elite from 1962 to 1964, still with the same running gear and B-series engine.

Riley 4/Sixty-Eight and 4/Seventy-Two (1959–69)

Like the MG Magnette, the Riley 'Farina' began life as a clone car of the rest of the range but did not receive the same modifications to bodywork in September 1961 (see MG Magnette Mk III and IV). As a comfortable car for toddling along, the car was a success, especially when fitted with the automatic gearbox, but as a car with sporting saloon pretensions, the car was no great shakes. Under-powered in 1500 4/Sixty-Eight form, the 1622 cc engine made a difference, but *The Motor* were protesting the car's lack of pace, refinement and sporting characteristics even in 1962. However, for those who liked the old-fashioned virtues of solidity and the feel of seats with leather covering, the 'Farina' Riley was an attractive, dependable car.

Wolseley Fifteen-Sixty and Sixteen-Sixty (1958–71)

The Wolseley 'Farina' models followed the Austin and Morris base models in terms of mechanical specification and body shape. The Wolseley was the first of the range to be introduced in December 1958.

A word here about grille identification of the 'Farina' models. The Austin Cambridge carried a mesh grille with heavy horizontal bar (the A55's lower portion consisted of a wide horizontal strip) while the Morris Oxford had eight horizontal bars which curved under the headlamps. The Wolseley had a central grille with vertical bars and separate side grilles with a central horizontal bar over mesh. Its Wolseley badge had a little light in it, which some people found most attractive. The Riley had a similar central grille but with a pronounced bump or upper lip at the top, while the MG's grille was wider than the others, echoing the shape but not the proportions of the MGB grille.

Wolseley 18/85 (1967–72)

(See Austin and Morris 1800.)

Wolseley 1500

Riley 4/68

Wolseley 15/60

Wolseley 18/85

Wolseley Fifteen-Fifty (1956–58)

In 1952, a new car appeared, designed by Gerald Palmer along the general lines of the Lancia Aurelia. It was fitted with the 1250 cc MG engine and was at first intended as an MG, but at the last moment it was turned into the Wolseley Four-Forty-Four. The body shell was later tampered with and in fact made much more attractive and became the first car to be fitted with the B-series engine (see MG Magnette ZA and ZB). The Wolseley, however, soldiered on with the old MG unit until, presumably, enough B-series engines became available in 1956. It was then renamed the Fifteen-Fifty, reflecting the car's engine size and bhp.

Nash and Austin Metropolitan (1954–61)

The Nash Metropolitan was conceived as a tripartite deal between Nash in the United States and Austin and Pressed Steel Fisher in the UK. By August 1953, BMC was formed with Pressed Steel as one of its component companies. The car was powered at first by the A40 1200 cc engine from August 1953 to July 1954, when the Series II took over with the B-series 1200 engine. It was first built with the 1500 engine in Series III then Series IV guise from August 1955 to 1961. The car was sold in non-US markets as the Austin Metropolitan 1500 from December 1956 to January 1959. Produced in coupé or drophead forms, the car was a disaster, like most of Leonard Lord's attempts to break into the US market. Its narrow wheelbase gave it dreadful roadholding and cornering abilities and its styling was strange to say the least! Today it is regarded as interesting because it is so unusual, but its passing was not widely lamented at the time.

Wolseley 15/50

Metropolitan

PART THREE

Mechanical repairs

1 Maintenance

Failure to maintain a B-series engine correctly is probably the only thing that stands between it and a life expectancy of over 100,000 miles, assuming that it has been run-in properly in the first place and that it has not been too severely thrashed. Fortunately, engine maintenance is simple, with the exception of points replacement, which is 'fiddly' rather than difficult, and with the aid of the following chapter any enthusiast should be able to maintain his or her own engine with the satisfaction that comes from knowing that a job has been well done. Most of the photographs for this section were taken in the service bay at John Hewitt's 'The MG Shop', Manchester, where impressively high standards seem to be the norm. The order of work shown is that carried out at 'The MG Shop' when undertaking a full service.

Job 1—Set tappets (recommended interval—6000 miles)

M1 B-series tappets are notoriously noisy and if the engine is worn, even more so. The problem is that the top of the valve wears into a small bump, while the rocker wears concave to match it. When the feeler gauge is inserted between the two, it bridges the concave, so the effective gap is larger than you can measure. In such cases, reduce the gap by 0.002 in. (2 thou) to quieten the tappets a little, but check them more often, as closed-up tappets cause rapid valve burning. Proceed as follows: Remove the rocker cover (*see* Cylinder head overhaul) and the spark plugs. Place the gearstick in neutral. Grasp the fan belt and, taking care not to pinch your fingers between belt and pulley, turn the engine over until number 1 rocker (the one at the front) just starts to move.

The mechanics of the engine are such that number 8 valve is now fully closed and its rocker ready for setting. Select a feeler gauge or combination of gauges with the correct gap (*see* Specification) and slide the gauge in between the top of the valve stem and the face of the rocker. If the gap is too tight, leave the feeler gauge to one side. The gap is altered by turning the screw at the other end of the rocker with a screwdriver, but first the locknut surrounding it must be slackened with a spanner as shown. Turn the screw until the feeler gauge can be withdrawn but there is a feeling of slight friction as it is barely gripped between valve and rocker. Hold the screw *tightly* in place with the screwdriver and retighten the locknut. You will find that the locknut tends to close the gap as it is given a final pinch of tightness, so check the gap after setting and readjust if necessary. Continue by turning the engine until number 2 rocker moves, then adjust number 7, number 3 goes with number 6, and so on to number 8 rocking while you adjust number 1.

NB. If you have to retighten the cylinder head after refitting, do so *before* you set the tappets because the gap will be altered

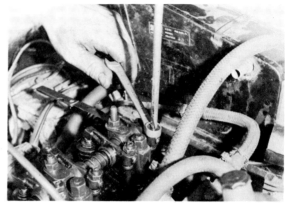

M1

M2

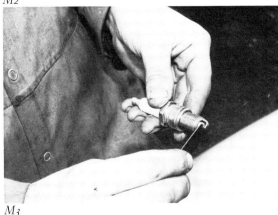

M3

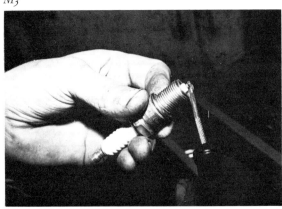

M4

M5

If the engine is difficult to turn over with the fan belt even with the spark plugs out, try placing the car in gear and, on a level slope, gently push or rock the car, turning the engine until the required rocker positions are found (*see* M35 for information on quieter worn tappets).

Job 2—Fit new rocker gasket (whenever necessary)

M2 The rocker cover gasket will leak badly whenever it becomes compressed or damaged and ought to be replaced after every service. Dig out the old one with a screwdriver if it is stuck in place and make sure that the rocker cover and top face of the head are perfectly clean where the gasket fits.

Job 3—Replace spark plugs (recommended interval—12,000 miles, but some owners prefer 6000 miles)

M3 Check the gap of the new spark plug, or the old one if it is being retained, with a 0.025 in. (25 thou) feeler gauge. If the old plug is at all dirty, clean it, preferably with a sand blasting machine at a garage. Remove only one plug lead at a time so that the firing order is not lost.

M4 If the gap is too narrow, lever the outer electrode against the outside of the plug (*not* the centre electrode or insulation) with a small screwdriver

M5 If the gap is too large, lightly tap the outer electrode on a clean, hard surface until the gap closes to the point where the feeler gauge can be inserted into the gap with just the slightest amount of frictional grip between the two electrodes.

Incidentally, an examination of spark plugs can tell you a lot about your engine. The electrode insulator should be a beige to light chocolate colour. If it is dark, the engine is running too rich; if white, the carburettor/s is/are set too weak or there is an air leak. If covered in oily deposits, the engine is worn and is burning oil.

Job 4—Replace or reset points (recommended intervals—6000 miles for adjustment and replacement if points are pitted. Replacement at no more than 12,000 miles)

M6 The distributor, which houses the points, is set low down on the rear-right of the engine.

M7 The distributor cap is held on by a pair of spring clips. This is a late model: earlier ones have longer clips.

M8 Lift off the rotor arm. It can only be replaced in one position.

M9 Unscrew the cheese-head screw that holds the points down and in adjustment.

M10 Because of the awkward situation of the B-series distributor, it makes sense to use a magnetic screwdriver to help prevent dropping the screw. Retrieve the spring washer and flat washer that sit under the head of the screw.

M11 On late-type distributors, unclip the wires from the points terminal as shown.

M12 On all the earlier-type distributors (the

M9

M6

M10

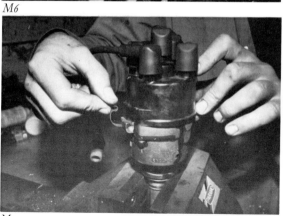

M7

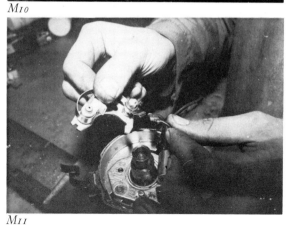

M11

M8

M12

M13

M14

M15

M16

majority) undo the nut from the top of the terminal bolt using a pair of pliers. It may or may not have a washer beneath it. The ring terminals from the condenser and low-tension leads fit *beneath* the flanged nylon cap, which in turn pushes into the eye on the end of the distributor spring.

M13 The condenser (which really ought to be replaced every 12,000 miles) is held down with a single screw.

M14 Again, use a magnetic screwdriver. Late-type condensers have a lead held under the screw: most do not.

M15 The condenser will now be free on earlier models: on late models the wire will have to be pulled through the distributor body.

M16 Wipe the base plate thoroughly to avoid the risk of damp formation and internal electrical tracking.

M17 After wiping all traces of old grease from the cams, put a smear of fresh grease on them. Also drop no more than two drops of oil on to the head of the screw beneath where the rotor arm sits (it will find its way down the spindle) and place another few drops down the hole at the side of the cams to lubricate the automatic timing mechanism. Too much oil or grease could contaminate the points.

M18 Fit the new points and turn the engine over until the heel of the points is on the highest point of one of the cams. Wipe the contacts with a petrol-dampened rag. Some have a protective coating which prevents the points from working properly until it is removed.

M19 Now tighten the cheese-head screw (arrowed) until it just nips the points in place, but still allows you to move them by levering them against the stop shown (later points) or by inserting the end of the screwdriver into the wing-shaped adjustment recess in about the same place on the earlier type of points.

M20 You can now slip the correct size of feeler gauge (15 thou) in between the two contacts. The gap is right when both contacts just stroke the sides of the feeler gauge as it is inserted and removed. You may have to use a flash lamp to illuminate the points well enough for you to see this.

M21 Now clean the lobe of the rotor arm on a piece of fine abrasive paper. If it is damaged or reduced in size, replace it. Refit the rotor arm, pushing it down on to its locating peg. Before replacing the distributor cap and high-tension

M17

M18

M19

M20

M21

plug leads, wipe them clean. After a period of time it is wise to replace both.

NB. See M36-on for information on changing the points on an earlier-type distributor.

Job 5—Set ignition timing (recommended interval—every 12,000 miles)

The ignition timing allows the spark to take place before the piston reaches the top of its stroke (Top Dead Centre, or TDC) so that the mixture ignites most powerfully at the correct time for pushing the piston back down again with maximum force, bearing in mind that ignition cannot be instantaneous. The faster the engine is running, the earlier the spark is required, which explains the function of the bob-weights inside the distributor which automatically advance the spark in line with the engine speed. Thus, the timing must be at normal tick-over speed with the engine at normal running temperature, so that neither bob weights nor vacuum advance are giving an artificial reading.

M22 On all B-series engines the crankshaft pulley has a pair of vees in the pulley perimeter (arrowed A), while the timing chain cover has two, four or sometimes five points on it (arrowed B). (NB. It is

M22

M23

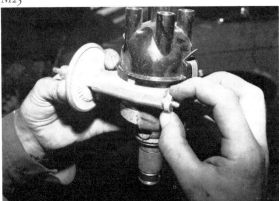

M24

M25

the ends of the pointers that are the relevant indicators not the vees in between.) Most B-series engines have their pointers at the bottom, seen from underneath the car; this late MGB engine has its pointers visible from inside the engine bay.

M23 Bearing in mind that the crankshaft pulley turns clockwise when viewed from the front and the fact that the *last* pointer it passes is at TDC, each pointer before the last equals $5°$ before TDC: thus, in M22, the timing is at $10°$ BTDC. There is only one way of checking this with the engine running and that is to use a timing light. This is connected with the special connectors supplied so that it flashes as the current travels to number 1 spark plug.

With the timing light connected up the engine is started. *Take care not to entangle the leads, lamp, hands or loose clothing with the cooling fan or fan-belt pulleys.* (The car pictured has an electric fan.) Point the light, which will now be flashing in time with the number 1 spark, at the timing marks on the timing chain cover. The stroboscopic effect will show the position of the crankshaft pulley marks in relation to the timing marks, but be sure that you have noted which one equals TDC. Timing tip: less expensive timing lights are not very bright. It helps to put a dab of white paint into the vees on the crankshaft pulley.

M24 This knurled wheel on the distributor advances or retards the ignition: anticlockwise to advance; clockwise to retard. If there is not enough adjustment available here, set the knurled wheel to its centre position and slacken the pinch bolt beneath the body of the distributor and turn the body of the distributor to adjust the timing, saving the vernier knurled wheel for fine tuning. (Eleven clicks of the knurled wheel = $1°$ of timing, by the way.) Keep your hands well clear of the plug leads when the engine is running to avoid a shock, especially in humid or damp weather. It is best to turn the distributor body with the engine stationary.

Job 6—Carburettor tuning (recommended interval—6000 or 12,000 miles, depending on how well or badly the engine is running)

Adjusting the carburettor is very simple on cars with a single SU or Zenith carburettor, but a little more complex where twin SU carburettors are fitted. Always correctly set the ignition before adjusting the carburettor/s and check the air filtration system is not clogged at all. *Zenith carburettor:* screw the mixture control screw right in but *do not* overtighten. Slacken it back $1\frac{1}{2}$ turns. Now turn the slow-running screw until it just touches the stop on the carburettor body and rotate it one complete turn.

M25 *Single SU carburettor:* the best DIY way of setting the mixture here is, in the author's view, with a Gunson Colortune. This fits in place of the spark plug and enables you to check visually the richness of the combustion process as it takes place. Follow the maker's instructions closely, but remember that the two outer cylinders will tend to be slightly weaker than the centre two.

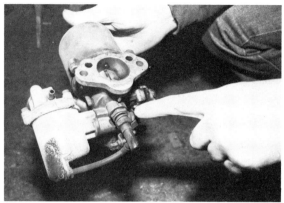

M26

M26 The hexagonal nut beneath the spring is the one for setting the mixture. Screw anticlockwise (down) to richen; clockwise (up) to weaken the mixture.

M27 Tick over is set by adjusting the screw arrowed A. When working with twin carburettors, it is essential to check that when the throttle cable is pushed as shown, the rod operates both throttles at exactly the same time. If it does not, slacken the operating levers (arrowed B) and retighten them at the position where they operate both carburettors simultaneously. Check also that both choke adjustment screws are set so that both chokes operate simultaneously, too. Ensure that the fast-running screw which operates off a cam as each choke is operated does not touch the cam when the choke is fully pushed in on the dash. With the linkages set correctly, the SUs can be set as for a single carb except that the colortune should be placed in the number 1 plug hole for adjusting the front carb and in number 4 for adjusting the rear carb. If either carb was a very long way out to start off with, you may have to check each one a second time.

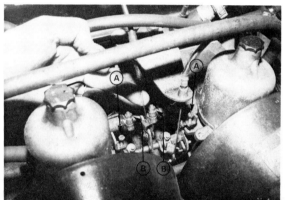

M27

M28

M28 Here's how you get at the adjusting nuts on most cars, those up to 1975: by grovelling beneath the air filters. You will probably be able to turn them by hand, but they may need spannering round.

M29 Latest SU carburettors of the HIF4 type have a screwed-type mixture adjuster in the side of the carburettor body. If there is a blanking plug above the adjuster, prise it out and discard it.

M29

M30

M31

M32

M33

Job 7—Oil and filter (recommended interval—at most 6000 miles)

M30 Viewed from beneath the rear of the car, the B-series oil drain plug is on the rear right of the sump, although its exact position may vary from engine to engine.

M31 Have a container ready to catch the old oil as it pours out. Draining is best carried out with the engine—and thus the oil—warm. Allow every drop to drain out.

M32 Clean the seal around the drain plug and replace it if it is split or damaged.

M33 There are several types of B-series oil filter. The most common is the canister with a disposable element. The canister is removed by undoing the long bolt through the middle of the canister, reached from beneath the car. After removing the canister and bolt as a piece, drain the old oil away, throw away the old element and clean out the inside of the canister. A later type used the same system, but the canister pokes upwards and is removed from inside the engine bay. After removal, using a stout pin, remove the rubber sealing ring that fits beneath the rim of the canister. Replace it with the new one that should be supplied in the box with the new element.

Later types have a disposable canister, removed from inside the engine bay with removing strap as shown, or by driving a long screwdriver into the side of it and unscrewing it using the screwdriver as a lever.

M34 Make certain that the seal beneath the base of the filter is cleaned thoroughly before the new filter is fitted. Fit the new filter hand tight only.

Job 8—Sundries (every 3000 miles)

(1) Unscrew the top(s) of the SU carburettor dashpot(s) and top up the dashpots with thin oil such as 3-in-1. Oil the carburettor controls.

(2) Change the oil in the air cleaners of early cars with oil bath-type air cleaners.

(3) Where a dynamo is fitted, place three drops of oil into the lubrication hole at the end opposite the pulley end. Check the fan-belt tension—there should be around $\frac{1}{2}$ in. of slack midway between the fan and the dynamo pulleys.

(4) Where the water pump has a grease nipple, give the water pump a single shot of grease.

Sundries (every 6000 miles all of the above, plus)

(1) Check the condition of all cooling system and heater hoses. Squeeze them hard and if any cracking can be seen, especially between the ribs

in convoluted hose, replace them.

(2) Remove and clean the fuel filters in carburettor or fuel pump, where fitted.

(3) Examine the exhaust system for leaks, especially around the manifold joint on those systems with a clamp joint. Ensure that all exhaust support straps are sound, too.

Sundries (every 12,000 miles, all of the above, plus)

(1) Clean any sediment out of the carburettor float chamber. Check the condition of the needle valve (SU-type) for marking and replace if necessary.

(2) Inspect ignition leads and replace if at all cracked or perished. Examine the ignition system *visually only* with the engine running at night. Look for sparking or tracking which would indicate faulty leads, plug caps or distributor cap.

(3) On later models fitted with positive crankcase breathing, change the oil filler cap and wash out the crankcase breather valve with detergent or methylated spirits. Over a period of time the running of the engine will become affected as the system becomes clogged.

(4) Look at the dynamo brushes (where fitted), replace them if necessary and clean the commutator. The same can be done with the starter motor, but only at every other 12,000 miles service. Clean the starter drive shaft at the same time.

(5) Remove the battery terminals, clean them thoroughly and check the cleanliness and tightness of the earth strap body connection.

M35 This is a view of the earlier-type distributor with the cap and rotor arm removed. The main difference between this and the later type is in the layout of the internal wiring.

M36 Use a pair of pliers to remove the nut which holds the low-tension and condenser leads in place.

M37 Beneath the nut is a flanged nylon washer and beneath *that* goes the two wiring terminals. The flange on the washer has to pass right through these terminals and into the eye on the end of the contact breaker spring.

M38 The points themselves are held down with a cheesehead screw, just as with the later-type points.

M39 Only use one-piece points. Points that comprise a Chinese puzzle of bits and pieces, if there are still any around, just aren't worth the hassle. When replacing the points, place the screw

M34

M35

M36

M37

M38

M39

into the hole in the points and hold it down with the screwdriver whilst holding the points in the other hand. Then lower the whole lot into place and do the screw up. This way allows you to support the screw, reducing the risk of dropping it into the murky depths.

M40 Having shown how to adjust the timing by the old-fashioned way, it must be said that the finest DIY approach is to use a dwell meter such as this Gunson's Sparktune 2. It measures the proportion of an engine revolution for which the points are open, rather than taking a measurement from one cam. This averages out the discrepancies that are bound to occur, especially with an older engine where a points gap measurement can be little more than a good estimate of the correct setting.

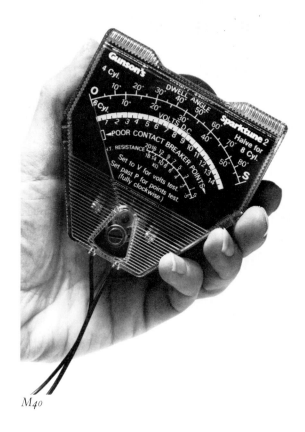

M40

2 Cylinder head overhaul—engine in car

The ritual of 'de-coking' an engine on a regular basis is, thankfully, no longer a regular service operation as it was for the users of pre-war and immediately postwar cars, but even so, a B-series cylinder head will normally have to be removed once or twice within the life-span of an unrebuilt engine. The earlier relatively unstressed engines do no more than lose the strength from their valve springs, lose the precision fit of their valve seats and suffer from a build-up of carbon deposits in the combustion chamber, but the more highly tuned engines often manage to burn out their exhaust valves, and the 1800s, especially in MGB early-1970s form, are prone to blowing a head gasket. While the mighty lump of cast iron from which the thing is hewn is not likely to warp (although it can in extremes), the narrow dyke between the 1800 cylinders can easily be damaged if the gasket is breached at this point. The good news in all cases is that the head comes off relatively easily, any fiddly bits being confined to the owners of 2-carb MGs and the 1800 and Princess models, whose exhausts are relatively inaccessible.

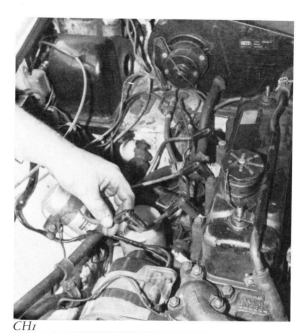

CH1

CH1 The first job is to disconnect the battery; then drain the radiator and block. Most cars have a drain tap on the bottom of the rad. and on the right-hand side of the block, near the distributor. Later models lost the block tap, then the radiator tap was left off. In such cases slacken the bottom hose, ease the hose away from the radiator stub with a screwdriver if it has bonded itself in place and place a tub to catch the splashes. Remove the plug leads and code them 1, 2, 3, 4 with dabs of paint, strips of insulation tape or by scoring the cap with a hacksaw blade so that you can easily replace them in the correct order.

CH2 With all the water drained out, remove the top hose and slacken and release the clips to the

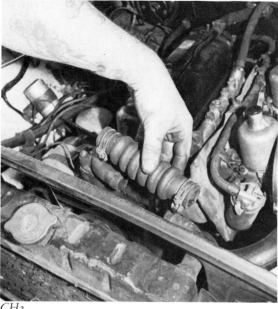

CH2

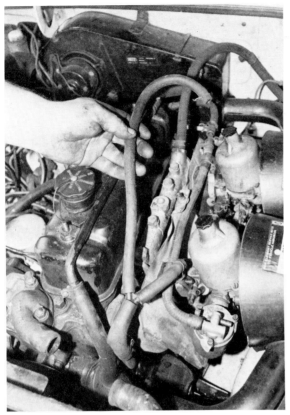

CH3

CH4

CH5

heater water pipe that passes down the side of the rocker box cover on most models and along the top of the rocker box on later models.

CH3 Later cars have various types of emission-control equipment fitted. This is the positive crankcase ventilation system: some of the fittings are push-on while others have simple spring clips. Jubilee clips are often substituted over the years. The Y-piece at the junction of these tubes is prone to fracture. Leave the pipes connected there if you can.

Models fitted with exhaust emission control: Also remember to disconnect:

(1) The automatic choke water hose from the cylinder head.

(2) The air pump. Take off the air cleaner (two nuts and bolts), disconnect the air hose. Slacken the pump bolts, remove the drivebelt. Remove the top adjusting link bolt and the mounting bolt, then remove the pump.

(3) Take the bottom hose off the water pump.

(4) Take off the hot-air duct. Loosen the air cleaner wing nut then swing the cleaner and air temperature control assembly out of the way. Take the hose off the duct then remove the duct by undoing the nut plus washer and bolt plus washer. Then unbolt the exposed inner duct.

(5) Disconnect and remove the air manifold rail.

CH4 Take off the heater hose shown from the heater unit. It is not necessary to take it off the pipe unless it shows signs of perishing and needs replacement. Unbolt the pipe from the top of the rocker box. If the pipe passes along the side of the rocker box, it will come away when the manifold nuts are removed.

CH5 Take the heater control tap off the block but leave the hose and control cable in place. Tie it back out of the way to something on the bulkhead. On transverse-engined models, you will also have to disconnect the feed pipe that runs the water supply around from the right-hand side of the engine (which faces the front of the car). Also take off the vacuum advance pipe that runs from the distributor to the carburettor(s). On earlier models a union has to be unscrewed from the distributor and a bracket disconnected from the head; on later models the plastic pipe is a push-fit.

CH6 On all models, the rocker box is held on by an internally threaded nut which screws down on to a stud in the head. Hang on to the washer and sealing washer beneath. If the rocker box doesn't simply lift off, give it a sideways tap with a rubber-faced mallet.

CH7 Some cars are fitted with a brakes servo unit, in which case disconnect the air pipe from the inlet manifold.

CH8 Pull off the electrical connection to the water temperature light (at the position shown here) or, if a water temperature gauge connection of the capillary type shown here is fitted, screw it out of the head.

CH9 The capillary pipe is prone to breakage, in which case the whole unit will have to be replaced at a specialist firm such as Spridgebits The M.G. Shop (see Suppliers section). Once unscrewed, the sender unit simply pulls out from the head as shown. As the first turns are given to the spanner, watch the pipe very closely at the point where it enters the nut. If the pipe turns with the retaining nut, it will quickly shear, so soak the area with releasing fluid in the hope that the nut will turn freely on the pipe.

CH10 Each carburettor is held on to a pair of studs with a plain washer, spring washer and nut. Earlier carburettors have their studs at the 12 o'clock and 6 o'clock positions, while later carburettors' studs are at 10 o'clock/4 o'clock.

CH8

CH9

CH6

CH10

CH7

CH11

CH12

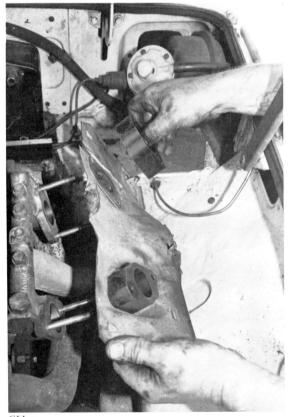

CH13

CH14

Whether dealing with a single or twin-carb set-up, it is not necessary to detach the choke connections, although it may be simpler to work on the twin-carb set-up after undoing the throttle cable. The fuel feed will have to be disconnected in all cases. The fuel feed pipe shown here is connected to the top carburettor studs on twin-carb cars.

CH11 The carburettors and air cleaners can be removed complete, as shown.

CH12 The two units are *not* held together in any way, the throttle and choke operating shafts just slotting into place. Note carefully where they go so that the carburettors can easily be reassembled.

CH13 With the carburettors in place, the four springs which pull the two throttles and two chokes back to their stops on twin-carb versions (two on single carbs) cannot be seen with the units in place. They must of course be removed before the carburettors are taken off, but they can be left connected to the heat shield or exhaust clamp bracket, as applicable. Note carefully where they go and replace them carefully, gripping the wire hooks with long-nosed pliers.

CH14 Beneath each carburettor will be a so-called emulsion block and, where twin carburettors are fitted, a heat shield. Both pull off the retaining studs.

CH15 MG heat shields often flex and break, right up to the point of disintegration. They can be bought new and sometimes second-hand from MG specialists.

CH16 All Austin and most Nuffield cars' manifolds are one-piece exhaust and inlet manifolds combined, with a hot-spot. MG manifolds are two-piece affairs, the inlet manifold being made of aluminium alloy while the three-into-two exhaust manifold is made of cast iron. When taking the head off an MG, take the manifold off the head but leave it connected to the exhaust. Two of the three bolts holding the parts together are difficult to get at and the bolts all too often shear off instead of unscrewing. On the other hand, Austin/Morris manifolds are held to the exhaust by a simple clamp. Slacken both nuts holding the bolt from turning with a second spanner, until the clamp is sufficiently loose for the exhaust pipe to slip out of it. When refitting this part, make sure that it is clean and not filled with exhaust leak 'goo', and lubricate the bolts so that the nuts screw up and down easily. Check also that the flare on the top of the pipe is not kinked— true it up carefully with pliers if necessary—and that the flare on the manifold is clean. Apply a bead of the white, hard-setting type of exhaust paste before refitting and make sure that the two flares are square against each other before tightening the clamp.

CH17 All types of manifold are held on by the same type of studs. With the split type of manifold, heavy-duty washers bear on the inlet and outlet fixing lugs, only the two outer ends of the exhaust manifold having complete holes which pass over the mounting studs.

CH18 Quite often, the stud comes out of the block while the nut stays resolutely in place. (The same often happens with the odd cylinder head stud.) You should hold the non-threaded part of the stud in a vice and remove the nut from the stud before putting the stud back in. If you try to use the stud plus nut as a bolt when reassembling, there is a strong risk that the stud will go a couple of turns into the head, then 'stick', allowing the nut to run further down the stud and tighten on to the manifold. There is then a strong risk of stripping the thread in the head.

North American models—manifold removal
(1) Disconnect the running-on control valve hose.

CH15

CH16

CH17

CH19

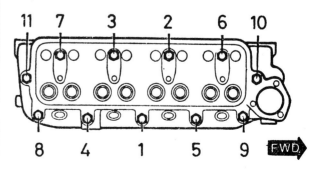

Cylinder head nuts – loosening and tightening sequence

CH19(A)

CH18

CH20

CH21

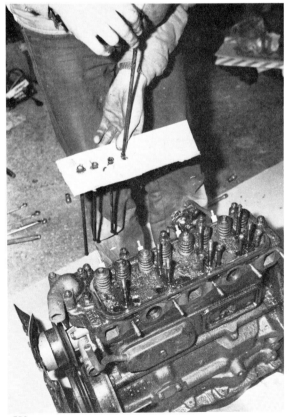

CH22

(2) Remove the gulp valve and hot-air shroud.

(3) Disconnect the exhaust pipe from the catalytic converter, where fitted.

CH19 You can now start to undo the cylinder head nuts, working in the order shown. Undo each nut half a turn at a time until none bears down upon the cylinder head . . .

CH20 . . . then remove the four nuts holding the rocker gear down to the head and remove the rocker gear by just lifting it off the studs.

CH21 Theoretically, the pushrods will pull straight out of the head. In practice, some of them may stick a little in deposits that have built up. If that happens, work the pushrod up and down vigorously until it comes loose.

CH22 Although this engine is out of the car, the principle is the same, of course. Keep the pushrods in the right order by poking eight holes in a piece of card and inserting the pushrods into them. Number the holes. The same idea can be used when you later strip the valves out of the head.

CH23 Now lift off the head—or try to! If it comes off first time, fine! Try to lift evenly, or the head will 'stick' on the studs, and have someone slide a piece of wood under it as you lift the first inch or so, so that if it does stick and you wiggle it free, it doesn't drop back down on to your fingers.

CH24 'CH23' sounded painful, but there's also the 'pain' of not being able to free the head! Leaving the manifold on Austin/Morris/Wolseley versions gives you something to shake; or you could tap the thermostat housing with a soft-faced mallet (a hammer could crack the cast iron head); or, *making certain that the plugs are disconnected* so that the engine cannot possibly fire up, turn the engine over on the starter—the pressure created could break the seal.

CH25 Lifting a heavy weight with your hands a long way away from your body can cause injury, so either have someone else give you a hand, or even try putting one foot in the engine bay so that you don't have to lean forwards. Even Rob, the mechanic shown here, is supporting an arm on the radiator shroud.

CH26 Use a flat-bladed scraper to lift off the old gasket from the block. Again, lift it off evenly or it will 'stick' infuriatingly on the studs.

CH27 Clean off the top face of the block with the flat-bladed scraper again, but first stuff rags into the bores to stop any rubbish dropping in. If the piston crowns are badly carbonated, turn the engine over until two pistons are at the top of

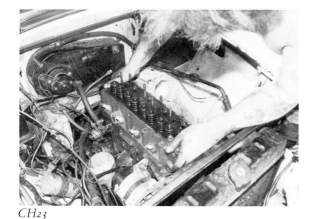

CH23

CH24

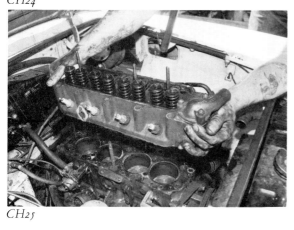

CH25

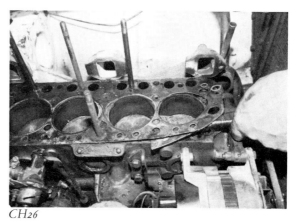

CH26

CH27

their stroke, stuff rags into the other cylinders, then insert an old piston ring into the bore of one of the top-dead-centre pistons. Now scrape the piston top with a hardwood scraper—but *don't* use a metal scraper, which could damage the aluminium piston. The ring of carbon left beneath the old piston ring will allow the carbon there to continue the seal that it will have tended to make, which can be especially beneficial on a worn engine. Protect the oil and waterways with small pieces of masking tape so that no carbon can fall into them.

CH28

CH29

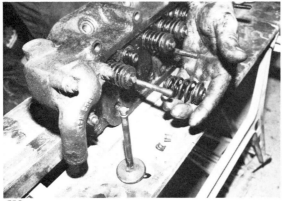

CH30

CH31

CH32

CH28 When you have cleaned the block, look very carefully for signs of water passage or, more likely, gas passage between numbers 1 and 2, or 3 and 4 on 1800 engines. If the block has been damaged, the top face will have to be skimmed, which is an engine-out job, unfortunately.

CH29 Also check the face of the head in the same way and, with the valves still in place to give protection to the seats, remove any carbon from the head with a scraper, finishing off with a wire brush held in an electric drill. Then remove the valves: start by compressing the valve spring as shown.

CH30 Most MGs have double valve springs, although this 1974 model did not. Remove by first taking off the hairpin-shaped spring circlips from the valve collets using a pair of pliers, then take out the collets (arrowed). The valve spring and shroud can be removed after the compressor has been freed.

You may have to push the compressor and valve spring to one side if it has not gone down completely evenly, because it can then bear on one of the collets and stop it from coming out. Simply pushing against it should do the trick but *don't*, whatever you do, lever the compressor so that it slips off the valve. The valve and shroud would fly like a very lethal bullet.

CH31 The exhaust valve on the left is reusable; the one on the right has been burned, so that there is no longer a usable valve head left and it will have to be replaced. Badly pitted valve seats can be refaced by a specialist, which can save ages of valve grinding. The valve seats in the head can be recut if they are damaged, although if the damage is very bad or the seat is cracked, your specialist may have to fit valve seat inserts.

CH32 Grind-in the valve by putting a light smear of 'fine'-grade grinding paste around the valve seat (only use coarse grade if there is some pitting present), applying the paste with the tip of a screwdriver. Keep it off your hands or they will rapidly become very sore with the next stage.

CH33 Buy a valve grinding tool from the accessory shop where you buy the paste. Make sure the head of the valve is clean and stick the sucker on the tool to it. (A little spot of 'spit' helps!) Pop the valve back in and work the tool back and forth between the hands like a caveman starting a fire. After a dozen or so 'twiddles', stop, lift the tool and valve a little, turn the whole thing round a part-turn so as to spread out the grinding effect, and grind again. You should aim to have a very narrow, bright ring around the face of the valve, the narrower the better. You may have to clean the paste off with paraffin and grind 'dry' to check this properly. When you have finished, wash the whole area very thoroughly with paraffin: grinding paste is one of the last things you should have inside your engine.

Valve guide replacement

If the valve can be moved with any side play at all the valve guides have worn and should be replaced. You can drift out the old ones and drift in new ones yourself, ensuring that the new valve guide is fitted from the top of the cylinder head with the large chamfer at the top. The new guide *must* be the correct height above the spring seat. It may be best to leave this to a specialist engine reconditioner, at least one of which can be found in most towns.

CH34 With everything wiped off clean, you can fit your new head gasket. *Never* reuse an old one and make certain that the face marked 'Top' is uppermost. Replace the head and ancillaries in the reverse order to that shown. Remember always to use new rubber seals (small black rubber rings) on the valve stems when refitting the valves and use a new heater tap gasket.

CH35 Remember to replace the shims on the rocker posts *but only on the posts and on the engines where they were fitted*; not in all cases.

Retighten the cylinder head nuts in the order shown below to the torque figure shown for your model of engine, shown in the 'Specifications' section. See the 'Maintenance' section for details of how to go about doing so. Remember to retighten the head to the correct figure and reset the tappets after around 500 miles of running.

Lastly, don't forget to change the rocker box gasket. Most B-series engines leak anyway, so there's no point in adding more drips of the dirt-attracting stuff. All the gaskets you will need will be contained in a so-called 'decoke' gasket set, obtainable from specialists or from a local motor factory or accessory shop.

CH33

CH34

CH35

3 Engine removal

The engines shown being removed here are MGB engines, but the removal of all B-series engines is carried out along similar lines. Any differences between model types are pointed out at the end of the text and, in fact, apart from the MGA, most models have much better access than the MGB, so the job should be somewhat easier.

ER1 The somewhat crowded engine bay of the MGB can be a daunting sight, but in fact the problems are of time rather than difficulty. The engine can be removed by itself or with gearbox attached. There is little in it in terms of time: the engine by itself is obviously more manoeuvrable but refitting it to the gearbox *in situ* can be tricky and carries a risk of damaging the clutch.

ER2 This is the Intec Engineering hydraulic engine hoist, one of which the author has bought for his own use. It makes engine removal so much easier, but it can only be justified if it will be used fairly regularly. You may be able to hire something similar or you could sling a hoist from a very well-supported beam—the B-series is a heavy engine so it may be best to support a beam with an extra vertical baulk of timber placed either side of the car.

ER3 After driving the front wheels of the car on to a pair of ramps or over a pit, disconnect the battery(ies) and drain the water and the oil from engine and gearbox, if the latter is to be removed.

ER4 Remove the bonnet but mark the exact positions of the adjustable hinges so that the bonnet can be lined up properly when it is refitted—there is a lot of adjustment there!

ER5 Unscrew the water temperature gauge sender unit (*see* 'Cylinder head overhaul') and place the bulb and tube well out of the way so that they cannot be damaged. Many models have a simple wire connection—disconnect.

After draining the coolant and engine oil,

ER1

ER2

ER3

ER4

ER5

ER5(NA)

disconnect the distributor cap and spark plug leads, remove the wiring from the distributor and generator—label it with masking tape tags so that it can be easily and correctly refitted—and remove the oil pressure pipe, where fitted—next to oil cooler union (see ER9)—or the electrical connection. Remove the heater tap, carburettors and manifold (*see* 'Cylinder head overhaul'). Take off the wiring to the starter motor and label it. Where a cable-drive rev. counter is fitted, unscrew it from the rear left of the block.

ER5(NA) On late North American MGBs, disconnect the wire from the induction manifold heater, the purge pipe from the top of the rocker cover and the manifold pipe from the running-on control valve. Take off the absorption canister hose connections from the rocker cover and carburettor.

ER6 You can, of course, leave the heater tap in place, disconnect the cable and remove the hose from the heater unit on the bulkhead.

ER7 If the engine is to be overhauled, reusing the old hoses would be false economy. Cut through the bottom hose at least with a hacksaw. The clips are not very accessible *in situ*.

ER6

ER7

ER8

ER9

ER10

ER11

ER8 The top generator mounting bolts are slackened with the aid of a pair of spanners, one to lock the bolt while the nut is removed.

ER9 The adjuster nut, however, does not require a locking spanner. It can be removed more quickly with a socket spanner and extension to clear the fan.

ER10 Both the generator and fan belt can now be lifted clear.

ER11 Where an oil cooler is fitted, you can either unbolt the oil cooler still fitted to the pipework (four vertical bolts into captive nuts beneath) or take off the pipes, which can be messier. Be certain to hold a spanner on the hexagonal boss beneath the union while undoing the union itself or you will probably rip the boss out of the oil cooler top.

ER12 Undo the two oil pipe engine connections.

ER13 Now, on MGBs, take out the whole radiator shroud with radiator still attached. There is nothing to be gained by taking out the radiator by itself since the shroud has to come out in any case.

ER14 Now the oil cooler radiator, cooling system radiator and shroud and oil cooler pipework can be lifted out as a piece with the minimum of dismantling or reassembly called for. NB. Non-MGBs also have to have their radiators removed, but the panel to which the radiator fits can be left in place. A tie bar across the front of the Magnette engine bay has to be removed as well as the radiator.

ER15 The clutch slave cylinder should be taken off the gearbox if the gearbox itself is being removed. The exhaust pipe mounting strap (arrowed A) should be taken off the rear of the engine and the gearbox cross-member mounts on both sides (arrowed B) soaked in releasing fluid ready to be removed later. From inside the car, again only if the gearbox is being removed, the gearstick grommet should be disconnected, the gearstick put into neutral and the three bolts holding the gearstick retaining plate removed, allowing the gearstick to be lifted away. The speedometer drive should be unscrewed from the gearbox. In the case of automatics, disconnect the manual control lever at the gearbox shaft and the wires from the inhibitor and reversing light switch. Disconnect the downshift cable at the carburettor.

ER16 Whether the gearbox is to remain in place or not, support it under the bellhousing, near the front, with a trolley jack.

ER17 The prop shaft can now be disconnected

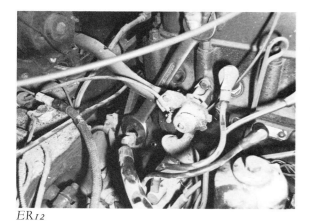

ER12

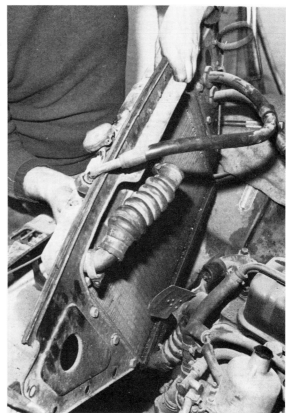

ER14

ER13

ER15

from the gearbox flange and the propeller shaft
withdrawn backwards. It can remain connected to
the rear axle.

ER18 Now, if the gearbox is to come out, undo
the cross-member fixing bolts and lower the
gearbox a little with the trolley jack. This gives
better access to the gearbox mountings, which can
be disconnected. The gearbox and engine
movement limiter cable which passes through the
cross-member can be disconnected. Also remove
the reversing light connection, when fitted.

ER16

ER17

ER18

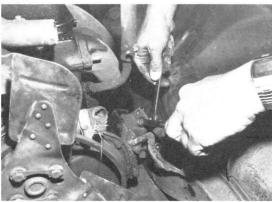

ER19

ER20

ER19 Undo and remove the engine mounting bolts: leave the rubbers connected to the engine plate and remove those that hold the rubbers to the chassis mounting. There are sometimes shims, especially under the left-hand engine mounting. Retain them for use later on.

ER20 This is the later type of MGB engine mounting, but the same principles apply.

ER21 Early engines had lifting hooks fitted to the rocker box bolts and this is a home-made version of such hooks. In the author's experience this type of mounting is a bit marginal in terms of strength and is not recommended, especially if both engine and gearbox are to be lifted together. A much better alternative would be a bracket made to bolt to a couple of cylinder head bolts. The point of balance, shown here, is a good one if both engine and gearbox are to be removed together.

ER22 Another approach is to place a rope sling around the engine, like this one being lifted at John Hill's. One problem is that the rope tends to stretch so you need plenty of height and be absolutely certain the rope is strong enough.

ER23 When the engine is removed by itself, the bellhousing bolts and starter motor have to be removed and the front of the gearbox lifted a little

ER21

ER22

ER24

ER23

with the trolley jack as the engine is lifted off its mountings with the hoist. The engine can be pulled forwards as shown in the previous shot, but the hoist should be used particularly carefully at first until the engine is free of the gearbox so that the weight of the engine does not damage the clutch or the first motion shaft which protrudes from the centre of the box. Make sure that no cables, connections, earth wires, etc., are still in place before finally attempting to pull the engine clear.

ER24 If the engine and gearbox are being lifted

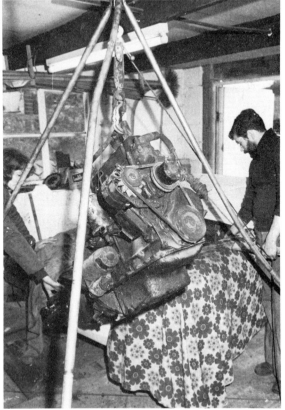

ER25

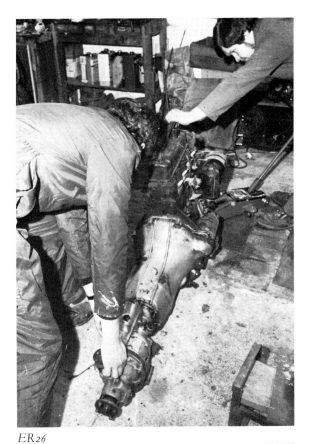
ER26

ER27

ER28

together, the gearbox has to be allowed to swing very low at the back to clear the bulkhead as it comes out.

ER25 The car can be pushed back from under the engine (sit in the driver's seat and apply the brake if the car is on ramps) and ease the gearbox/engine over the front of the car.

ER26 You will find the whole thing very heavy to move around in the workshop. One approach is to lift the front of the engine with a trolley jack and lift and 'steer' the lighter gearbox end, taking care not to tip the whole thing over.

ER27 If the gearbox has been left in place, lash it up with a piece of rope before removing the trolley jack to avoid straining the mountings. This shot shows, incidentally, how the MGB exhaust manifold is best left connected to the exhaust pipe as described in 'Cylinder head overhaul'.

ER28 Although nothing to do with the engine as such, if you want to clean out the engine bay, there's no time like now! Note that the body panels have been protected with cloths.

ER29 Your biggest problem when refitting the engine is in lining the clutch plate up correctly so that the first motion shaft will go into it and also fit the end of the crank correctly. A clutch aligning tool bought from a motorists' shop would be a very worthwhile investment. As when removing the engine, don't allow its weight to rest on the first motion shaft.

ER30 Line the engine and gearbox up as accurately as you can with a combination of engine hoist and trolley jack under the gearbox and if you're incredibly lucky, the two units will slip together like velvet. (It has never yet happened to the author with a B-series engine!) The weight of the engine means that it is far more difficult to 'jiggle' the engine on to the gearbox. Try placing a spanner on the crankshaft end nut, or use the starting handle on some earlier cars, to turn the engine over a little whilst pushing. *Nil desperandum*, it *will* go in eventually, but this is one good reason for removing the engine and gearbox as a unit. Reconnect the components as a reversal of the dismantling procedure and remember to refill both engine *and gearbox* with oil.

Austin A40, A50, A55

(1) When removing the radiator, also remember to remove the bonnet release cable and remove the wiring harness from the clip on the cylinder.

(2) Disconnect and remove the battery completely.

(3) Before disconnecting the fuel line from the carburettor close the petrol shut-off cock.

(4) Disconnect the column change shifter/selector rods from their respective levers on the gearbox.

(5) Remove the parking brake connection from its bracket and push it clear of the gearbox support.

Alternatively the engine can be removed along with the front suspension, as follows:

(1) Take off the distributor cap and remove the rotor.

(2) Disconnect the track-rods from their arms and disconnect the brake lines.

(3) Undo the four suspension unit-to-body nuts and disconnect the clutch.

(4) Raise the front of the car's body with a block and tackle or with some hefty person power and wheel the suspension, engine and gearbox away.

Morris Cowley, Oxford, Traveller, ½-ton commercials

As Austin A40, A50, A55 except that in:

(1) It is not essential to remove the battery.

(2) There is an oil pressure gauge connection to disconnect at the union.

(3) There may not be a petrol shut-off cock.

(4) The parking brake connection does not have to be removed. The engine, gearbox and front suspension *cannot* be removed as a unit.

ER*29*

ER*30*

'Farina' Cambridge-type cars

As MGB except that the radiator alone has to be removed without its shroud. The gearstick is removed by taking out the large circlip from around the gearstick retaining plate with a pair of long-nosed pliers. Retain the spring found beneath it.

MGA—pre-15GD engine (see engine number)

(1) Mark rear flangs of propeller shaft and disconnect from the axle. Drain gearbox and engine of oil.

(2) Mark the handbrake cable operating lever and splined shaft so that they can be correctly refitted. Remove nut and bolt and prise lever off shaft.

(3) Remove the reinforcement bracket from inside the propeller shaft tunnel—held on with nuts, bolts, spring washers. Remove seats and frames, floorboards and toe boards. Remove gear lever knob, draught excluder cover and propeller shaft and gearbox covers.

(4) Remove the six bolts holding the gearbox remote control assembly and pull off, manoeuvring the remote control lever from the selectors.

(5) Take the weight of the engine on the hoist and remove the engine mountings. Pull the engine and gearbox forwards, level, a little way. Then the rear of the gearbox can be tipped sharply down and the engine lifted out at an acute angle.

MGA—15GD engines on

As pre-15GD engines, except that the propeller shaft can now be disconnected from the gearbox flange, not from the rear axle. (See ER17.)

MGA Twin-Cam

As MGA, but with the following differences:

(1) Take out the screws holding the gearbox cover to the frame and remove the left-hand sides of the cross-brace plates to the cover. Remove the cover by springing out the rear end to allow the cross-brace plates to be pulled past the prop shaft.

(2) Remove header tank and thermostat housing cover.

(3) Take out the steering column.

(4) Take off the dipswitch mounting, the petrol pipe from the steering column seal plate, the throttle cable and the toeboard support plate.

(5) Remove the four nuts, bolts and spring washers that secure the mounting plates to the sides of the engine.

4 Engine stripdown

ES1

ES2

This section shows a stripdown on an MGA engine, which is typical of all sub-1800 three-main bearing engines, and a selection of shots from stripdowns on various MGB engines which applies also to Marina 1.8, 1800 car and, to a large extent, 1800 diesel engines. The following stripdown shows how far you can go in preparing your engine for the reconditioners prior to their machining and your reassembly.

ES1 This MGA engine was stripped at Moss Engineering Ltd of Ledbury, having first been mounted on one of their 'patent' engine stands. The engine had been removed as detailed in the 'Engine removal' section.

ES2 This engine stripdown, carried out at John Hills, was done on the floor on an opened-out sheet of card from a cardboard box. For the home restorer/repairer, this is the safest place to work with such a heavy lump of metal.

ES3 Both early and late types of oil filter removal are described under 'Maintenance'. This is the 'intermediate' type of filter shown here being removed complete with housing by undoing the angled bolt into the block from beneath.

ES4 Cylinder head removal and stripdown are described fully in 'Cylinder head overhaul'.

ES5 So that the head can be refaced, the head studs must be removed. You can use a special stud remover like this . . .

ES6 . . . or lock together a pair of nuts with two spanners as shown and spanner the stud off with a spanner on the bottom nut. Studs often stick badly on old engines. Use a self-grip wrench or even a pipe wrench on the *bottom* of the stud (to cut down on torque and risk of breakage) and use both spanner and wrench simultaneously. You may have to renew the stud if it is badly damaged.

ES7 On the side of the block, the external oil feed main pipe can be unscrewed from the back of the

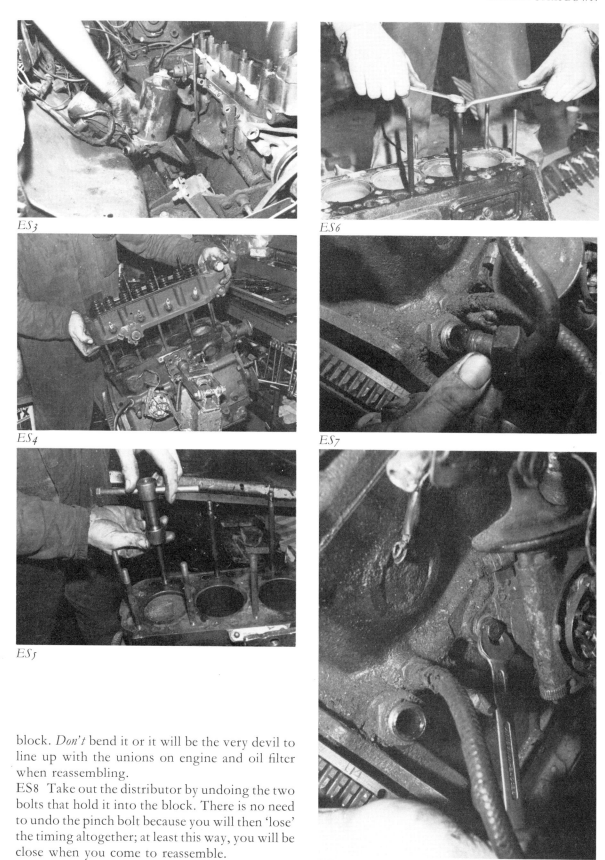

ES3

ES6

ES4

ES7

ES5

block. *Don't* bend it or it will be the very devil to line up with the unions on engine and oil filter when reassembling.

ES8 Take out the distributor by undoing the two bolts that hold it into the block. There is no need to undo the pinch bolt because you will then 'lose' the timing altogether; at least this way, you will be close when you come to reassemble.

ES8

ES9

ES10

ES11

ES12

ES9 The distributor just pulls out of the block, as shown.

ES10 The distributor housing is removed after unscrewing the countersunk screw shown, then prised out of the block.

ES11 Screw a $\frac{5}{16}$ in. UNF bolt or stud down into the hole where the distributor goes, into the end of the distributor driveshaft, then lift out the drive shaft, turning slightly to free the skew gear.

ES12 Undo the crankshaft pulley nut after knocking back the tab washer. One way of stopping the engine turning is to get someone to lock the flywheel with a flat bar held against the starter ring, through the starter motor mounting hole.

ES13 Another way is to take off the sump and lock the crank with a piece of wood. It may even be helpful to tap your tommy bar with a mallet—although you could easily ruin a ratchet wrench in this way.

ES14 After the nut (a starter dog, too, on some early engines) comes the tab washer, then the pulley itself.

ES15 To remove the fan, knock back the tab washers and undo all four bolts.

ES16 The fan and distance piece . . .

ES13

ES14

ES15

ES16

ES17

ES18

ES19

ES20

ES21

ES22

ES23

ES24

ES17 . . . then the water pump can be removed.

ES18 A ring of bolts holds the water pump to the block.

ES19 It may need tapping clear with a soft-faced mallet or the end of a hammer if you don't mind knocking the handle about.

ES20 The timing chain cover is held on with a ring of bolts, spring washers and special flat washers.

ES21 If, as in this case, the cover has been stuck on with 'gasket goo' you may have to use a screwdriver in an unconventional way to get it free.

ES22 Beneath the cover, an oil thrower sits on the crank nose. The concave dished part of this particular thrower faces outwards.

ES23 The timing chain tensioner, if scrap, can be removed without the following steps being carried out. If taut, the lock washer holding the adjuster plug should be tapped flat . . .

ES24 . . . the plug removed . . .

ES25 . . . and the adjuster turned clockwise while the tensioner is retracted inwards against the spring. This 'exploded' picture shows how it works.

ES26 This engine is the other way up! After tapping back the tab washers, the two retaining bolts can be unscrewed from the block . . .

ES27 . . . and the adjuster removed.

ES28 At Moss Engineering, the MGA engine was turned on the stand so that the timing chain faced upwards. The camshaft nut lock washer was tapped down flat . . .

ES29 . . . and the retaining nut removed.

ES30 The camshaft sprocket often jams. Here it is being tapped with an aluminium drift, but a soft-faced mallet would break the seal just as well.

ES31 The crankshaft sprocket just pushes on, although it's a tight fit. With a pair of screwdrivers, lever it off a little way, then transfer

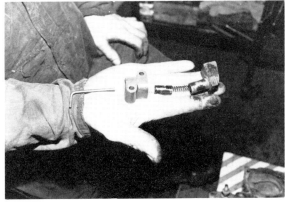

ES25

ES26

ES29

ES27

ES30

ES28

ES31

ES32

ES33

ES34

ES35

to the camshaft sprocket and then back to the crankshaft sprocket until . . .

ES32 . . . the two sprockets and chain come away. This is a later type cost-reduced (which means 'cheap') 1798 cc single chain. The older, stronger duplex chain, sprockets and tensioner can be used when reassembling, which is an especially useful mod if you are tuning.

ES33 Behind the camshaft sprocket is the locating plate, held on with three retaining bolts.

ES34 The front plate is held to the block with a series of bolts, but leave in place the nuts and bolts holding the engine mounting plates to the front plate.

ES35 Now undo the two bolts holding the engine mounting plate to the block . . .

ES36 . . . and remove the lot complete.

ES37 In this vicinity is the generator mounting bracket, which is held to the block with two bolts.

ES38 The flywheel is taken off by knocking back the six tab washers . . .

ES39 . . . and undoing the six nuts. To stop the flywheel from turning have a helper lock the flywheel starter ring with a screwdriver through the starter motor mounting hole.

ES40 Take off the tab washers to enable the flywheel to come off easily.

ES41 Remember that the flywheel is particularly heavy, so take care not to drop it: it often comes free quite suddenly.

ES42 Later 1800 engines' flywheels are held on with six bolts, the flywheel being located on two studs. It is wise to use a new one-piece tab-washer when refitting.

ES43 The end plate is often covered in an accumulation of dirt which obscures the bolt heads, many of which are recessed into the end plate.

ES44 The rear oil seal retainer, on later engines, is removed after knocking back the tab washer . . .

ES36

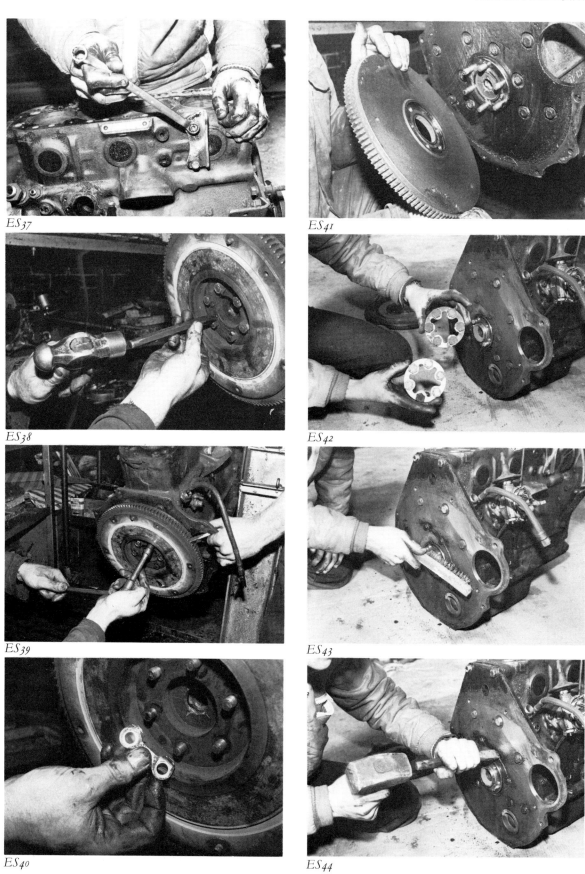

ES37

ES38

ES39

ES40

ES41

ES42

ES43

ES44

ES45

ES46

ES47

ES48

ES45 . . . unscrewing the four bolts . . .

ES46 . . . after which you can remove the retainer.

ES47 The end plate is removed after undoing the two sizes of endplate bolt. (This is a 1622 cc engine.)

ES48 The endplate will probably have to be tapped to free it. It is made of steel, so an ordinary hammer can be used.

ES49 The three-main bearing 1798, 1622, 1500 and 1200 endplate comes off as a simple plate.

ES50 Five-main bearing 1800 endplates have the integral oil seal mounted like so.

ES51 Both tappet covers are held on with a central bolt. The breather tube from the rear cover may be clipped to the block.

ES52 Pre-1800 valve tappets have a tapered top, so the tappet can often be lifted out with a pair of long-nosed pliers.

ES53 Later types have a thimble-type tappet and it can be removed—like a thimble. In either case, if the tappet won't come out easily at this stage don't worry. It is best to get most of them out now, but the rest can come out later.

ES54 If you haven't already removed the sump, undo the ring of bolts, spring washers and special washers around the sump.

ES55 If the sump sticks, tap it around the sides with a soft-faced mallet.

ES56 When this fails, use the screwdriver pushed into the gap as a last resort. There should be no need to use the sort of gasket cement used here to prevent leaks!

ES57 Having freed the sump, it just lifts off.

ES58 If the gasket was glued down it will have been split when the sump was removed, so clean the waste gasket from the block and sump.

ES59 Three nuts hold the oil pump down . . .

ES60 . . . after which it lifts off its three long studs.

ES49

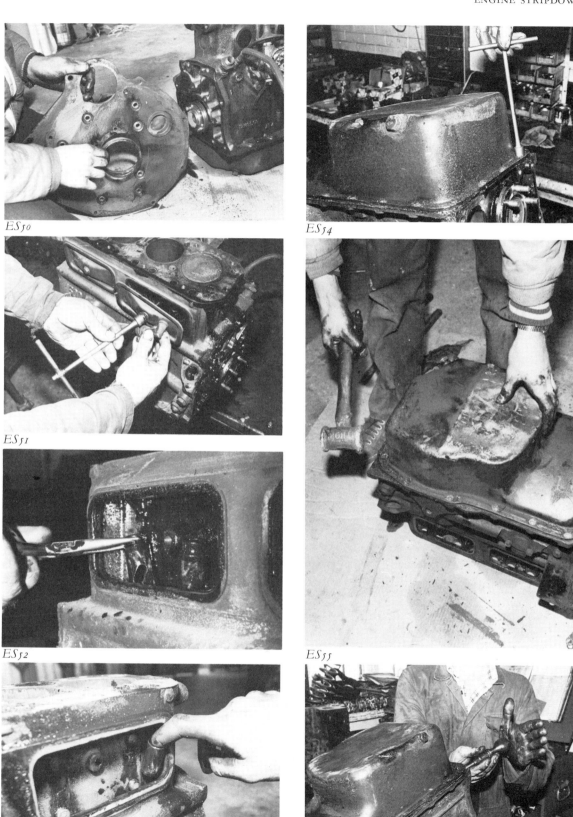

ES50

ES51

ES52

ES53

ES54

ES55

ES56

ES57

ES58

ES59

ES60

ES61

ES62

ES63

ES61 The pump drive can be lifted up and out of the block with a pair of long-nosed pliers used with the same sort of twisting lift as was used to remove the distributor drive.

ES62 Now, with the block upside down so that any remaining tappets drop out of the way and with none of the camshaft-driven components connected up, the camshaft can be withdrawn.

ES63 No, it's not a mystery engine component being withdrawn, it's a rod pushing the 'stuck' tappets out through the top of the block!

ES64 Before disconnecting any of the crankshaft bolts, put a light chisel mark on each of the big-end bearing caps to indicate, from the front, 1,2,3,4. Then knock the big-end tab washers back.

ES65 Five-main bearings are the same, but there are, naturally enough, more main bearings. Undo one big-end bearing cap at a time . . .

ES66 . . . and lift the cap away. If it sticks because of the surface tension of the oil, tap the cap lightly to release it whilst lifting it.

ES67 The pistons should just push out through the tops of the bores, but because of the wear in the bores leaving an unworn ridge around the top, they undoubtedly won't. Tap them sharply from beneath with a hammer handle then, once the

ES66

ES64

ES67

ES65

ES68

ES69

ES70

ES71

ES72

piston rings are free, pull them out.

ES68 As soon as each piston is removed, fit its cap back in place the right way round in order to eliminate the risk of confusion.

ES69 Next, undo the main bearing nuts.

ES70 A good way of removing the main bearings, which are a very tight fit into the block, is to make up a slide hammer as shown with a thread brazed to the end that will fit into the thread in each main bearing cap.

ES71 You may just get away with tapping with a soft-faced mallet. But it's not very likely to work. You could make a special tool which consists of a stout 'bridge' over the bearing cap, a bolt passing through a clearance hole in the top of the 'bridge' and into the thread in the cap and a nut run down the bolt to bear downwards on the 'bridge', thus pulling the bearing cap out.

ES72 The centre main has a semicircular thrust washer in a recess on each side with another matching pair in the block. Retrieve them all: they will undoubtedly need replacing.

ES73 The crank can now be lifted right out of the block.

ES74 Due to the surface tension of the oil, the only way to remove the bearing shell is to slide it out, in the direction of the locating lug.

ES75 A worn engine will have shells which are worn through to the copper base beneath the white metal bearing. Look for reddish colour showing clearly through.

ES76 Rather less usual is this type of wear, where water has made a complex maze of wear lines in the surface of the shell. It pays to keep the stuff out of the sump!

ES77 Disconnect the piston from the con-rod by undoing and removing the clamp bolt up inside the piston.

ES78 The three parts go together in this order, the clamp bolt going through the groove in the gudgeon pin. (The washer placed next to the gudgeon pin in this photograph is *not* part of the assembly.)

ES79 With the clamp bolt undone, the pin can be driven out over an open vice as shown. *Don't* grip the piston or con-rod in the bare jaws of the vice.

ES80 A specialist can measure the crank journals for wear using a micrometer, taking measurements from several different angles. (It is unlikely that the home enthusiast will have the correct size of micrometer.)

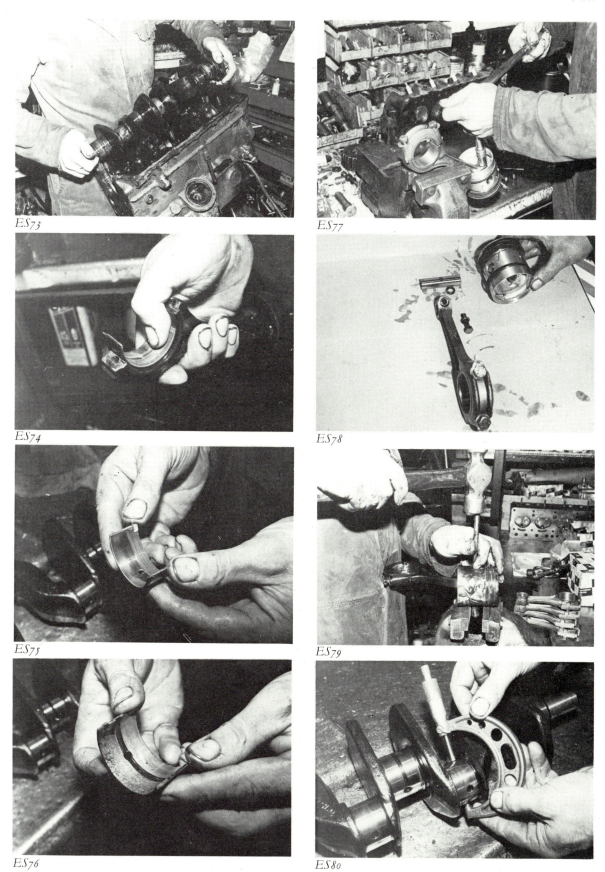

ES73

ES77

ES74

ES78

ES75

ES79

ES76

ES80

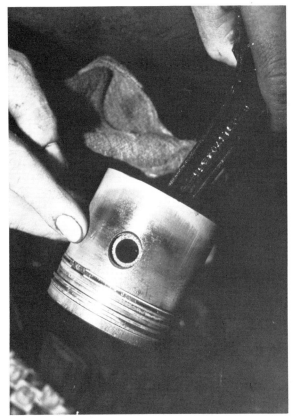

ES81

ES82

ES83

ES81 Dark marks on the side of the piston indicate blow-by caused by worn rings and bore giving a poor seal.

ES82 Examine the very tips of the cams for any sign of damage. A reprofiled cam can be used, but its life is rarely as great as that of a new cam.

ES83 The cam followers, or tappets, are also prone to wear: look for pitting on the surface of the cam.

ES84 With the block stripped, chisel into each of the core plugs.

ES85 When you lever the old one out, you could be amazed at the amount of rubbish beneath. A good engineering firm like Moss Engineering will clean out and blow out all the water passageways to ensure cooling performance up to the maker's intentions.

ES86 Engines fitted with a mechanical tachometer (rev. counter) drive: undo the two nuts that hold it in place and lift it away.

ES87 A large domed nut on the left-rear of the block contains the oil pressure valve spring and assembly.

ES88 The valve itself will probably stay put. This is the Moss Engineering 'special tool' for removal: the end of a valve-lapping tool.

ES89 At the top is a new 'bottom-end' gasket set (or 'conversion' set) and a 'decoke' set. Beneath are (left) an oil pump, flywheel tab washer and bolts, timing chain tensioner and (right) tappets, rocker shaft and rockers, valve springs and valves. You will also need main and big-end bearing shells, pistons and rings and gudgeon pins, and possibly an oil pressure release valve if the old one is damaged and not seating properly. Other areas to check with the engine stripdown, shown here in no particular order, are:

ES90 Oil pump: Undo the bolts that hold the casing together.

ES84

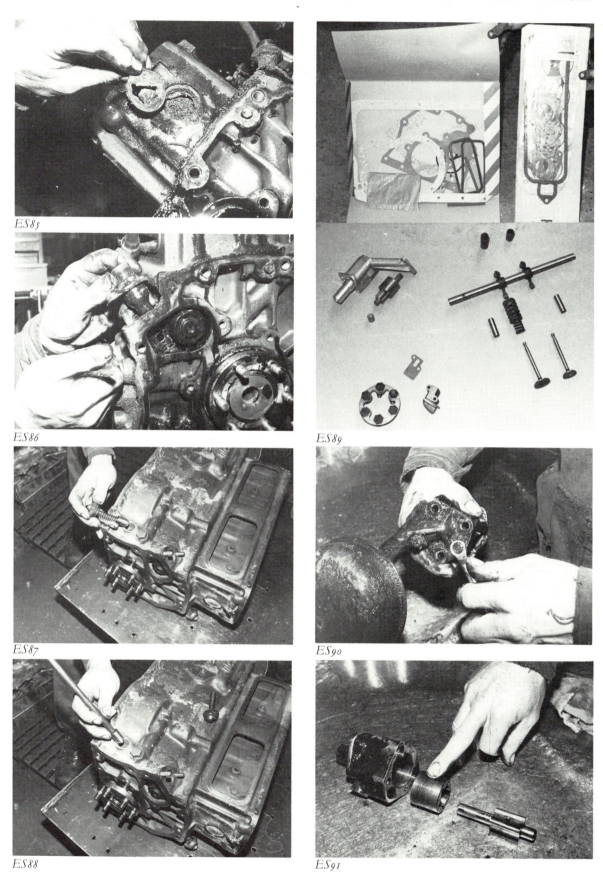

ES85

ES86

ES87

ES88

ES89

ES90

ES91

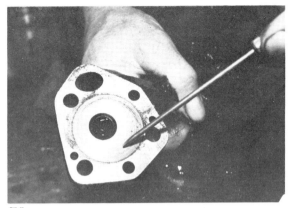

ES92

ES93

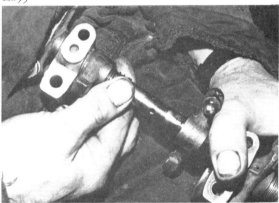

ES94

ES95

ES91 Check the outer rotor both inside for signs of scoring and examine the inner rotor housing too. Also look at the peg on the end of the drive shaft where it locates into the slot on the inner rotor shaft. Severe wear can sometimes take place there.

ES92 Scoring on the end plate in particular will cause a loss in oil pressure. if you are rebuilding an engine, you should always fit a new oil pump as a matter of course.

ES93 The rocker shaft can wear quite badly after a very high mileage. Check bushes and shaft by taking hold of a rocker and attempting to rock it at 90 degrees from its normal action, i.e. in line with the shaft itself.

ES94 Also push the rockers down the shaft against the springs and examine the shaft for wear. Any wear present will mean that a new shaft is necessary.

ES95 Look at the ends of the pushrods and at the ends of the rockers where they fit into the other ends of the pushrods to check for pitting or other signs of wear.

ES96 The camshaft bearings are often stained but not often worn. New bushes will have to be pressed in only if the bearings are scored.

ES97 Check the timing chain for wear by holding one end and comparing it with a straight edge. This is the amount of deflection you get with a new chain.

ES98 Bore wear can be checked visually by looking and feeling with your finger nail for the presence of a wear ridge in the top of the bore.

ES99 Bore ovality and precise measurements can only be taken with an internal micrometer or a dial gauge such as this one, neither of which is likely to be found outside a specialist engineering workshop. The workshop responsible for machining your engine will undoubtedly own such equipment.

ES96

ES97

ES98

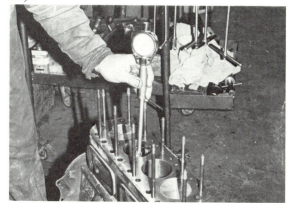

ES99

5 Engine reassembly

EA1

EA2

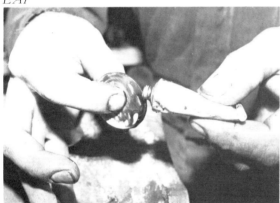

EA3

As you can see from the previous section, dismantling an old engine is not necessarily as simple as the official manual would have you believe. Reassembling it after the major components have been machined is a job with just as many 'tricks of the trade' involved, and there is undoubtedly a good deal more skill required, too. Don at Moss Engineering of Ledbury very kindly divulged *most* of the trade secrets practised by that excellent firm and also showed the sorts of hidden improvements that a restorer can incorporate into his or her engine rebuild. However, it may be best to use this book alongside a workshop manual when reassembling the engine.

EA1 This is a block being refaced at Moss Engineering. Naturally, the cylinder head is also faced to ensure a perfect seat, the crank is reground and the valve seats recut or replaced if necessary. Otherwise, parts such as pistons, rings, oil pump and shells are replaced with new items. Replacement of valves and camshaft depends on the amount of wear that has taken place, the B-series camshaft in particular often lasting more than one rebuild. Blow the rebored block out with an air line before fitting it up.

EA2 New core plugs can replace the old ones after the seats have been thoroughly cleaned off. Use a good-quality sealing compound all around the edge and bottom surface of the new core plug.

EA3 Place the plug convex side up into its seat in the block . . .

EA4 . . . and hammer or drift the plug with three or four good hammer blows to concave and spread the plug, seating it tight.

EA5 Blow through all the crank oilways with an airline to ensure that there is no swarf trapped in there.

EA6 Check that the size stamped on the new shells tallies with the amount you have had ground off the crank. (Incidentally, make *certain* that the crank fillets have been properly radiused, otherwise crank strength will be severely diminished—not all reconditioners seem to appreciate this.

EA7 Before putting the new main bearing shells in place check that the shell seatings in the block and caps have not got a build-up of carbon on their outer edges. If necessary, scrape any carbon that may be present away or the shell will be lifted slightly out of place, causing uneven wear and crank binding.

EA8 Slip the shells into place in the block and squirt engine oil on to the shell, wiping it all round the shell with the back of your index finger.

EA9 Carefully put the crank in place then fit the caps with shells in place, also fully oiled.

EA10 Insert the thrust washers, with the white-metal bearing surface facing outwards.

EA11 Slide the bottom ones around until they sit with their two ends lying horizontally.

EA12 Place the two thrust washers one on each side of the centre cap and fit it into place.

EA13 Now tap the nose of the crank with a soft-faced hammer or drift, so that it is fully back, and measure the gap between the thrust face and the

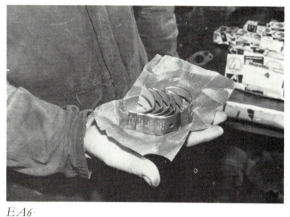

EA6

EA7

EA4

EA8

EA5

EA9

EA10

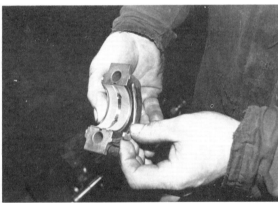

EA11

EA12

EA13

bearing surface on the inside of the crank web. Check that the gap (indicated by the largest feeler gauge that can be slipped in) corresponds to the manufacturer's tolerances. If not, go back to the reconditioners and complain that either the regrind is out or the thrust washers supplied are incorrect.

EA14 You can tell if the regrind is too tight, because the crank won't turn after the bearings have been tightened. Too loose, and you could have even more problems when you come to use the engine. Slip a piece of thin plastic around 3 or 4 thou thick between one of the journals and the shell.

EA15 Now tighten the main bearings with a torque wrench to the specified figure.

EA16 When you try to turn the crank it should be too tight to turn with the strip of plastic in place but free to turn without it. Additionally, the plastic should be spread out in appearance when it is removed. If the crank is tight *without* the plastic in place, check scrupulously that there is no carbon build-up beneath the shells nor a speck of dirt there, that the bearing caps are the right ones (especially important with numbers two and four on the five-main bearing engines) and that they are the right way round. The same is true when checking the big-end bearings using the same technique. *Each bearing cap is individually machined to fit only in one place—they are not interchangeable or reversible.*

If the crank still turns even with the plastic strip in place, then too much has been taken off the crank or—less likely—there is a fault with the shell sizes.

EA17 Put a large dab of grease on to the oil pump drive shaft to hold it into the pump body so that it does not drop down while the pump is being lowered into place.

EA18 Fill the pump with oil before bolting it into place.

EA19 Place the front plate gasket in place, locate the cork seal on top of the front main bearing . . .

EA20 . . . then bolt the front plate in place holding the cork seal down until it is gripped by the front plate. It is extremely difficult to fit the cork seal after the front plate has been bolted up.

EA21 After liberally oiling the camshaft bearings, fit the camshaft from the front of the engine and bolt it into place as a reverse of the dismantling procedure. Take care not to damage the relatively soft camshaft bearings with the cam lobes. Rotate it slightly to ensure that it has meshed with the oil pump drive.

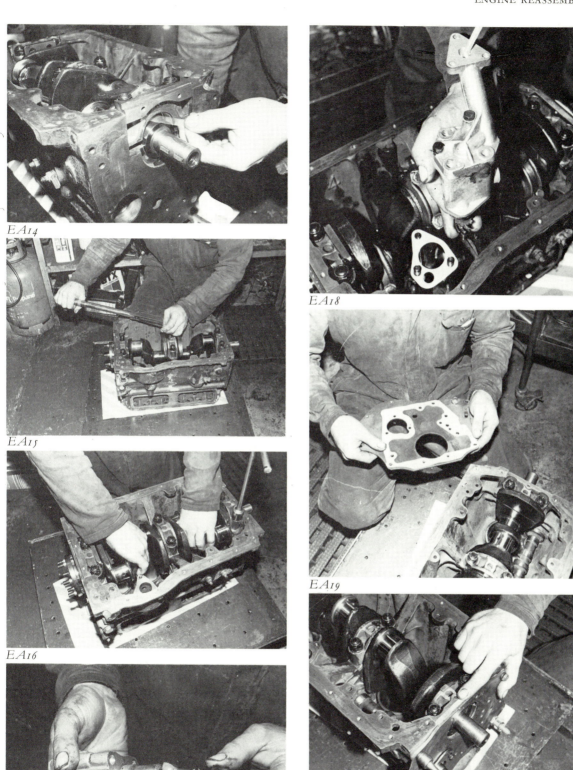

EA14

EA15

EA16

EA17

EA18

EA19

EA20

EA21

EA22

EA23

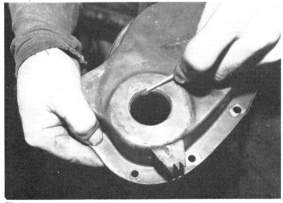

EA24

EA22 First fit the two timing gearwheels without the chain, place the edge of steel rule across them both and measure any discrepancy between the levels of the two gearwheels using feeler gauges. Add or take away packing shims from beneath the crank nose until the two line up exactly. Make sure that the woodruff keys (steel guide pegs) are in place on both crank and camshaft noses and turn them until the crankshaft woodruff key is at the 12 o'clock position and the camshaft key is at 2 o'clock, both when viewed from the front with the engine upright. Now place the timing gears into the timing chain in such a position that the dimple on each wheel lines up with the other and the gearwheel centres, as shown. The two gearwheels should now slide straight on, lining up correctly with the woodruff keys, although it may be necessary to turn the camshaft a touch to get them to line up. Fit the retaining nut and tab washer.

EA23 The early type of tensioner is fitted by screwing the tensioner inwards as shown under 'Engine stripdown' and then freeing the tensioner again, but the later type is simply compressed in the hand before being fitted.

EA24 The early type of timing chain cover incorporates a felt oil seal which has to be dug out and painstakingly replaced if it is to be retained.

EA25 A better solution is to fit the front cover from a later scrapyard engine with the far more efficient rubber type of oil seal.

EA26 The later type of front cover, shown left, has to be used with the correct type of crank nose oil thrower. The early type, fitted concave side outwards, is shown alongside.

EA27 The later type of oil thrower is fitted with the side marked 'Front' facing outwards.

EA28 Drift the new oil seal *evenly* into place using a soft drift such as a piece of wood. Oil it thoroughly as well as the timing chain and tensioner before refitting the front cover.

EA29 Wash the con-rods in paraffin or cleaning fluid and blow out the oilways with an air line before use.

EA30 The gudgeon pin should be a tight sliding fit into the piston. Try to match new pistons with new gudgeon pins so that the best fit is obtained. However, if you can't avoid having a tight gudgeon pin, heat the piston in hot water so that the piston expands, allowing the pin to slide in more easily. Line up the indentation on the front of the gudgeon pin *exactly* with the line of the clamp bolt, otherwise the clamp bolt threads can be damaged.

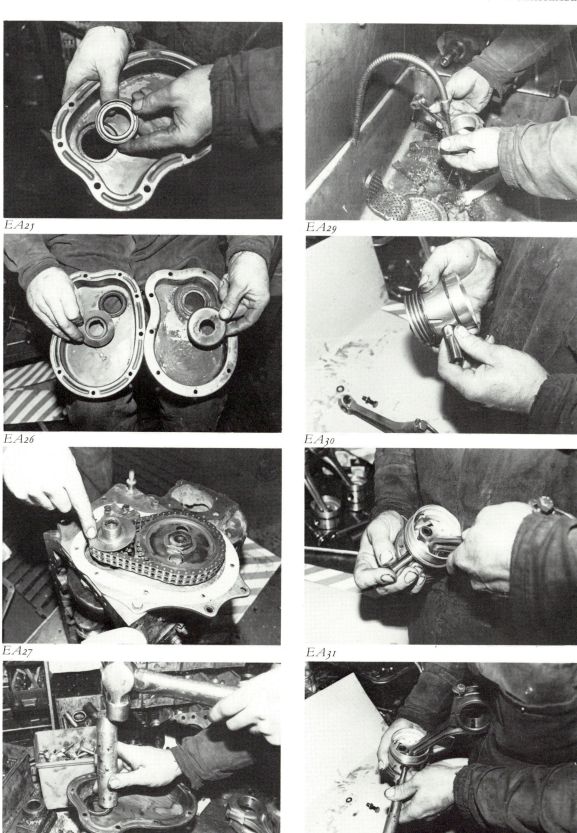

EA25

EA26

EA27

EA28

EA29

EA30

EA31

EA32

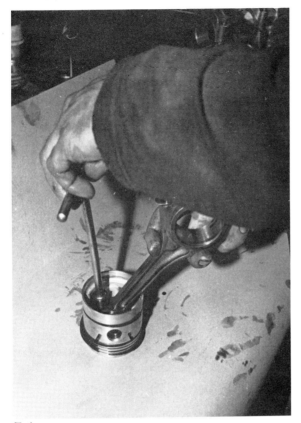

EA33

EA34

EA35

NB. In the unlikely event that you will reuse pistons, fit the same pistons, gudgeon pins and con-rods as an assembly: mixing worn parts is not at all a good idea!

EA31 Now hold the con-rod in the piston and slide the gudgeon pin right in.

EA32 Look down the clamp bolt hole and tap the gudgeon pin until it lines up exactly, using a suitable drift.

EA33 Tighten up the clamp bolt, making the final turn with the torque wrench to the recommended figure. If necessary, hold the con-rod in the vice after protecting the jaws with a couple of strips of wood. There is no need to tighten the vice up a great deal.

EA34 Thoroughly clean out the bores with a fresh rag.

EA35 Ensure that the con-rod offsets are correctly positioned: these are numbers three and four piston assemblies.

EA36 Lubricate the big-end shells . . .

EA37 . . . and the piston rings. Don't be mean with the oil at this stage!

EA38 Place the con-rod into the bore, clamp the oil control ring with a piston ring clamp and tap the bottom of the piston into the bore. Then clamp the top rings and do the same until the piston is fully home. Don't push the rings out of the bottom of the bore because they can then be extremely difficult to clamp and return up the bore.

EA39 After fitting, torqueing-up and testing the fit of the big-end bearings just as you did for the mains, turn the tab washers over with a wrench. Provided that the tabs are sound, once-used tab washers are even better than new ones because they have already fully compressed under the big-end bolts and so cannot become microscopically loose in future.

EA40 Place the front main cork oil seal in place . . .

EA41 . . . then the sump gasket (check that it's the right one because late types are sometimes supplied in error, it seems) . . .

EA42 . . . and bolt the sump down, tightening from the centre outwards and not forgetting the special washers (not fitted to later engines).

EA43 Lubricate the oil pressure release valve before refitting, then bolt in the whole assembly.

EA44 If you can have the cylinder head sandblasted or bead blasted, so much the better. Do blow it out thoroughly with an air line before fitting up so that you get rid of any abrasive particles.

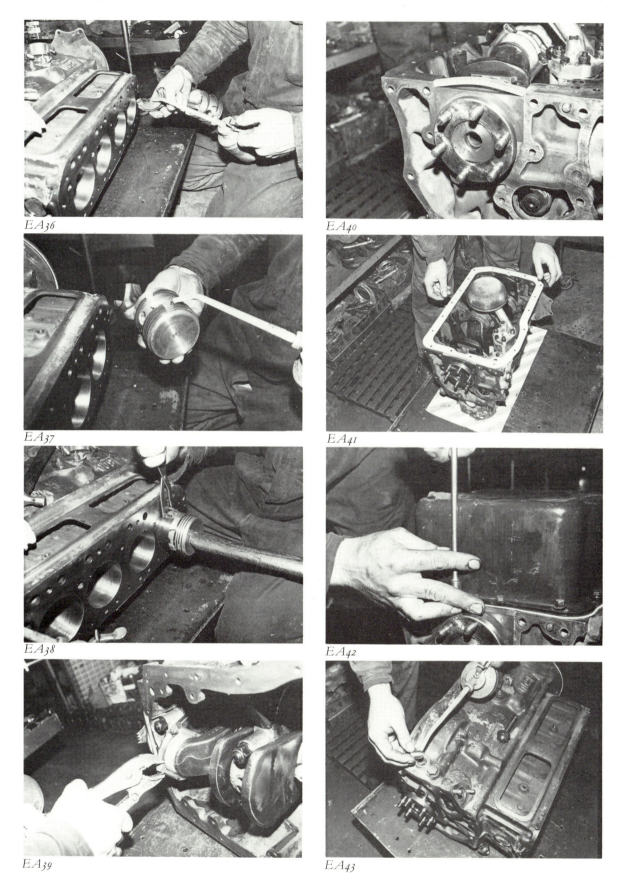

EA36

EA37

EA38

EA39

EA40

EA41

EA42

EA43

EA44

EA45

EA46

EA47

EA45 In any case, clean out the combustion chambers really well to get rid of any carbon and discourage the build-up of new deposits.

EA46 Fit the valve spring seat over the stem of the valve, then the valve seal (illustrated: the later type of seal).

EA47 The early type of valve seal is fitted preferably after the valve springs are compressed, but certainly before the cotters go on. Both types of seal fit into the bottom of the recess for the cotters.

EA48 The circlips which fit into the grooves in the cotters will probably have opened up a little with age. Pinch them closer together then clip them to the valve cotters as shown.

EA49 Finally, give each valve a clout with a soft drift just to make sure that everything is seated properly and that nothing is sticking.

EA50 Replace the cam followers, lubricating the cams and the tops of the cam followers. Refit the tappet covers with new gaskets.

EA51 After refitting the head studs (fit all the short ones first so that the long ones don't get in the way when tightening the short ones down) and placing a new head gasket in position the correct way up as marked, refit the cylinder head. Incidentally, no gasket cement or oil should be applied to the face of the cylinder head gasket.

EA52 Replace the pushrods and oil them.

EA53 Replace the rocker gear, carefully seating each rocker into its pushrod before tightening it down. Don't forget to fit the important locating plate on top of the rear rocker pedestal.

EA54 Pull down the four rocker pedestal nuts but without tightening them up. Then torque the head down. First, tighten each head nut up slightly in the order shown in 'Engine stripdown' (NB. *Not* the reverse order). Next, torque each one down to 5 lb below its fully tightened figure, then go round them all tightening down to the correct figure.

EA55 Lubricate all the rocker gear thoroughly before refitting the cover.

EA56 This top backplate gasket is only used with later, 1798 cc engines with the full-height backplate.

EA57 Refit the main oil pipe but don't tighten any of the connections or the filter itself until all are in place.

EA58 Check that No. 1 cylinder is at Top Dead Centre *and* on the firing stroke by either: (1) checking that both No. 1 cylinder valves are closed.

EA48

EA52

EA49

EA53

EA50

EA54

EA51

EA55

EA56

EA57

EA58

EA59

(2) Also, the valves on No. 4 will be 'rocking'—inlet valve just opening, exhaust just closing.

(3) The marks '1/4' on the flywheel are at TDC or the dimple on the crankshaft pulley is in line with the end or largest pointer (*see* 'Maintenance').

(4) The dots on the timing chain gears are lined up. Insert a $\frac{5}{16}$ in. bolt into the distributor drive and reinsert the drive so that the slot is in the position shown with the slightly larger segment to the left.

EA59 It would seem that modern gasket sets do not include a gasket for the mechanical (early) type of tachometer drive. Make your own from gasket paper by placing the paper over the mounting studs and marking the stud positions carefully with a hammer.

EA60 Enlarge the holes with a ball-ended drift and the paper held over a nut or tube held in the vice.

EA61 Slip the paper over the studs and, hammering lightly with the ball end of a ball-pein hammer, cut through the outline of the hole in the block. Then place the paper over the drive fitting itself, draw around the outline of the flange with a Biro and cut around the outline of the gasket with scissors.

EA60

EA61

6 Engine tuning

The B-series engine is not, by its nature, a high-performance engine at all. It is heavy, it has a long stroke and the siamesed ports in particular place limitations upon it. However, most people interested in tuning their B-series engine would not be too worried about ultimate performance because if they *were* interested in snarling acceleration and a car that 'wheelies' away from the traffic lights, they would not be driving, say, an Austin A55 in the first place, at least not one without a drag strip racer's interior hidden beneath the skin! Basically, this chapter will look at ways of making the B-series engine more efficient and perhaps a little faster with the aid of bolt-on goodies, taking the advice of John Hewitt of The MG Shop, Manchester, who knows a thing or two about tuning and racing MGBs, having done extremely well on the track with his Standard-Plus MGB, which is basically a road-going car with 'blueprinted' engine—a standard unit that has been meticulously assembled with every component hand-shaped to fit its fellows to give excellent gas flow and efficiency. This type of work—second nature to John with his background of Formula One racing team management—is actually a great deal more expensive to have carried out than the options shown here.

Before going into engine tuning at all, two more points must be made. The first is that extra performance can often be obtained just by a change of head and manifold or even a complete engine, while the second point is that the safety and stability of the car's chassis, structure and tyres must be considered before any engine mods are even contemplated. Modifications to the chassis (by which is meant suspension, steering and brake assemblies) are beyond the scope of this book, but books on the subject, particularly with relevance to the MGB, are available. Needless to say, the structure of the car should be very sound before any modifications are carried out and the brakes should work as well as they are able. If you consider uprating the performance of your car by changing it to the higher specification of another model, find out what alterations, if any, were made to the donor car when compared with your own. An example is the Wolseley 1500, which can easily be fitted with the head, manifold and carburettor mods from a Riley 1.5, but the faster car's brakes should also be fitted to match the extra performance. There were really too many production modifications for anyone to be able to say which heads and manifolds will work successfully on which cars, but the choice of an alternative for tuning purposes is a matter of applied common sense and some detective work. Use the specifications given in this book to check things like valve sizes, combustion chamber sizes where given and compression ratios (though remember that if you fit a head with a cr of, say, 8:1, but to a smaller engine, its combustion chamber may be larger than that of the head it replaces and so the cr could actually end up lower). Fitting twin carburettors from, say, an MG Magnette Mk IV to an Austin Cambridge will allow the Cambridge to 'breathe' more efficiently and won't necessarily worsen fuel consumption if the carbs are set up accurately. Apart from fitting twin carbs or a better head from the appropriate model, the next step up is to fit a larger complete engine. It has been known for people to fit an MGB engine into a Cambridge, but unless the car is sound to a degree now rare and unless considerable and expensive modifications are carried out to the chassis, the conversion could be unsafe. *De*-tuning the engine by fitting a standard Austin/Morris 1800 or Marina cylinder head to it would help, but it is

The K & N filters utilise part of the existing MGB air filter base plate and bolt-on in the normal way. The filtering principle is totally different, however: the 'holes' in the filter are much larger than those in a paper filter but they don't clog up, nor do they let dirt through. An electrostatic charge in the filter makes dust and dirt build up on the outside of the filter rather than in its pores. The suppliers say the filters only need cleaning every 100,000 miles, after which they are ready for use once again. They could conceivably be the longest-lasting component on a car!

The exhaust system placed in front of John Hewitt's 'B is the sort that would easily extract more power again from any B-series engine. It has a long centre-branch manifold and no centre box. It may be possible to fit the manifold to other B-series engined cars (it all depends upon the structure of the engine bay and floorpan) but deletion of the centre 'box is possible on all, with the added advantage for MGA and MGB owners that the exhaust system is less likely to 'ground' and become damaged

This is the exhaust manifold in place. It is essential that the thickness of the mounting flanges exactly matches those of the inlet manifold or the washers which tighten both manifolds on the centre four studs will not pull down evenly leading to air leaks into or exhaust leaks out of the engine

Alongside the Dell'Orto is a pair of standard carbs with pancake air filters. These actually lose you a few brake horsepower compared with the standard air filters

vitally important not to push an old car beyond its safety limits.

Obviously, neither the 1800 nor Princess B-series can be fitted to cars with their engines in the north-south direction, but the MGB three-main bearing engine will fit the gearboxes of earlier cars, including the MGA, although it may be necessary to fit the front plate and engine mountings from the engine being replaced. When the MGB engine went to five-main bearings, the end diameter of the gearbox spigot shaft was enlarged to fit a larger bush in the end of the crank and the number and size of the splines on the shaft and in the clutch were also altered. If a five-main bearing engine from an MGB or from a Marina 1.8 is to be fitted to an earlier car, it will be necessary to fit the backplate and clutch centre-plate of the earlier engine on to the flywheel and clutch cover of the five-main bearing engine (and if the five-main bearing engine has a pre-engaged starter, fitted from October 1967, it will be necessary to fit the early starter, too) and it will also be necessary to have a special bush made to fit inside the end of the crank. The early spigot shaft, which enters the end of the crank, has to fit in a running clearance inside the phosphor bronze bush and the outside of the bush has to push into the end of the crank. Any engineering works should be well capable of producing such a bush. So, in general, the component-swap approach to 'tuning' (although it's not really tuning at all, of course) is based around fitting a better cylinder head and carburettors, preferably from the same engine size (i.e. a ZB Magnette, Riley 1.5 or MGA 1500 cylinder head to a 1500 engine; a Mk IV Magnette, 'Farina' Riley, or an MGA 1600 Mk II head to a 1622 cc engine or an 1800S or MGB head to an 1800 engine) or by going up a whole engine size, but remembering the whole time not to stretch the car's performance beyond the competence and reliability of its chassis components. Another way of extracting more power, and one that can be rather less troublesome, is by making what you have already got in the car go faster.

The John Hewitt approach to tuning is, in its early stages at least, surprisingly simple and relatively inexpensive to carry out. His concern is mainly with the MGB engine, but the same advice would apply also to the MGA unit. Cars fitted with non-MG (or Riley or 1800S) cylinder heads could be fitted with the appropriate MG, Riley or 'S' head and carburettor and then tuned in the following ways, but as mentioned towards the start of this chapter, any saloon would have to be made structurally strong enough and sufficiently well sorted in the brakes and suspension areas to make the engine-tuning exercise safe to carry out.

Before fitting any tuning 'goodies', put your car through a simple acceleration test. On a really quiet, safe and level stretch of road, take some accurate acceleration figures with a stop-watch. Then 'tune' the engine meticulously, setting the ignition and carburettor(s) as shown in the Maintenance chapter. (Don't forget to change the condenser, distributor cap and plug leads, too, if they look at all ratty.) Take your acceleration figures again—you could be pleasantly surprised.

Stage One

The first step as suggested by John Hewitt is to throw away the Coopers type of air filter (or oil bath type on earlier models) and fit a K&N high-flow type of air filter. Any air filter tends to reduce the efficiency of the engine by reducing the amount of air that can readily be drawn through it. However, to run an engine without an air filter at all can reduce its life by a frightening amount, which is OK for short-lived racing engines but too expensive to contemplate where the engine is to be used for everyday use. Fitting pancake air filters is actually a retrograde step, according to John Hewitt, because they can actually *lose* you around 3 bhp from an MGB engine! K&N filters seem to be the best compromise because they give an increase in maximum bhp of 4 to 5 bhp (to the MGB engine), they only require cleaning—not changing—every 100,000 miles and they still provide a source of all-important clean air to the engine. The increase in bhp at the rear wheels (and remember that the MGB only develops 60-odd bhp at the wheels: the 95 bhp factory figure is given at the flywheel) is a very noticeable difference and is in the same sort of order as fitting a 45 DCOE Weber carburettor to an otherwise standard engine.

Having got the air *in* to the engine more easily, it makes sense to get it out again more easily as well. John Hewitt recommends fitting an exhaust system without a centre box, or cheaper still, trip down to your friendly local exhaust centre and ask them to substitute a piece of plain pipe for the centre of your existing system if it is basically sound. Now that the air is flowing more freely through the engine, you may gain power by fitting richer needles to the carburettors. Standard MGB needles are No. 5, while No. 6 needles are

On 'rubber bumper' MGBs, the engine mountings are prone to breakage and the rubbers to becoming soft. If the latter happens, the Dell'Orto trumpet will foul the flitch plate (inner wing)

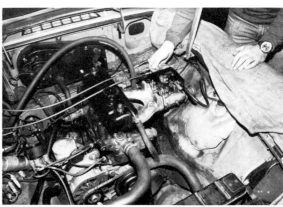

In place, the carburettor looks most businesslike. It's certainly easier to get on and off than a pair of SUs! It really ought to be set up on a rolling road to be certain that it is turned properly and it would be sensible to fabricate a support bracket running from under the body of the carburettor back to the engine to take account of the extra overhang

The old 'Special Tuning' booklet recommended fitting these twin $1\frac{3}{4}$ in. SUs at Stage One, but they are not as easy to get hold of as they used to be nor are the correct parts to go with them and in any case, they do not give a very large increase in power

Going to the other extreme, if you have carried out an enormous amount of work to the head, the cam and the engine capacity, you may want to go as far as to fit 2 in. SUs which can often be cannibalised from a scrapyard Jaguar. All the needle swaps should be available, but manifolding would be, er, interesting!

the next richest. On the other hand, MGBs are often on the rich side to start off with, so you need to check the system over very carefully with a Gunson Colortune to find out whether you ought to go to richer needles or not. (Later cars with HIF carburettors often have a 'lean' setting and may well benefit from a richer needle.) In fact you must set the engine up carefully after fitting these simple modifications because the extra ease with which the air can pass through your engine will have altered the fuel–air ratio on the carburettor settings that you were using before. As a rule of thumb, John Hewitt points out that the HS4 and earlier type of carburettor, with hexagonal nut adjustment on the jet, would probably need to be richened (screwed anticlockwise) by one or two flats of the adjuster nut. (Later HIF4 carburettors are adjusted with a screwdriver (*see* Maintenance section).) Incidentally, even at this stage—or even before it!—copper cored spark plugs can be recommended, many racing drivers swearing by NGK plugs BP6ES (for MGB) or the rather expensive platinum-tipped plugs BP6EV. The only way of being certain that more power has been obtained and that all is well is to run the car on a dynamometer.

Stage Two

This is the stage where you are not just concerned with making what you have got work better, but you are actually changing one or two simple bolt-on components. The John Hewitt approach is to fit a side-draught Dell'Orto carburettor (and appropriate inlet manifold) which works on a twin-choke basis: there's the first choke for more economical driving and then, when you put your foot down, the second choke comes in, giving a surge in performance (and petrol consumption!) which is so dramatic that it's almost like an instantaneous down-shift on an automatic. Once again, the improvement in 'input' needs to be matched by 'output', and the best way is to fit a Janspeed 'extractor' exhaust manifold with long centre branch. This is a particularly useful piece of tuning equipment in view of the B-series' siamesed centre exhaust ports in the head because the extra-long centre helps to get the extra gases away more quickly. As with Stage One, a one-box exhaust system is recommended as a way of reducing back pressure to the engine.

An alternative to the use of a Dell'Orto is to fit a pair of $1\frac{3}{4}$ in. SU carburettors with KP needles, blue spring and 0.100 in. jets. This was the traditional way of uprating the B-series engine, but these carburettors and their manifolds are not as easy to get hold of as they were and neither are the correct needles, jets and springs. If you do come across some, they give a more economical alternative to the Dell'Orto, but they certainly do not give as big an improvement in power, nor do they give the extra throttle 'snap' a 48 Dell'Orto set-up will give you. On the other hand neither Dell'Orto nor Weber carburettors can be set up satisfactorily at home as an SU can.

Stage Three

You can now no longer get away with bolting off-bolting on some external bits, but instead you need to start getting more deeply into the engine. And what's more, the changes made from now on will give extra performance but at the expense of low-range tractability. The Newman 271 cam-shaft is recommended as 'a reasonable road cam' (camshafts designed purely with high-speed power in mind make an engine highly inflexible and *very* difficult and frustrating to drive in town traffic) and John also recommends fitting a 'competition'-type distributor at this stage to make the most from the extra power given by the Dell'Orto plus Newman camshaft. The chart below shows how the competition distributor gives more advance at speeds over 2200 rpm but less at lower speeds. Incidentally, some competition distributors have a vacuum advance unit and others do not. If you fit one without vacuum advance, remember to blank off the inlet on the manifold so that no unwanted air is drawn in.

Some people may be surprised that the B-series cylinder head has not yet been the subject of attention. After all, when tuning Minis, the cylinder head is one of the first areas to be modified or replaced. The truth is that the B-series head is pretty efficient to start off with, so you can gain most by making changes in the areas already mentioned. Head swaps are the next thing to go for, however. As far as 1798 cc engines are concerned, the best heads with the biggest inlet valves are those fitted to engines whose engine number begins with 18V and the Austin and Morris 1800S engines (although the latter has a slightly lower compression ratio than the MGB). As far as pre-1800 engines are concerned, simply go for the best head applicable to your engine type but used on a faster version of the car. 18V engines partly did away with the Weslake promontory between the valves, and owners of

At the top is an 18V head with smoother combustion chamber shapes and larger inlet valves, while at the bottom is a pre-18V head with a sharp promontary between the valves and at the edge of the spark plug hole

Owners of earlier heads can improve matters by shaping the area shown here, as described in the text. Remember to have, say, 25 thou. taken off the head to restore the compression ratio

If you were determined to extract large quantities of power from your B-series engine, you would find that the rocker shaft support posts, set inboard of the outer pair of rockers because of the sheer problem of fitting everything in on this head, were not up to the job of preventing the shaft from flexing. The overhung supports keep the shaft in place outside the outer pair of rockers too. They are examples of the fairly esoteric stuff that John Hewitt can supply alongside the more mundane bits and pieces

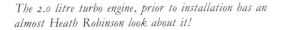

The 2.0 litre turbo engine, prior to installation has an almost Heath Robinson look about it!

pre-18V engines can use the drawing below as a guide to cutting a little of it away using a small grinding wheel held in the chuck of an electric drill. The same tool will have to be used to grind a recess in the top of the block when an 18V head is fitted to a non-18V block because otherwise the larger inlet valves will foul the block. When fitting a replacement or reshaped cylinder head, it would make sense to have the head face skimmed to ensure that it remains true. 0.025 in. can be taken off an MGB cylinder head to give a slight increase in compression ratio and John Hewitt says that up to 0.050 in. could be taken off, but that that would be taking the compression ratio up to the limit imposed by Four Star petrol.

Incidentally, post-1975 18V cylinder heads were built with extra 'meat' so that the air injectors used in the US market could be fitted. Of course, the injectors were not fitted in the UK, but the extra metal remains and makes the heads less prone to lifting in the centre, which is a common cause of a blown head gasket on the MGB.

Appetizers

If the tuning bug really gets to you, there is an almost endless range of things you could try doing to your engine. (At the ultimate, what about trying out the modification suggested by Eric Bareham himself back in the 1950s, when he put forward a method of breaking the exhaust port into two halves—see text for details.) But there is usually one limiting factor, quite apart from the limitations of the weight of the engine and the inefficiencies of its breathing apparatus: and that is cost. The simplistic little graph below shows how the law of diminishing returns works when it comes to tuning—so much so that you can pay a fortune and end up in the 'experimental' area shown shaded-in, where you may actually end up with *worse* performance if the experiment you try does not work out.

Some modifications which are sure to work would include lightening and balancing the engine's intervals, boring the engine out to give higher capacity (around 1750 cc from a 1622 cc unit and 1950 cc from a 1798 cc), reworking and gas flowing the head, fitting a pair of Dell'Orto 48s, just using one choke of each and then going on to fit a stronger steel crankshaft to cope with the extra power. If you're something of a beginner but you have the money to spend on super-tuning or even going to turbocharging, you will need the specific advice of someone like John Hewitt at

The MG Shop in Manchester who can supply all the tuning bits and tuning advice right through from mild to wild.

MGB Turbo

Fitting a turbocharger to an MGB (or any similarly engined car) is one way of increasing its performance up to or beyond that of what one would expect a modern sports car to have.

Adrian Tyndale worked over a five-year period from 1979 to build himself a pair of MGBs with the ultimate in road-going performance. One MGB was fitted with a standard B-series 1800 engine, while the other was a bored-out B-series giving 2 litres. (At least one 2-litre MGB was actually built, probably at Abingdon, and tested at Longbridge around 1976, but it was fitted with the O-series engine, which was derived from B-series of course.)

The results of Adrian Tyndale's endeavours have been catalogued elsewhere in very great detail but it is sufficient to say here that the results obtained were very impressive indeed! The tables that follow show just what can be achieved by turbocharging an MGB but the cost of having the work carried out can seem rather high—until you consider how much more you would have to pay to buy a modern car with matching performance.

Turbocharging kits and installations have to be done properly if you're not to end up with a car that is undriveable at low revs or that melts its pistons the first time it is taken on the motorway. The author knows personally of a highly reputable supplier for fitting a turbo in Manchester, another in the Midlands while Adrian Tyndale himself has set up a business supplying and fitting turbos to MGBs in the south of England. John Hewitt's The MG Shop Manchester, Rolling Road Auto Tune, and Carspares in London are all detailed in the Suppliers section.

Specifications	1.8-litre engine	2-litre engine
Head/block	Cast iron/cast iron	Cast iron/cast iron
Cylinders	4-in-line	4-in-line
Main bearings	5	5
Cooling	Water	Water
Cooling fan	Twin electric with fixed thermostat	Single electric with adjustable thermostat
Bore	80.26 mm (3.16 in.)	83.24 mm (3.27 in.)
Stroke	89.90 mm (3.50 in.)	89.90 mm (3.50 in.)

The special exhaust system joint, shown here holding the extra-big-bore pipework together, is described in Adrian Tyndale's text

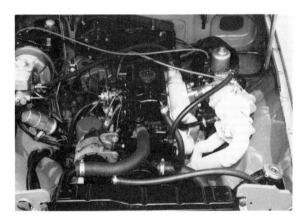

Inside the engine bay, the 1.8 turbo engine looks really purposeful and most attractive when the whole thing has been prepared to such high standards as these

Capacity	1798 cc	1935 cc
Valve gear	ohv	ohv
Camshaft drive	Chain	Chain
Ignition	Turbo distributor	Contactless turbo distributor
Spark plugs	RN7Yc	RN7Yc
Compression ratio	9.0:1	7.4:1
Octane rating	97 RM (minimum)	97 RM (minimum)
Turbocharger	IHI (II 15R1393B/RHB5 045117)	Rajay 377B25
Carburation	Suck-through a single SUHIF4 with 0.1 jet, needle BCE, red spring	Suck-through a single SUHIF6 with 0.1 jet, needle BDE, green spring
Boost pressure	6 psi	12 psi
Peak (flywheel) power (DIN)	130–140 bhp at 5000 rpm	140–150 bhp at 4800 rpm
Peak (flywheel) torque	136–147 lbf. ft. at 4500 rpm	180–190 lbf. ft. at 3500 rpm

Speed (mph)	Standard MGB GT	Standard MGC GT	MG Metro Turbo	Turbo MGB GT	Standard MGB GT V8
0–30	3.6	4.0	3.1	3.0	2.9
0–40	5.6	5.6	4.6	4.3	4.3
0–50	8.2	7.6	6.5	6.3	5.9
0–60	11.6	10.0	9.4	8.4	7.7
0–70	15.9	13.8	13.0	11.2	10.5
0–80	21.4	18.0	17.0	14.8	13.0
0–90	30.2	23.1	24.3	19.9	17.3
0–100	46.3	29.3	38.3	26.8	23.4

Top speed (mph)

105	120	111	120	125

Fourth gear acceleration (sec)

20–40	9.2	9.6	11.4	9.9	6.4
30–50	8.8	9.1	10.0	9.0	6.2
40–60	8.9	10.0	9.6	7.7	6.2
50–70	10.5	10.7	10.3	6.4	6.3
60–80	12.7	11.1	12.8	6.7	6.6
70–90	16.1	12.8	16.7	9.0	7.6
80–100	—	15.4	22.1	13.6	9.8

Overall petrol consumption (mpg)

27.4	17.5	30.3	25.0	19.8

Appendix

Specialist suppliers

The following list is mostly compiled from the author's personal knowledge of particular specialists where it has been found that good quality and good service are important to the supplier. There are large numbers of other specialists and most if not all can be found through the recommendations of the appropriate one-make club for your car—and all B-series-engined cars now have a UK club that caters for their needs.

The MG Shop (proprietor: John Hewitt), 82 Hewitt Street, Knott Mill, Manchester, England.

The MG Shop caters mainly for MGB owners but examples of earlier B-series cars can often be seen lurking in their huge premises. General mechanical and bodywork repairs undertaken, all MGB parts supplied (northern agents for the MG Owners' Club), MGBs bought, sold and there is a special interest taken in tuning—and since John and brother Bill are frequent MGB race winners, they prove their own points! Must provide the widest range of services to the MGB owner and to the B-series engine tuner. Catalogue available. BL Heritage approved.

Spridgebits (proprietors: Graham Sykes/Jed Watts), 54 St. Peters Road, Handworth, Birmingham B20 3RP, England. As the name suggests, Spridgebits started off as specialists in Sprite and Midget parts but they have since diversified into MGB parts, too. Worldwide mail order with discount scheme a speciality. Free catalogue. Recommended for friendly service, free advice.

Sprite, Midget, B, C & V8 Centre (proprietor: Graham Paddy), 22–28 Manor Road, Richmond, Surrey TW9 1YB, England. Quite apart from having the longest name in the business, Graham Paddy's company supplies parts for all the makes listed. Ideal for southern MGB owners. Friendly service.

MGA Centre (proprietor: Simon Robinson), Cleveland Street, Darlington, England DL1 2UL. The MGA Centre know just about all there is to know about all four engine types of MGA and provide the full range of services for MGA owners internationally. BL Heritage approved.

John Monkman, 90 Cardoners Road, Sheffield S10 5RU. Although not known personally by the author John is said to provide a good service to owners of MG Magnettes ZA and ZB.

University Motors Ltd. (proprietor: John Twist), 614, Eastern Avenue, SE, Grand Rapids, Michigan, 49503, USA. John Twist was trained on MGs in the UK and is the American MGB Association's technical secretary. His knowledge of MGA and MGB mechanics is vast! Mail order service available.

Moss Motors Ltd, PO Box MG, Goleta, Ca 93116, USA. Moss Motors, range of spares is nothing short of staggering! They sell parts for all postwar MGs, especially MGA and MGB. Their catalogue is worth having whichever side of the Atlantic you live—BL Heritage Ltd authorized.

Carspares Turbocharger Conversions (proprietor: Adrian Tyndale), 18 Clifton Road, London SW19 4QT, England. Adrian's data on the MGB Turbo in this book speaks for itself. Carspares market four 'stages' of MGB tune from a mild turbo on the 1.8 MGB to an electronically controlled turbo on a 2-litre MGB.

Rolling Road Auto Tune, Maylite Trading Estate, Martley, Worcestershire. Very high standards of road and race preparation with rolling road, dynamometer and good experience.

Don't forget that the majority of standard engine parts are still available through BL parts outlets and through normal local motor factors.

The following companies' products are mentioned in this book. They should be available from leading accessory shops but if difficulty is experienced in finding them contact the makers at the addresses below. (K&N filters are obtainable through 'tuning' experts such as John C. Hewitt's The MG Shop.)

K&N filters—Advance Products, Owen Street, Warrington WA2 7PA, England.

SPQR tappet adjusters—Rowlands Castle, Havant, Hants, England.

Gunson Colourplugs and Sparktune—40 Warton Road, London E15 2JU.

John Hill's MG Centre, Arthur Street, Redditch, Worcs. Suppliers of a very large range of MGB parts.

Moss Engineering, Lower Road Trading Estate, Ledbury, Herefordshire HR8 2JG. Engine reconditioners with a strong interest in older vehicles, the capacity to adapt or make parts as necessary, a wide range of engine parts and higher standards than most.

Intec Project Engineering, Unit 1, North Moon's Moat, Redditch, Worcs. Makers of inexpensive but good quality hydraulic engine hoists.

Clarkson Puckle (West Midlands) Ltd., Martin Cooke, PO Box 27, Falcon House, The Minories, Dudley DY2 8PF. Insurance brokers with a range of policies especially tailored to the owner of classic cars.

One-make clubs
Please remember to enclose an sae when writing to membership secretaries for information and membership forms.

MG Owners' Club, 2/4 Station Road, Swavesey, Cambs CB5 8BR. Formed in 1973, the MG Owners Club has grown to become 'the worlds largest one-make motor club'. From its offices in Swavesey and St Ives a staff of 54 administer and cater for the needs of a membership of around 50,000. The club has 140 Areas, throughout 14 Regions in the United Kingdom, with further affiliates and Areas in over twenty different countries throughout the world.

For a modest annual membership fee, members receive each month a lavish, full colour magazine—*Enjoying MG* of some 70 pages, containing features, articles, tips and technical aid, plus superb colour shots of all types of MGs. Also shown in the magazine is the wide range of quality special offers the club provides for the membership, plus a complete round-up of events and happenings throughout the club.

The MG Owners Club is unique in that it has negotiated and administers its own insurance scheme exclusively for MGs, at very competitive rates, with cars receiving full comprehensive cover and agreed valuation. To date over 13,000 members have taken advantage of the MGOC Insurance Scheme.

Other benefits include free technical advice for all MGs from 1925 to the latest Austin Rover products bearing the famous initials, also available to members is the opportunity to purchase or lease, at discount, the new breed of MG such as the Metro, Maestro and Montego. Each member receives annually the MGOC Club's Hand Book containing, in addition to many technical tips, a comprehensive listing of MG spares and restoration specialists.

MG Car Club: Direct descendant from original, factory-supported club. Excellent for racing connections. Polished monthly magazine with good historical, technical content. Secretaries for areas and also for most models of MG.

MG Car Club, 67 Wide Bargate, Boston, Lincolnshire PE21 6LE, England. Not commercially minded.

American MGB Association (AMGBA): 'It's so far spread, it's a bit like running a club to cater for all the peoples of Europe,' says Steve Glochowsky, president. First-rate quarterly magazine with excellent technical service. National Annual Convention. Area coordinators. Discounts on key products and publications.

AMGBA, PO Box 11401, Chicago, Illinois, 606011, USA. UK chapter—Ken Smith, Broomhill Villa, 185 Broomhill Road, Old Whitington, Chesterfield, England.

The Cambridge–Oxford Owners Club: The Cambridge Oxford Owners Club, which was formed by a group of enthusiasts in 1980, exists to help the owners of the range of BMC saloons, generally known as Farinas and based on the Austin A55 Mk II/A60 Cambridge and series V and VI Morris Oxford models. The club also caters for the 1954–59 A40, A50 and A55 Cambridge cars, in addition to the Farina-based MG, Wolseley and Riley cars.

Technical advice and information are available from the Marque Secretaries, and they operate a spares service, which includes the manufacture of replacement panels etc. The club holds local meetings, together with regional and national rallies. Current membership is in excess of 1000 and continues to grow at a healthy rate. The club welcomes anyone who owns or has an interest in this type of car. Write enclosing an sae to The Membership Secretary, 10 Harewood Place, Upton Road, Slough, Berks SL1 2AB.

Membership Secretaries, Terry and Mandy Spearing, 2 Bloomfield Close, Timsbury, Bath.

Austin Counties Car Club (a club for pre-B-series Austin Eight, Ten, Twelve, Sixteen, A40, A70 and A90). Philip Carpenter, 68 Upper Road, Plaistow, London E13 0DH

Metropolitan Owners Club for owners and enthusiasts of Nash and Austin Metropolitan. W. E. Dowsing, 4 Burnham Road, Knaphill, Woking, Surrey.

Morris Cowley & Oxford Club: For Oxfords, Cowleys and Isis (i.e. the last Morris designed cars; pre-Farina). D. J. Garrett, 28 Dermott Avenue, Comber, Co. Down BT23 5JE, Ireland.

Riley Motor Club Ltd: Advice, spares, library for all Rileys. J. S. Hall, 'Treelands', 127 Pen Road, Wolverhampton WV3 0DU, England.

Wolseley Register: General enquiries—Hon. Sec., Glerville, Glynde Road, Bexleyheath, Kent DA7 4EU, England.

Gilbern Owners' Club: Richard Bonnie, 'Four Seasons', Sutton Hill Road, Bishops Sutton, Bristol, Avon BS18 4UT.